A BOOK OF NEW ZEALAND

A BOOK OF
NEW ZEALAND

edited by

J. C. REID

with 54 photographs

COLLINS
GLASGOW · LONDON · AUCKLAND

GENERAL EDITOR: J. B. FOREMAN, M.A.

First published 1964
Reprinted 1971

CONTENTS

5

The Land

Amusements and Sports

Poems, Songs and Ballads

LIST OF ILLUSTRATIONS

ACKNOWLEDGMENTS

The publishers gratefully acknowledge the co-operation of the following authors, owners of copyright and publishers who have given their permission for poems, prose extracts and dramatic passages to appear in these pages.

Every care has been taken to trace the holders of copyright for the pieces used in this anthology. Should any have been overlooked, the publishers hope that the information will be communicated to them so that appropriate acknowledgments may be made in future editions.

MRS. J. A. ABSOLOM for the extract from *Tutira* by W. H. Guthrie-Smith.

GEORGE ALLEN AND UNWIN LTD. for the poems "The Tides Run Up The Wairau", "New Zealand" and "New Zealand Art" from *Poems* by Eileen Duggan; and "Sculptress" from *The Sunlit Hour* by Ruth Gilbert.

AUCKLAND ART GALLERY for the extract from *The Far-Away Hills* by M. T. Woollaston.

E. H. AUDLEY for the story "Third Step".

JAMES K. BAXTER for the poems "The Mountains", "Farmhand", "Brown Bone", and "Lament for Barney Flanagan"; and the extract from *Jack Winter's Dream*.

BEGGS LTD. for the extract from *Music and the Stage in New Zealand* by Maurice Hurst.

THE BODLEY HEAD LTD. for the poem "Leaving New Zealand" by W. D'Arcy Cresswell.

CHARLES BRASCH for the poems "A View of Rangitoto" and "The Islands" from *Disputed Ground*.

R. M. BURDON for the extract from *Outlaw's Progress*.

ALISTAIR CAMPBELL for the poems "Coming of Spring" and "At the Fishing Settlement" from *Mine Eyes Dazzle*.

JONATHAN CAPE LTD. and DAVID HIGHAM ASSOCIATES LTD. for the extract from *The Young Have Secrets* by James Courage.

PETER CAPE for the poems "Taumarunui", "Down the Hall on Saturday Night" and "Nativity".

CAPRICORN PRESS for the poems "Suburban Train" from *New Worlds for Old* by Louis Johnson and "Teddy Boy" by John Boyd and "River Land" by Peter Bland, from *Three Poets*.

CASSELL AND COMPANY LTD. for the extract from *Present Without Leave* by W. D'Arcy Cresswell.

CAXTON PRESS for extracts from *Life and Time of Julius Vogel* and *New Zealand Notables*: *11* by R. M. Burdon and for the poems "The Mountains" from *Beyond the Palisade* and "Farmhand" from *Blow, Wind of Fruitfulness* by James K. Baxter; "In the Cotswolds" from *Words for Music* by J. C. Beaglehole; "Southerly Sunday" and "The Long Harbour" from *Collected Poems* by Mary Ursula Bethell; "Country Road" and "Farmyard" from *Country Road* by Ruth Dallas; "The Early Days" and "The Morepork" and "Scything" from *Signs and Wonders* by Basil Dowling; "Arrowtown" and "The Road Builders" from *The Wind and the Sand* by Denis Glover; "Hydro Works" and "She was my Love" from *She Was My Spring* by J. R. Hervey; "On the Swag" from *This Dark Will Lighten* by R. A. K. Mason; "Island" from *Fire Without Phoenix* by W. H. Oliver; "Ballad of Halfmoon Bay" from *Strangers or Beasts* by Keith Sinclair; "The Cloud, The Man, The Dream" and "Walk Past Those Houses" from *The Blind Mountain* by Kendrick Smithyman.

R. M. CHAPMAN for the extract from "Politics and Society", in *Landfall*.

ALLEN CURNOW for the poems "The Unhistoric Story" from *Sailing or Drowning* and "Jack-in-the-Boat" from *A Small Room With Large Windows*.

PETER DAVIES LTD. for the extract from *Tangahano* by Frances Keinzly.

DEPARTMENT OF INTERNAL AFFAIRS for the extracts from *Settlers and Pioneers* by James Cowan; *The Women of New Zealand* by Helen Simpson; *Journey Towards Christmas* by S. P. Llewellyn; *22nd Battalion* by Jim Henderson.

ANDRE DEUTSCH LIMITED, IAN CROSS and HARCOURT, BRACE & WORLD, INC. for the extract from *The God Boy* by Ian Cross.

CHARLES DOYLE and QUADRANT for the poem "Phials".

EILEEN DUGGAN for the poems "The Tides Run Up The Wairau", "New Zealand" and "New Zealand Art".

W. R. EDGE for the poem "Prayer for a Young Country" and the extract from *Check to Your King* by Robin Hyde and the poems "Spring Fires" and "The Grey Company" by Jessie Mackay.

FABER AND FABER LTD. for the extracts from *The Story of New Zealand* by W. H. Oliver and *Backblocks Baby-Doctor* by Doris Gordon.

JOHN FARQUHARSON LTD. for the extract from *Paradise Bay* by John Guthrie.

RODERICK FINLAYSON and THE UNICORN PRESS for the extract from "The Tangi" in *Brown Man's Burden*.

H. G. FORDER and THE UNIVERSITY OF AUCKLAND for the extract from *1840 and After*.

DENIS GLOVER for the extract from *Hot Water Sailor* and the poems "Arrowtown", "The Road Builders" and "Conversation Piece".

HODDER AND STOUGHTON LTD. for the extract from *High Adventure* by Sir Edmund Hillary.

HUTCHINSON AND CO. LTD. for the poem "Prayer for a Young Country" and the extract from *Check to Your King* by Robin Hyde;

the extracts from *Allen Adair* by Jane Mander and *The Whalers* by Felix Maynard and Alexandre Dumas.

A. F. JACKSON for the extract from "Gus Buys a Bull" by F. S. Anthony.

LOUIS JOHNSON for the poems "Mating Call" and "Suburban Train".

M. K. JOSEPH for the poems "Secular Litany" from *Imaginary Islands* and "A Riddle: Of the Soul" and "Distilled Water" from *The Living Countries.*

MICHAEL JOSEPH LTD. for the extracts from *Farewell Campo 12* by James Hargest and *Green Kiwi* by Temple Sutherland.

MICHAEL JOSEPH LTD. and DAVID HIGHAM ASSOCIATES, LTD. for the extract from *Roads from Home* by Dan Davin.

LANDFALL for the poem "In my Country" by Colin Newbury and the extracts from "Politics and Society" by R. M. Chapman and "Fretful Sleepers" by W. H. Pearson.

JOHN A. LEE for the extracts from *Shining With the Shiner* and *Children of the Poor.*

HORACE MARSHALL & SON LTD. and MRS. A. B. WHITE for the extracts from *The Long White Cloud* by W. Pember Reeves.

BRUCE MASON for the extract from *The Pohutukawa Tree.*

E. H. McCORMICK for the extract from *New Zealand Literature.*

ALAN MITCHELL for the extract from *Cricket Companions* by Alan Mitchell.

COLIN NEWBURY for the poem "My Country".

THE NEW ZEALAND COUNCIL FOR EDUCATIONAL RESEARCH for the extracts from *Littledene* by H. C. D. Somerset and *Some Modern Maoris* by Ernest and Pearl Beaglehole.

THE NEW ZEALAND LISTENER and the authors for the extracts from "Sir Ernest Rutherford" by R. A. Knox, "New Zealand and Politics" by D. D. Raphael and "Race Day" by Maurice Duggan.

NORTHLAND MAGAZINE for the poem "Sea Call" by Hone Tuwhare.

W. H. OLIVER for the poem "Island".

OSWALD-SEALY LTD. for the extract from *Puborama* by Ian Mackay.

OXFORD UNIVERSITY PRESS for the extracts from *The Exploration of New Zealand* by W. G. McClymont, *New Zealand Literature* by E. H. McCormick and *Report on Experience* by John Mulgan.

PAUL'S BOOK ARCADE for the poems "Charity" from *This Slender Volume* by Helen Blackshaw and "Any Complaints?" from *The Best of Whim-Wham* by "Whim-Wham"; and the extracts from *A Shepherd's Calendar* by Oliver Duff; *The Signature Was Joy* by Iris Hughes-Sparrow; *Man Alone* by John Mulgan, and *Our Own Country.*

W. H. PEARSON for the extracts from "Fretful Sleepers" in *Landfall.*

PEGASUS PRESS for the extracts from *Early New Zealand Families* by Douglas Cresswell and *A Gun in My Hand* by Gordon Slatter; and the poems "Brown Bone" by James K. Baxter from *N.Z. Poetry Yearbook 1962*; "At the Fishing Settlement" and "Coming of Spring" from *Mine Eyes Dazzle* by Alistair Campbell; "Norfolk Pines" from *Norfolk Island* by Merval Connelly; "Conversation Piece" from *Arawata Bill* by Denis Glover; "Mother" from

Starveling Year by Mary Stanley; "River Bed" from *The Falcon Mask* by Hubert Witheford.

A. D. PETERS for the extract from *A Year of Space* by Eric Linklater.

PENGUIN BOOKS LTD. for the extract from *Pelican History of New Zealand* by Keith Sinclair.

THE PROPRIETORS OF PUNCH and SIR ALAN HERBERT for the extract from "Mr. Punch Goes A-Roving: Rotorua" by A. P. Herbert.

A. H. & A. W. REED LTD. for the extracts from *A Good Keen Man* by Barry Crump; *Hot Water Sailor* by Denis Glover; *Tavern in the Town* by James McNeish; *The Making of a New Zealander* by Alan Mulgan; *Strait of Adventure* by Stephen Gerard; *High Country Days* by Peter Newton; *The Maori People and Us* by Norman Smith.

THE RICHARDS PRESS and MRS. A. B. WHITE for the poems "New Zealand" and "The Passing of the Forest" by W. Pember Reeves.

GLORIA RAWLINSON for the poem "The Old Coach Road" from *Of Clouds and Pebbles*.

SAMPSON, LOW AND MARSTON LTD. for the extracts from *Waitaruna* by Alexander Bathgate.

J. H. E. SCHRODER for the extract from "The Otira Gorge Coach" in *Remembering Things* and the poem "The Song of the Boob" from *The Street*.

SIDGWICK AND JACKSON LTD. for the extract from *The Greenstone Door* by William Satchell.

THE SOCIETY OF AUTHORS and ALFRED A. KNOPF INC. for the extract from "At The Bay" in *The Short Stories of Katherine Mansfield*.

F. ALEXA STEVENS for the poem "Modern".

DOUGLAS STEWART and the *Bulletin* for the poem "Watching the Milking".

HARRY H. TOMBS for the extracts from *Hero-Stories of New Zealand* by James Cowan and *Sheep Kings* by Joyce West.

P. A. TOMORY for the extract from *New Zealand Painting*.

UNICORN PRESS for the extract from *Katherine Mansfield* by Arthur Sewell.

ARNOLD WALL for the poems "The City from the Hills" and "The Full Cup".

T. WERNER LAURIE LTD. for the extracts from *Paradise Bay* by John Guthrie and *Cricket Companions* by Alan Mitchell.

WHITCOMBE AND TOMBS LTD. for the extracts from *King Dick* by R. M. Burdon; *Dance of the Seasons* by M. H. Holcroft; *Grand Hills for Sheep* by Georgina McDonald; *Dim Horizons* by Jean Boswell; *Remembering Things* by J. H. E. Schroder.

R. WRIGHT-ST. CLAIR for the extract from an unpublished letter by W. E. Aytoun.

MRS. A. P. YOUNG for the poems "Old Woman", "These Islands", "Winter Night", "In the Younger Land", "Tom's A-Cold", "Reverie on the Rat" by A. R. D. Fairburn.

ILLUSTRATIONS

Grateful acknowledgments are made to the following for permission to reproduce photographs:

THE ALEXANDER TURNBULL LIBRARY, WELLINGTON for "On the Grass Plain below Lake Arthur" and "Kauri Forest, Wairoa River."

THE ALEXANDER TURNBULL LIBRARY and the REX NAN KIVELL COLLECTION, CANBERRA for "A Tabood Store-house", "Scouting Party", "Wanganui" and "Auckland, 1858".

THE AUCKLAND CITY ART GALLERY and the artists named for "Hot Springs, Whakarewarewa", "Mt. Tarawera and Lake", "Otira Gorge", "The Birthday Party" (Bryan Drew), "Sir Edmund Hilary" (Alison Duff), "From a Landscape Series" (Colin McCahon) and "Pipawharuaroa, Late Summer" (Don Binney).

V. C. BROWNE, CHRISTCHURCH for "The Octagon, Dunedin."

T. W. COLLINS, WARKWORTH for "Modern Auckland."

FENWICK PHOTOGRAPHY, ROTORUA for "Kawerau, a Modern Timber Town".

GREIG ROYLE LTD., WELLINGTON for "Jerusalem".

NEW ZEALAND GOVERNMENT PUBLICITY STUDIOS for "Arrowtown" and "Deer-hunters".

GREEN AND HAHN, CHRISTCHURCH for "A Sheep Sale" and "Roman Catholic Cathedral, Christchurch".

OLAF PETERSEN, SWANSON for "A West Coast Beach" and "Wattle in Bloom".

ROBIN SMITH PHOTOGRAPHY LTD., CHRISTCHURCH for "New Zealand Bush".

LINDBERG PHOTO PRODUCTIONS, HAMILTON for "Yachting at Hamilton".

NEW ZEALAND HERALD for the remaining 30 photographs.

Mr. D. W. Lochore of the *New Zealand Herald* and Mr. Hamish Keith of the Auckland City Art Gallery staff are especially thanked for their assistance and advice in selecting these illustrations.

INTRODUCTION

In line with the general intention of this series of
National Anthologies, *A Book of New Zealand* attempts
to indicate the special character of a land and its people.
In a brief compass, a compiler can hope to represent
only a few of the values, attitudes, traditions and
aspirations of any community; even from a more
generous selection, important distinguishing nuances
are likely to escape. My aim has been to make a pleasant,
readable book which will, as fairly as possible, also
convey some sense of the history, physical environment
and culture that make up the New Zealander's world
of experience.

As New Zealand has had such a short European
history by comparison with the other lands represented
in this series, and its Polynesian past is still shrouded
in the fog of legends and speculations, it is inevitable
that most of the extracts should have been chosen from
the writing of the last half-century. There is no lack
of records of early days—of the sealers and whalers who
preceded the colonists, of the first missionaries, of the
turbulent days at Kororareka (Russell) in the Bay of
Islands, where British rule began, of the struggles of
pioneers against primitive conditions, of the various
planned settlements, of the soon-superseded Provincial
Governments, of the land-wars with the Maoris, and
of the gradual emergence of the modern State-structure.
The pioneers were indefatigable writers; their letters,
diaries, reminiscences, didactic novels, reports, journals
and newspapers all testify to a passion for factual
records which their modern descendants have retained.

Early creative writing, however, carried over from
England the forms and subjects of minor Victorian

literature; the most popular writers were those who imitated the rough jocosity and simple sentimentality of current English sub-literary modes. Thomas Bracken, the author of New Zealand's most re-printed poem, "Not Understood" and of our national song, "God Defend New Zealand", was typical of his times in his ingenuous sentiment, his poeticising of the common-place and his slapdash facility. An interesting patch of Scottish vernacular literature flourished briefly in Otago until annihilated by the polyglot influx of the gold-rushes. Just a handful of indigenous ballads and occupational songs survive from earlier days; in this respect, New Zealand comes a poor second to Australia, from whose rich store of bush and other ballads many of our "folk-songs" were borrowed virtually unaltered.

In the nineties came the first signs of a native as opposed to an immigrant literature. Partly because most of the inhabitants were now not expatriates but native-born, and partly because the economic depression of the eighties had focused attention on live issues close at hand, a new awareness of independent identity and of national purpose began to be expressed, not without stridency, in the work of such writers as Jessie Mackay and W. Pember Reeves. But, although the sentiments were different, the literary stereotypes remained much the same as in the past. And so it was for the next forty years, despite the high gifts of some writers, especially the women, during the first three decades of this century.

It was in the 1930's that New Zealand writing came of age. In part, this was the natural result of the evolution of a colonial literature, the new talent springing from among third and fourth generation New Zealanders; in part, too, it was the effect of a more devastating economic depression, whereby writers were prevented from sinking into stultifying comfort and had their attention wrenched away from remote and often trivial themes linked with "Home" (the hard-dying older New Zealander's name for a land 12,000 miles away) to matters of immediate and challenging concern. A new relevance in writing that gave voice to the conflicts, troubles and aspirations of the whole people led to an enhanced status for the writer. No longer was poetry, for instance, the preserve of the concert entertainer and the talented lady of leisure, as it had been largely in Victorian times. While the practical man is still more highly regarded than the poet in New Zealand's pragmatic society, the vision, vigour and craftsmanship of the writing of the 1930's forced the acceptance of the writer as a person of some significance. The self-conscious nationalism of some of the work of this period and its spirit of revolt against the tyranny of the concept of an idealised Britain have been modified by time to produce a local literature that no longer feels obliged to proclaim its indigenous specialness. The Wordsworthian note has always been strong in our poetry, and contemporary writers share with their predecessors a fondness for meditations on the hills, plains, mountains, glaciers, sounds, rivers and forests of this land, different though the spirit and emphasis now are. A poetry of urban life in New Zealand is, in fact, of comparatively recent growth.

In the 1930's, poets like A. R. D. Fairburn, Allen Curnow and Denis Glover, and short story writers like Frank Sargeson spoke in a tone of voice, which, while universally apprehensible, was recognisable by other New Zealanders as distinctive to this land. During the past thirty years, more and more writers have followed this lead; with the overlapping today of several generations of active poets and novelists of remarkable diversity and quality for a country with a population of but 2½ millions, the present literary scene is singularly lively. The novel, which also grew up in the depression years, with the books of "Robin

Hyde", John A. Lee and John Mulgan, was slower than poetry to come to maturity, but in the past decade, by exploring varied subjects and forms, has at last caught up.

Recent decades have witnessed another significant change. In the early years of the century, the typical New Zealand writer was an expatriate like Katherine Mansfield who left her native country never to return. In older societies, such talents found a more congenial atmosphere for creativity than in the undeveloped New Zealand one where sportsmen and successful businessmen were more readily applauded than artists of any kind. While their example has been followed up to the present time, nowadays a high proportion of writers and artists return after the conventional pilgrimage overseas to live and work contentedly in New Zealand. The expansion of New Zealand publishing and the greater readiness of publishers in Great Britain and America to issue New Zealand books give contemporary writers assurance of an audience such as was often denied to their fathers.

Because in its origins our society was comparatively homogeneous, with settlers overwhelmingly English-speaking, from English, Scots and Irish stock, it has been spared the racial conflicts of some other colonial communities; but, lacking fruitful cultural tensions, it has also been subject to a deadly uniformity and mediocrity of outlook. To some extent the Maori has provided a leavening influence, tempering New Zealand materialism with an exuberant awareness of natural living, and, since the Second World War, an influx of settlers from Denmark, the Netherlands, Poland and elsewhere has led to a slight, but important, modification of New Zealand stodginess.

On the surface, our society today appears aggressively egalitarian, with its contempt for English class divisions and snobberies, its stress on equality of opportunity in

education, its Socialist legislation, its distrust of the
oddity, the gifted individualist and the more articulate,
its propensity for "cutting people down to size", its
strong sense of personal resourcefulness. In our literature such characters as the "man alone", the old gold-
miner, the "gentleman of the roads" and the independent
deer-stalker are regarded by some as archetypal New
Zealanders, and as representing, like such typical customs
and attitudes as the addiction to football and horse-
racing, the informality of social relations, the "booze-
party" and the attitude towards women, for instance,
the legacy of a not-too-distant pioneering past. But this
is to simplify the picture. Quite as significant are such
things as the passionate regard for the Royal Family,
the competitive snobberies that cluster around Royal
visits and Vice-Regal functions, the status-symbols that
haunt professional men and expense-account executives,
the differing mores of town and country, the increasing
interest in ballet, opera and chamber-music, the steady
growth of private schools in a land where education up
to the highest levels is free—all forming a pattern about
which it is difficult, not to say rash, to generalise.
Beneath the surface of seeming conformity and uniformity, there are many interesting diversities in modern
New Zealand society. In this anthology, I have tried
to show something of this variety.

Despite their smugness, too, about the felicities of
"God's Own Country" ("Godzone" simply, to the
irreverent) and their resentment at the well-intentioned
criticisms of visitors, New Zealanders are not completely
lacking in the virtue of self-criticism. Although an
occasional intellectual talks as if serious self-appraisal
exists neither in America nor New Zealand, the fact
is that not only have many acute anatomisings of our
society appeared in, for example, the finest and longest-
established of our literary journals, *Landfall*, but even
more is implicit in the work of poets and novelists. If

New Zealand has not yet produced its substantial
criticism of Welfare State boredom, as Britain has, the
beginnings of such an appraisal can be seen in the poems
of Louis Johnson. The extent to which such attitudes
have percolated through the community at large is,
of course, another matter.

In this book I have aimed at bringing together
passages that give a frank impression rather than a
uniformly flattering one, that show the warts as well
as the handsome features, that present the crudities,
the banalities, the mediocrity and the self-satisfaction
as well as the courage, dignity, integrity and vitality
of our people. I trust that readers will find an additional
piquancy in some of the juxtapositions.

Many of our best writers, past and present, are
represented here. Yet, since this is not primarily a
literary anthology, sometimes first-rate pieces of
writing have been by-passed in favour of others that
happen compactly to express a particular attitude. This
does not mean that literary quality has not been one
of my guiding principles; I hope that sufficient work
of real merit has found its way in adequately to indicate
the vision and skill of New Zealand writers. It goes
without saying that I have no intention of specifying
which extracts I have chosen primarily for their docu-
mentary character.

Some pieces have been included because their continued
popularity with a New Zealand audience testifies to
their having expressed something real in the national
sensibility; others because they reveal unexpected in-
sights in out-of-the-way places.

The design of the anthology follows the general
pattern laid down by the earlier volumes in the series.
I have modified one or two general headings the better
to fit the characteristics of New Zealand life and I have
added a section on the Maori, since no New Zealand
compilation can pretend to even relative completeness

without a recognition of the special role played in our society by its Polynesian members.

Every anthologist runs the risk that the mirror he fashions for others will serve in the end merely to reflect his own face. I can only hope that my prejudices and preferences are shared sufficiently by my fellow-countrymen to enable them to see in this book several of their national characteristics as caught in the work of indigenous and foreign writers, and to allow others to recognize that in this country lives a community that, while sharing ancestors, institutions, certain values and part of its history with other members of the British Commonwealth, possesses its own individuality and is aware of its separate destiny.

J. C. REID
Professor of English,
University of Auckland

AUCKLAND, 1963

Prologue

NEW ZEALAND

God girt her about with the surges
  And winds of the masterless deep,
Whose tumult uprouses and urges
  Quick billows to sparkle and leap;
He filled from the life of their motion
  Her nostrils with breath of the sea,
And gave her afar in the ocean
  A citadel free.

Her never the fever-mist shrouding,
  Nor drought of the desert may blight,
Nor pall of dun smoke overclouding
  Vast cities of clamorous night,
But the voice of abundance of waters,
  Cold rivers that stay not or sleep,
Greets children, the sons and the daughters
  Of light and the deep.

Lo! here where each league hath its fountains
  In isles of deep fern and tall pine,
And breezes snow-cooled on the mountains,
  Or keen from the limitless brine,
See men to the battlefield pressing
  To conquer one foe—the stern soil,
Their kingship in labour expressing,
  Their lordship in toil.

Though young they are heirs of the ages,
  Though few they are freemen and peers,
Plain workers—yet sure of the wages
  Slow destiny pays with the years.

Though least they and latest their nation,
  Yet this they have won without sword—
That Woman with Man shall have station,
  And Labour be lord.

The winds of the sea and high heaven
  Speed pure to her kissed by the foam;
The steeds of her ocean undriven,
  Unbitted and riderless roam,
And clear from her lamp newly lighted
  Shall stream o'er the billows upcurled
A light as of wrongs at length righted,
  Of hope to the world.

WILLIAM PEMBER REEVES (1857-1932)

THE ISLANDS

Always, in these islands, meeting and parting
Shake us, making tremulous the salt-rimmed air;
Divided and perplexed the sea is waiting,
Birds and fishes visit us and disappear.

The future and the past stand at our doors,
Beggars who for one look of trust will open
Worlds that can answer our unknown desires,
Entering us like rain and sun to ripen.

Remindingly beside the quays, the white
Ships lie smoking; and from their haunted bay
The godwits vanish towards another summer.
Everywhere in light and calm the murmuring
Shadow of departure; distance looks our way;
And none knows where he will lie down at night.

CHARLES BRASCH (b. 1909)

History

NEW ZEALAND HISTORY

The raw facts of New Zealand history are these: a habitat quite hospitable to human life, two races of men who have arrived from the north at different times, two sets of social usages and economic demands carried by the men who looked for a home in New Zealand. Maori society grew in numbers but slowly, and made minimal demands upon the habitat; European society grew with great speed and could tolerate neither the Polynesian settlers nor the habitat in its primitive condition. New Zealand's history, since the arrival of the Europeans, has been a history of struggle; a struggle between Polynesia and Europe, the first and second wave of colonisers; a struggle between the European settlers and the environment; a struggle between groups and interests within the European population. In this history can be seen, very dimly, brown Polynesians making their home, coming to terms with the environment, fighting among themselves for food and honour. With greater clarity may be observed the hitherto unchallenged Polynesians retreating before the muskets, the diseases, the sheer numbers of the new men from Europe, who journeyed out to New Zealand from the eighteenth century on, out of curiosity, out of greed, out of an ambition for security.

Europeans met two adversaries, the Maori and the land. They fought both, and quickly enough they overcame both. New Zealand became a European country; it was found to be a country that responded quite well to European demands. It would grow crops and support animals, it could feed men. But Europeans had greater and more complex demands to make than

31

the Maoris. They were not content to fish and hunt, to eat the food they grew. Before long they were too numerous for such a primitive economy even if they had had a mind for it. They were accustomed to clothes and implements of some complexity, to diversions and luxuries of some sophistication; they sent to England for them, where factories constantly turned them out in great quantity. They had to pay for them; they sold seal skins, whale oil, kauri gum and timber, wool, meat, butter and cheese. These were articles that could be extracted from the grass which had replaced the forest—articles which the English were prepared to buy.

To settle into such a pattern, exchanging food and wool for manufactures, meant the transformation rather than the end of the struggle. Tied, by the demands of her people and the capabilities of her soil, to international markets, finance and commerce, New Zealand had accepted a perpetually precarious position, one of dependence upon overseas markets, creditors and shipping. In these spheres she has been and remains engaged upon a struggle less simple than the business of shooting Maoris and burning bush, a struggle which she can, by the nature of things, never quite win. New Zealand can never stop a market from contracting, a creditor from turning sour, a ship-owner from raising his charges.

W. H. OLIVER (b. 1925)
The Story of New Zealand

THE UNHISTORIC STORY

Whaling for continents suspected deep in the south
The Dutchman envied the unknown, drew bold
Images of marketplace, populous rivermouth,
The Land of Beach ignorant of the value of gold.

ON THE GRASS PLAIN BELOW LAKE ARTHUR (1846)

The early colonisation years produced many water-colour records of the raw New Zealand landscape as it appeared to European eyes. Sir William Fox (1812-1893), who became Prime Minister, expressed his sense of the land's solitudes in several water-colours like this one.

HOT SPRINGS AND GEYSERS, WHAKAREWAREWA (1888)

The areas of intense thermal activity attracted the attention of many nineteenth century New Zealand artists. This water-colour by William Boodle, who lived in Auckland in the 1880's, depicts a scene such as can still be found in many places in the centre of the North Island.

KAURI FOREST, WAIROA RIVER, KAIPARA (1840)
This water-colour depicting logging operations was painted by Charles
Heaphy (1822-1881) who came to the country as artist for the New
Zealand Company. He received the V.C. for bravery in the Maori
War, became an M.P., Commissioner of Native Reserves, and Judge of
the Native Land Court.

Morning in Murderers' Bay,
Blood drifted away.
It was something different, something
Nobody counted on.

Spider, clever and fragile, Cook showed how
To spring a trap for islands, turning from planets
His measuring mission, showed what the musket
    could do,
Made his Christmas goose of the wild gannets;
        Still as the collier steered
        No continent appeared;
        It was something different, something
        Nobody counted on.

The roving tentacles touched, rested, clutched
Substantial earth, that is, accustomed haven
For the hungry whaler. Some inland, some hutched
Rudely in bays, the shaggy foreshore shaven,
        Lusted, preached as they knew,
        But as the children grew
        It was something different, something
        Nobody counted on.

Green slashed with flags, pipeclay and boots in the bush,
Christ in canoes and the musketed Maori boast;
All a rubble-rattle at Time's glacial push:
Vogel and Seddon howling empire from an empty coast
        A vast ocean laughter
        Echoed unheard, and after
        All it was different, something
        Nobody counted on.

The pilgrim dream pricked by a cold dawn died
Among the chemical farmers, the fresh towns; among
Miners, not husbandmen, who piercing the side
Let the land's life, found like all who had so long

Bloodily or tenderly striven
To rearrange the given
It was something different, something
Nobody counted on.

After all re-ordering of old elements
Time trips up all but the humblest of heart
Stumbling after the fire, not in the smoke of events;
For many are called, but many are left at the start,
    And whatever islands may be
    Under or over the sea,
    It is something different, something
    Nobody counted on.

ALLEN CURNOW (b. 1911)

TASMAN ENCOUNTERS THE MAORIS
1642

On the 19th d° early in the morning a boat of these
people with thirteen heads in her came within a stone's
throw from our ship. They called out several times,
which we did not understand, the language bearing no
resemblance to the vocabulary given us over there by
the Honourable Governor General and Councillors of
the Indies, but this is not to be wondered at as it contains
the language of the Solomon Islands, etc. As far as
we could see these people were of average height but
rough of voice and build, their colour between brown
and yellow. They had black hair tied together right on
top of their heads, in the way and fashion the Japanese
have it, at the back of the head, but their hair was
rather longer and thicker. On the tuft they had a large,
thick, white feather. Their boat consisted of two long,
narrow praus joined together, over which a number
of planks or seating of a kind had been laid, in such a
way that above the water one can see underneath the

boat. Their paddles were a little over a fathom in length, narrow and pointed at the end. They could handle these boats very cleverly. Their clothing, so it seemed, consisted with some of them of mats, with others of cottons; almost all of them had the upper part of the body naked. We made signs to them several times to come on board, showed them white linen and some knives which had been given to us as cargo. They did not come nearer, however, but at last paddled back. Meanwhile the officers of the Zeehaen, following our summons of the previous night, came on board our ship upon which we convened a council and decided to go as close to the shore with the ships as we could, since there was good anchoring-ground and these people (as it seems) are seeking friendship. Shortly after drawing up this resolution we saw seven more boats put off from the land, of which one (high in front and sloping sharply towards the back, manned by seventeen heads) paddled round behind the Zeehaen and a second one (in which thirteen able-bodied men) came to within half a stone's throw of our bows. Both called out to each other every now and then. We showed them (as with the previous one) white linens, etc., but they remained where they were. The skipper of the Zeehaen sent his quartermaster back to his ship with their cockboat, in which six rowers, in order to instruct the junior officers not to let too many on, should the people want to come on board, but to be cautious and well on their guard. As the cockboat of the Zeehaen was rowing towards her, those in the canoe nearest to us called out and waved with their paddles to those lying behind the Zeehaen but we could not make out what they meant. Just as the cockboat from the Zeehaen put off again, those who were lying in front of us, between the two ships, began to paddle towards it so furiously that when they were about halfway, slightly more on the side of our ship, they struck the Zeehaen's cockboat

alongside with their stern, so that it lurched tremend-
ously. Thereupon the foremost one in the villains' boat,
with a long blunt pike, thrust the quartermaster,
Cornelis Joppen, in the neck several times, so violently
that he could not but fall overboard. Upon this the
others attacked with short, thick, wooden clubs (which
we at first thought to be heavy blunt parangs) and their
paddles, overwhelming the cockboat. In which fray
three of the Zeehaen's men were left dead and a fourth
owing to the heavy blows, was mortally wounded. The
quartermaster and two sailors swam towards our ship
and we sent our shallop to meet them, into which they
got alive. After this monstrous happening and detestable
affair, the murderers left the cockboat drift, having
taken one of the dead in their canoe and drowned another. We and those of the Zeehaen, seeing this, fired
heavily with muskets and guns, but, although we did
not hit them, they withdrew and rowed to the shore,
out of reach of our fire. With our fore, upper and
bow guns we fired many shots near and around their
boats but hit none. Skipper Ide Tercxsen Holman, with
our shallop, well manned and armed, rowed to the
Zeehaen's cockboat (which, fortunately for us, these
accursed people had left adrift) and forthwith returned
with it to our ship, having found therein one of the
dead and the one mortally wounded. We weighed our
anchors and set sail, since we were of opinion that no
friendship could be made with these people, nor water
nor refreshments be obtained.

ABEL JANSZOON TASMAN (1603-1659)
*Journal of a Voyage Made from the City of Batavia in the East Indies for
the Discovery of the Unknown South Land in the year Anno 1642.*
translated by M. F. VIGEVENO

CAPTAIN COOK

The ruder Italy laid bare
    By that keen Searcher of the Seas,
Whose tempest-baffling, never baffled keel,
Left half our planet little to reveal;
    But restless roaming everywhere
Zigzagged the vast Pacific as he prest
With godlike patience his benignant quest;
True hero-god, who realized the notion
Its races feign of mythic Maui still,
And plucked up with a giant might of will
A hundred islands from Oblivion's ocean!
Sea-king and sage—staunch huntsman of pure Fame,
Beating the waste of waters for his game,
Untrodden shores or tribes without a name;
    That nothing in an island's shape,
    Mist-muffled peak or faint cloud-cape,
Might his determined thoughtful glance escape;
    No virgin lands he left unknown,
    Where future Englands might be sown,
    And nations noble as his own.

ALFRED DOMETT[1] (1811-87)
from *Ranolf and Amohia*

COOK'S FIRST LANDING IN
NEW ZEALAND

Monday, 9th October, 1769
. . . I went ashore with a Party of men in the Pinnace
and yawl accompanied by Mr. Banks and Dr. Solander.
We landed abreast of the Ship and on the E. side of the
River just mentioned; but seeing some of the Natives

[1]Domett, Browning's "Waring", spent several years in New
Zealand, where he became Prime Minister (1862).

on the other side of the River of whom I was desirous
of speaking with, and finding that we could not ford
the River, I order'd the yawl in to carry us over, and the
pinnace to lay at the Entrance. In the meantime the
Indians made off. However we went as far as their
Hutts which lay about 2 or 300 Yards from the water
side, leaving 4 boys to take care of the Yawl, which
we had no sooner left than 4 men came out of the woods
on the other side of the River, and would certainly have
cut her off had not the People in the Pinnace discover'd
them and called to her to drop down the stream, which
they did, being closely persued by the Indians. The
coxswain of the Pinnace, who had charge of the Boats,
seeing this, fir'd 2 Musquets over their Heads; the
first made them stop and Look round them but the
2nd they took no notice of; upon which a third was
fir'd and kill'd one of them upon the Spot just as he
was going to dart his spear at the Boat. At this the
other 3 stood motionless for a Minute, wondering, no
doubt, what it was that had thus kill'd their comrade;
but as soon as they recovered themselves they made off,
dragging the Dead body a little way and then left it.
Upon our hearing the report of the Musquets we
immediately repair'd to the Boats, and after viewing
the Dead body we return'd on board. In the morning,
seeing a number of the Natives at the same place where
we saw them last night, I went on shore with the
Boats, mann'd and Arm'd, and landed on the opposite
side of the river. Mr. Banks, Dr. Solander, and myself
only landed at first, and went to the side of the river,
the natives having got together on the opposite side.
We call'd to them in the George's Island Language,
but they answer'd us by flourishing their weapons over
their heads and dancing, as we suppos'd, the War
Dance; upon this we retir'd until the Marines were
landed, which I order'd to be drawn up about 200 yards
behind us. We went again to the river side, having

Tupia (a Tahitian. Ed.), Mr. Green, and Dr. Monkhouse
along with us. Tupia spoke to them in his own Language, and it was an agreeable surprise to us to find that
they perfectly understood him. After some little conversation had passed one of them swam over to us,
and after him 20 or 30 more; these last brought their
Arms, which the first man did not. We made them
every one presents. But this did not satisfy them; they
wanted everything we had about us, particularly our
Arms, and made several attempts to snatch them out
of our hands. Tupia told us several times, as soon as
they came over, to take care of ourselves for they were
not our friends; and this we very soon found, for one
of them snatched Mr. Green's hanger from him, and
would not give it up; this encouraged the rest to be
more insolent, and seeing others coming over to join
them, I order'd the man who had taken the hanger to
be fir'd at, which was accordingly done, and wounded
in such a manner that he died soon after. Upon the
first fire, which was only 2 Musquets the others retir'd
to a Rock which lay near the middle of the River, but
on seeing the man fall they return'd, probably to carry
him off or his Arms, the last of which they accomplished,
and this we could not prevent unless we had run our
Bayonets into them, for upon their returning from off
the Rock, we had discharged off our Peices, which were
loaded with small shott, and wounded 3 more; but
these got over the River and were carried off by the
others, who now thought proper to retire. Finding
nothing was to be done with the people on this side,
and the water in the river being salt, I embarked with
an intent to row round the head of the Bay in search
of fresh water, and if possible to surprize some of the
Natives and take them on board, and by good Treatment
and Presents endeavour to gain their friendship with
this view.

JAMES COOK (1728-1779)
Journal of the First Voyage of Captain James Cook

OLD KORORAREKA

The evil deeds of some of the Kororareka settlers in the Bay of Islands were the chief causes of the missionary opposition to the immigration of Europeans. Ever since the commencement of the century, ships frequenting the northern island touched at the Bay of Islands in preference to all other places, in consequence of the excellence of its harbours, the abundance of pigs and potatoes, and the numerous native population living on the banks of the many rivers falling into the bay. In 1825 a few Europeans had peacably located themselves in the bay, and in 1830 Mr. Benjamin Turner opened the first grog-shop. In these days the settlers lived apart in remote inlets, until experience taught them that the most convenient place for erecting huts was around the deep-water beach at Kororareka, in close proximity to the native village.

In these beautiful inlets, the free-trading flax schooners and whalers rode out gales in safety, and their crews, although leading a piratical sort of lives themselves, objected to all intruders. One morning, in 1827, a Sydney vessel anchored in the bay with eighty men on board. An old New Zealand trader named Duke invited the captain on board, and discovered that he and the crew were convicts who had overpowered the guard, and seized the vessel, during their voyage from Sydney to Norfolk Island. Duke hoisted two guns out of the hold, and with the aid of several Maori war canoes, he commanded the convicts to surrender; this being refused, an engagement ensued, which ended, after considerable loss to the convicts, in Duke's victory. The vessel was taken back to Sydney, when nine of the mutineers were hung, and the others again shipped to Norfolk Island.

In 1832, there were one hundred white settlers permanently located in Kororareka, and the place was then described as the Cyprus of the South Ocean, in which life was one unceasing revel. Chiefs in the neighbourhood lived in affluence by pimping for the crews of whale ships, and Pomare kept a harem of 96 slave girls for the pandemonium. . . .

Meanwhile Kororareka prospered. In 1838 it was the most frequented resort for whalers in all the South Sea Islands; and its European population, although fluctuating, was then estimated at a thousand souls. It had a church, five hotels, numberless grog-shops, a theatre, several billiard tables, skittle alleys, and hells. For six successive years, a hundred whale ships anchored in the bay, and land facing the beach sold at three pounds a foot. 36 large whale ships were anchored at Kororareka at one time in 1836; and in 1838 56 American vessels entered the bay, 23 English, 21 French, one Bremen, 24 from New South Wales, and six from the coast.

It was impossible that a community composed of sailors of different nations, runaway and liberated convicts, traders, beach-combers, sawyers and New Zealanders could live together, either drunk or sober, without quarrelling, more particularly when revelry and brawling are what British sailors come on shore to enjoy. Disputes between white men and natives were often settled by the missionaries; quarrels confined to white men generally ended in combats which occasionally terminated in bloodshed. There was no authority to grapple with these disturbances.

ARTHUR S. THOMSON, M.D. (1816-60)
The Story of New Zealand

THE GREY COMPANY

O the grey, grey company
Of the pallid dawn!
O the ghostly faces,
Ashen-like and drawn!
The Lord's lone sentinels,
Dotted down the years,
The little grey company
Before the pioneers!

Dreaming of Utopias
Ere the time was ripe,
They awoke to scorning,
The jeering and the strife.
Dreaming of milleniums
In a world of wars.
They awoke to shudder
At a flaming Mars.

Never was a Luther
But a Huss was first—
A fountain unregarded
In the primal thirst.
Never was a Newton
Crowned and honoured well
But first alone, Galileo
Wasted in a cell.

In each other's faces
Look the pioneers;
Drank the wine of courage
All their battle years.

For their weary sowing,
    Through the world wide,
Green they saw the harvest
    Ere the day they died.

But the grey, grey company
    Stood every man alone
In the chilly dawnlight.
    Scarcely had they known
Ere the day they perished,
    That their beacon-star
Was not glint of marsh-light
    In the shadows far.

The brave white witnesses
    To the truth within
Took the dart of folly,
    Took the jeer of sin;
Crying "Follow, follow,
    Back to Eden-gate!"
They trod the Polar desert,
    Met a desert fate.

Be laurel to the victor,
    And roses to the fair,
And asphodel Elysian
    Let the hero wear;
But lay the maiden lilies
    Upon their narrow biers—
The lone grey company
    Before the pioneers.

JESSIE MACKAY (1864-1938)

EDWARD EDWARDS

Edward Edwards was a castaway sealer,
Edward Edwards was a runagate sailor.
He fled from the pressgang or a midland slum,
Slunk from the bilge of a sharp right whaler.

Fed on bully-beef and mutton bird,
Smelling to heaven of his salty board,
He dressed in the slops of the prideless poor,
Walked in the eye of a watchful Lord.

Edwards and his woman lived in sin,
Briding and breeding just the same
And caring for two orphans that seamen left,
Twenty years until the bishop came.

Mary Hinekino was white as a half-caste,
Gentle as the daughter of a Kentish priest.
She spoke the King's English like a currency lass,
    though
Born to the flavour of a cannibal feast.

Mary and her man had two squeakers to raise—
Throats of conch unless stopped on her breast,
And the sun called them mess-mates, the moon to tea.
Days at the double and at night no rest,

Still she managed and mothered the orphans—
Friday, the foundling, a right tight lad,
The son of a sealing-gang that stayed for a season,
Long in the nose like his unseen dad;

Sarah the other was the moon in the spindrift,
Bright for a lady-love and not sixteen,
As dark as the last light held in a rock pool,
Begotten by her mother for a yard of jean.

Edwards had an island for his back-yard,
Edwards had a whare with a roof of thatch,
A Brown Bess, a go-ashore, a print of the *Savannah*,
Six fat grunters and a small spud patch.

One day he built a cutter on the beach,
Next day he worked in his potato patch,
Another he sold fresh victuals to a whaler,
Sometimes he fished in an evening slatch.

Friday and he were the terror of the blue cod.
Where they sailed the groper fled,
From the Land of the Living round to Ruggedy;
Hounded the green-bone past Red Head.

Monday to Saturday he farmed, skinned seal,
Sunday he hoisted his red sprit-sail
And walked his cutter to Halfmoon Bay,
Fair or weather or a two-reef gale.

KEITH SINCLAIR (b. 1922)
from *The Ballad of Halfmoon Bay*

WHALERS IN PEGASUS BAY

As soon as the weather permitted, we, in our turn, went to cruise in Pegasus Bay. All the ships anchored in the various inlets of the peninsula had arranged a meeting-place there.

What a magnificent spectacle it was! Pegasus Bay was a hippodrome, where the cars progressed without axles or wheels, where the reins were more than four hundred feet long, and the coursers were urged by the spur which kills them, and paused only to die. The sun appeared from the open sea; it rose from the far horizon of this ocean which, in these latitudes, sweeps its waves over an expanse of two thousand leagues, from Banks Peninsula to the shores of South America, without one island, one islet, or one rock showing above its surface. . . .

Yesterday evening we anchored all alone in the centre of the great bay. This morning we can count fourteen ships in sight. No doubt all the barometers announced this beautiful weather, and the vessels which were sheltering from the south-west winds, in the various covers of the peninsula, hastened to come out and make up for lost time. Some are clewing up their sails and allowing themselves to drift, while their boats, which left with the dawn, are prowling along that strip of sand which unites the peninsula with the mainland. Others, at anchor, have despatched their boats towards the cliffs of Tavai, and almost as far as Table Island. Still others, under full sail, but with their boats ready for launching, cruise at the entrance to the bay, ready to intercept the passage of the mother whales returning from the open sea. . . .

Each masthead carries its look-out, and the crews wait impatiently for the American cry to resound: "She blows! She blows!" Everywhere, north, south, east and west, to every quarter of the compass appear isolated boats, tossing on the swell, the peaked oars of which resemble, at a distance, some spider lying on its back with its feet in the air. The hours which pass in this manner seem very long, with not one whale spouting its double plume of water in the sight of the fishers. Then yonder, yonder, a dark speck appears and disappears on the surface of the water, and the tail or fin of a cetacean describes an enormous curve above the water. Immediately the peaked oars fall into the water, the ships lay their main topsails aback and launch their boats, and the chase begins, obstinate, relentless, with no truce until the death of the animal, or at least until night falls.

The poet accorded a triple breastplate of brass only to the man who first, unfalteringly, dared to confide himself to the mercy of the waves. That is not sufficient for him who gave the first stroke of a harpoon to these giants of nature; no longer are they sailors, men, beings like ourselves, who thus launch themselves into this morning arena, already in itself so full of strange dangers; they are rather madmen, I dare even say they are heroes.

DR. FELIX MAYNARD[1] and ALEXANDRE DUMAS
The Whalers
translated by F. W. REED

A WHALING STATION

The little harbour in which the boats of the whalers lie in security, and from which they sally forth in pursuit of their game, in under the rocky peninsula I have mentioned, is formed by the mouth of the Waikouaite River—an inconsiderable stream, which expands in its lower part into a large, salt-water lagoon, which discharges itself into and fills itself again from the sea by a narrow passage. . . . As we entered it we passed the shears by which the whales are hoisted up in the operation of stripping them of their blubber. Further on was a large shed, in which the oil is tried out, greasy in the extreme, and smelling like a thousand filthy lamps. The whole beach was strewed with gigantic fragments of the bones of whales, and flocks of gulls,

[1]Felix Maynard, a French surgeon, visited New Zealand on the whaling-ship, *Asia* in 1837 and 1838, 1845-1846. He spent seven years on such vessels throughout the world. His book, written in collaboration with Alexandre Dumas, was first published in 1858.

cormorants and other sea-birds and savage-looking pigs prowled about to pick up the refuse. The place altogether, like other whaling-stations, is a picture of the most perfect neglect of anything like order or neatness. The huts in which the men live—rickety things—are stuck about in all directions, and not one of them possesses a garden. There seemed, however, to be abundance of poultry, as well as dogs and pigs; and another common feature of whaling-stations was also to be seen there in perfection, in the shape of a variety of dirty native women—half-dressed in tawdry European clothes, with a proportionate number of half-caste children.

DR. DAVID MONRO (1813-77)
Nelson Examiner, 1844

"THAT ATROCIOUS COUNTRY"

But what are you doing in the native land of Cockatoos? I can hardly suppose that you are practising the Esculapean art upon the natives, except at times a little bit of vivisection for the sake of keeping in your hand. The colonists by all accounts have as little about them to plunder as so many gutter bloods of the antique High street. Flax won't do, and sheep seem shorn of their value. Are you really serious in remaining in that atrocious country, now that you have tried the merits of the natural against the civilised state, or will you not take second thought and return before your best years have slipped by you like water, and some fine morning the coup de grâce inflicted on your hampan by the blow of a boomerang? I really do think you might do worse. Exile yourself by all means if you are getting an equivalent for it, but if not, you will never persuade me that you are happier in a wooden hovel of New Zealand among the rough, hairy, and

coppercoloured, than you would be here beside the
pianoforte with waxlights above and a Brussels carpet
below, albeit you had just enough silver in your pocket
to afford a eleemosynary oyster before retiring comfortable to roost. Damn independence and freedom
and all that sort of thing! You know very well, now
that you have tried it—don't you?—that these visions
are composed of the entirest gammon, and that sometimes it is more for a man's advantage to submit to
straps and tight boots, than to walk about the jungle
with a patch over his posteriors and a chevelure unconscious of Macbryde! What the devil, man! don't be
ashamed tho' the experiment has not succeeded, and
don't in obstinacy waste any more time in thrashing
out fushionless straw. Stick up handbills, call the
whole colony together, submit your supernumerary
goods and chattels to the venture of Dutch auction, and
come back here, where, heaven be praised, there is still
roast hare and stuffing, and, as this was a decentish year
for the berries, currant jelly also.

PROFESSOR W. E. AYTOUN
in an unpublished letter to
Dr. David (later Sir David) Monro.
From Edinburgh, September 2, 1844

THE NIGHT-WATCH SONG OF THE
"CHARLOTTE JANE"

'Tis the first watch of the night, brothers,
  And the strong wind rides the deep;
And the cold stars shining bright, brothers,
  Their mystic courses keep.
Whilst our ship her path is cleaving
  The flashing waters through,
Here's a health to the land we are leaving,
  And the land we are going to!

First sadly bow the head, brothers,
    In silence o'er the wine,
To the memory of the dead, brothers,
    The fathers of our line.
Though their tombs may not receive us,
    Far o'er the ocean blue,
Their spirits ne'er shall leave us,
    In the land we are going to.

Whilst yet sad memories move us,
    A second cup we'll drain
To the manly hearts that love us
    In our old homes o'er the main.
Fond arms that used to caress us,
    Sweet smiles from eyes of blue,
Lips that no more may bless us,
    In the land we are going to.

But away with sorrow now, brothers,
    Fill the wine-cup to the brim!
Here's to all who'll swear the vow, brothers,
    Of this our midnight hymn:
That each man shall be a brother,
    Who has joined our gallant crew;
That we'll stand by one another
    In the world we are going to!

Fill again, before we part, brothers,
    Fill the deepest draught of all,
To the loved ones of our hearts, brothers,
    Who reward and share our toil.
From husbands and from brothers,
    All honour be their due,—
The noble maids and mothers
    Of the land we are going to!

The wine is at the end, brothers;
    But ere we close our eyes,
Let a silent prayer ascend, brothers,
    For our gallant enterprise—
Should our toil be all unblest, brothers,
    Should ill winds of fortune blow,
May we find God's haven of rest, brothers,
    In the land we are going to.

JAMES EDWARD FITZGERALD (1818-96)

TRIALS OF THE PIONEERS

If the Nelson settlement was born amidst sunshine and laughter, its infancy was surrounded by tears, gloom, and tragedy. The long-expected *Lloyds* arrived on the 15th of February, 1842, a ship of lamentation and woe—65 children thrown overboard—"Rachel mourning for her children and would not be comforted"—and all "the sad tales of that disastrous voyage." The tragedy of the Wairau massacre stunned the infant settlement in June, 1843. Within two years, in March, 1844, the New Zealand Company collapsed, and soon after starvation time began.

From the day they sailed out of the Thames in a small, overcrowded vessel, forced in rough weather to spend days below, cooped in stuffy cabins with the deadlights closed—in pitch darkness save for ill-smelling oil lamps—the long monotonous voyage, especially to women and children, was a prolonged misery. Then, on arrival, the settler found the lands he had paid for were not even surveyed, and after weary waiting, slender savings had been expended, and he found his section a barren hill-side, perhaps 30 miles from Nelson, reached only by an almost impossible track. Many a settler, struggling hopelessly in a strange environment, died of a broken heart, dispirited by the task of scraping

a living for his family from the section he was allotted.
In the "Starving time" children went hungry to bed,
night after night, and never knew what a satisfying
meal was like. Men were glad to work for two shillings
a day. Bread, flour, milk, fresh meat, tea and sugar—
the mere necessities of life—were luxuries seldom tasted
by the majority of settlers. Storekeepers could not get
a bag of flour for their own families, and despairing
settlers dug up the very seed potatoes to feed their
starving children.

At the end of May, 1842, over seventeen hundred
persons were crowded round the town of Nelson and
not an acre of country land had been distributed. It
was not until August 21 that suburban lands were open
for selection, and another season was gone before fern
land could be got ready for sowing or swamp lands
drained. The Wakefield system of colonisation was
blamed, but it was no part of Wakefield's published
theory to send thousands of penniless emigrants where
no one could obtain possession of the land on which
to employ them. "It was," wrote one settler, "all
unfulfilled promises, shuffling procrastination and
hopeless executive incapacity." "Early in March, 1842,"
said Mr. Alfred Saunders, "another calamity was
inflicted on Nelson by the arrival of a man appointed
to nearly all the Government offices. . . . He was
immediately seen to be very eccentric. . . . Many will
remember how he ordered all the settlers off the Government reserves the very day he landed, and cried and
stamped when they refused to go. . . . How he poisoned
his own imported fowls the next morning, and swore
at them for eating poison intended for rats."

Nelson Evening Mail
Oct. 17, 1923

THE TREATY OF WAITANGI
1840

Her Majesty Queen Victoria, Queen of the United Kingdom of Great Britain and Ireland, regarding with Her Royal favour the Native Chiefs and Tribes of New Zealand, and anxious to protect their just Rights and Property, and to secure to them the enjoyment of Peace and Good Order, has deemed it necessary, in consequence of the great number of Her Majesty's Subjects who have already settled in New Zealand, and the rapid extension of Emigration both from Europe and Australia which is still in progress, to constitute and appoint a functionary properly authorised to treat with the Aborigines of New Zealand for the recognition of Her Majesty's Sovereign Authority over the whole or any part of those Islands. Her Majesty, therefore, being desirous to establish a settled form of Civil Government with a view to avert the evil consequences which must result from the absence of the necessary Laws, and Institutions alike to the Native population and to her Subjects, has been graciously pleased to empower and authorise me, William Hobson, a Captain in Her Majesty's Royal Navy, Consul, and Lieutenant-Governor of such parts of New Zealand as may be, or hereafter shall be, ceded to Her Majesty, to invite the confederated and independent Chiefs of New Zealand to concur in the following Articles and Conditions.

Article the First
The Chiefs of the Confederation of the United Tribes of New Zealand and the separate and independent Chiefs who have not become members of the Confederation, cede to Her Majesty the Queen of England, absolutely

and without reservation, all the rights and powers
of Sovereignty which the said Confederation or Individual Chiefs respectively exercise or possess, or may be
supposed to exercise or to possess, over their respective
Territories as the sole Sovereigns thereof.

Article the Second

Her Majesty the Queen of England confirms and
guarantees to the Chiefs and Tribes of New Zealand,
and to the respective families and individuals thereof,
the full, exclusive, and undisturbed possession of their
Lands and Estates, Forests, Fisheries and other properties which they may collectively or individually
possess, so long as it is their wish and desire to retain
the same in their possession; but the Chiefs of the
United Tribes and the Individual Chiefs yield to Her
Majesty the exclusive right of Pre-emption over such
Lands as the proprietors thereof may be disposed to
alienate, at such prices as may be agreed between the
respective proprietors and persons appointed by Her
Majesty to treat with them in that behalf.

Article the Third

In consideration thereof Her Majesty the Queen of
England extends to the Natives of New Zealand Her
Royal protection and imparts to them all the Rights
and Privileges of British subjects.

W. HOBSON
Lieutenant-Governor

Now therefore, we, the Chiefs of the Confederation of
the United Tribes of New Zealand, being assembled in
Congress, at Victoria, in Waitangi, and we, the Separate
and Independent Chiefs of New Zealand, claiming
authority over the Tribes and Territories which are
specified under our respective names, having been made
fully to understand the provisions of the foregoing

Treaty, accept and enter into the same in the full spirit and meaning thereof.

In Witness whereof, we have attached our signatures or marks at the places and dates respectively specified.

Done at Waitangi, this 6th day of February, in the year of our Lord 1840.

(512 signatures follow.)

HOW THE SOUTH WAS SAVED
FOR THE EMPIRE

This poem gives a fanciful account of an incident connected with the French Settlement in 1840 at Akaroa, on Banks' Peninsula, in the South Island. The facts as given by Dr. Keith Sinclair in his *History of New Zealand* are: "Knowing of the French plans for a settlement on Banks' Peninsula, and suspecting that to be the destination of (a French corvette), he (Governor Hobson) instructed the captain of a British ship, H.M.S. *Britomart*, to hurry there in order to consolidate British claims by establishing effective occupation. The British flag had been hoisted when the French gunboat followed immediately by a ship bringing a handful of French colonists, arrived at Akaroa. There was, however, no 'race' to Akaroa, for the French captain had no intention of contesting the British claims." Adams' poem preserves a popular tradition still current among New Zealanders.

The French corvette on a weary wing
Down the quiet waves came fluttering
    To her nest in the bush-rimmed bay.
The waters list to the anchor's kiss,
The cable spun with a gladsome hiss,
And the captain spake, "'Tis a fair land this,
    At the end of our ocean way!"

There were eager eyes that looked from France,
Her huddled Empire to enhance
    By a way in the Southern Sea.

There were vacant islands, free and fair,
That were booty rich for the Powers to share,
And brides for the first adventurer,
   And France to the fore would be. . . .

The British Governor greeting sent—
With a grim smile hid 'neath his kind intent—
   And the captain leapt ashore.
At the Governor's house with friendly zest
They feasted long and drank the best,
And the courteous host and his gallant guest
   A firm-clasped friendship swore!

But the *Britomart* in the bush-rimmed bay
Astrain on her cables waiting lay,
   With her old war-blood aglow.
She had looked contempt with her eye askance
At the trim rigged grace of the ship of France;
And her timbers thrilled for the glorious chance
   That should yield her the throat of the foe!

And Stanley, her captain, lingered yet
And toasted his friend of the French corvette
   Where the revelry rippled high,
But he rose when the riotous night was new,
And strode to the door at a hidden clue;
"I must go," he cried, "I have work to do,"
   And he laughed them a light "Good-bye."

The darkness drowsed on the bay that night,
The *Britomart* lay with never a light.
   And the *Aube* did not see the while
A black shape slip through the quiet tide—
A bird that hovered on pinions wide—
But the British ship was a' wing outside.
   Full flight for the Southern Isle!

The finger of dawn from the far east swept,
And the *Aube* alone in the harbour slept.
　　Her burden a squandered chance!
But her captain laughed with a boastful heart,
"Can our *Aube* not yield to our foe a start?
To-morrow we catch the *Britomart*
　　And win the South for France!"

Then she circled once like a flying thing
And swooped for the South on a silver wing,
　　In her beauty lithe and brave;
Like a swaying bloom to the breeze she bent,
She spurned the spray that the waters sent
And away on a freshening wind she went
　　The honour of France to save!

With the morn she saw on the main afar
Where the *Britomart*, maimed with a broken spar,
　　Fluttered a helpless thing!
And the British faces grimly set
The tricolour's flaunting challenge met,
And they heard, close abreast, from the slim corvette,
　　A roar of triumph ring!

But by sweat and will the wound was healed,
And close in the chase of the *Aube* she reeled,
　　With a crew of fierce hearts manned.
And away through a windy day and night
The two ships sped in their southward flight,
The *Aube* in the van till there leapt in sight
　　The bluff of the longed-for land.

Then, was it skill or a simple chance?
For the fair wind failed the ship of France
　　As she hugged the bluffs too near.

The *Britomart* caught the breeze she lost,
And farther out to the front she crossed,
And she passed the *Aube* at the winning-post
    To the tune of a British cheer!

Like a Queen she triumphed up the bay,
A boat from her davits dropped away
    And sped for an inlet straight.
A staff was raised on the sombre shore,
And a British flag like a flame it bore—
And the South was the Empire's evermore—
    As the *Aube* came up—too late.

                              ARTHUR H. ADAMS (1872-1936)

THE LAY OF THE DIGGER

This is the lay of the digger, the song of the seeker of
        gum,
Sung in a kerosene twilight, to the tune of the kerosene
        drum;
The lay of the sick and the sorry, the men who have
        drawn God's wrath,
Warbled in tent and whare everywhere over the North.

Chorus

The new-chum and the scum,
And the scouring of the slum,
And the lawyer and the doctor and the deaf and halt and dumb,
And the parson and the sailor and the welsher and the whaler,
    When the world is looking glum,
        Just to keep from Kingdom Come
    Take to digging kauri gum.

In the slighted, blighted North, where the giant kauris
      grow,
And the earth is bare and barren where the bush-bee
      used to hum,
When the luck we've followed's failing, and our friends
      are out of hailing,
And it's getting narrow sailing by the rocks of Kingdom
      Come,
There's a way of fighting woe, squaring store bills as
      you go,
    In the trade of digging gum.

Chorus

In the scrubby, grubby North, when the giddy sun is set,
And the idiot-owl cicada drops the whirring of his drum;
When the night is growing thicker and the bottled
      candles flicker,
And the damned mosquitoes bicker in a diabolic hum,
There's a way of ending fret and of pulling down a debt
    In the task of scraping gum.

Chorus

In the sloppy, floppy North, through the dismal winter
      rain,
When the man is merely muscle and the mind is nearly
      numb,
When the old, old pains rheumatic fill the bones from
      base to attic,
And a sound of words erratic sets the pannikins a-thrum,
There's a way of killing Cain and an antidote to pain
    In the task of hooking gum.

Chorus

And the man of law has gambled through another man's
      estate,

And the doctor's special weakness at the present time
is rum,
And the parson loves the clocking on a pretty maiden's
stocking,
And his sermons (mostly shocking) scare the neophyte
new-chum;
By the smouldering tea-tree fire, when the wind is
blowing higher,
They are cracking jokes that blister the Recording
Angel's slate,
And the matters that they mention are too primitive
to state
    At the scraping of the gum.

Chorus

But the new-chum and the scum,
And the scouring of the slum.
And the lawyer and the doctor and the deaf and halt and
dumb,
And the parson and the sailor and the welsher and the
whaler,
When the Day of Judgment's come,
Oh, won't they be looking glum,
And the mighty trumpets thunder and the harps go
tinkle-tum,
And they've finished with the digging and they've scraped
the final crumb,
And the bottom's gone for ever from the trade of kauri gum.

WILLIAM SATCHELL (1860-1942)
The Land of the Lost

A GREAT EXPLORER

In December, 1846, Thomas Brunner left again for the coast with E Kehu, Epikiwati, and their respective wives. The newspapers of the time said he was going to look for a route to Port Cooper[1] from Lake Rotoroa. If he failed to find one he was going to follow the Buller River to the coast and come back over the Alps to Port Cooper. From there he might explore the east-coast rivers, even the Molyneux. He might take five months; he might be back next spring. He was going to live on the country, and it was thought that the expedition was as difficult as any that could be well conceived.

He began by looking for the route south of Rotoroa and, failing to find any, went down the Buller to the sea. For three days they were without food and Brunner had to eat his favourite dog, which in better country would have been an invaluable hunter of birds. For this desperate act the Maoris named him Kai Kuri (dog-eater). Even when he reached the mouth of the Buller he had to worry about food. A sealing party had visited the place and the potato-gardens were empty. However, he reached the Grey and the Tara-makau and waited for the natives to finish work at their gardens. Then he was taken south to the Arahura, to the Hokitika, and to the Wanganui. It was October 1847 by then and he could use flax sandals, walk barefoot, and live on fern roots. He went on to Okarito and had a surfeit of eels. Today the view from here is unsurpassed in New Zealand, and Brunner thought so too. The rata gave a touch of flaming red to the dark bush, and above it were the great peaks of the Alps, rose-red in the morning sun, glistening white at midday, red again at sunset, cold and hard at night.

He still went on, crossing the Waiho at some risk,

[1] See map on page 62.

and yet not mentioning the Franz Josef glacier which
flows down into the bush. Brunner, like Captain Cook,
is notable for this surprising omission. At Tititira Point
he twisted his ankle on the boulders of the beach and
at last turned back to avoid spending another
winter on the coast. Besides he wanted to go up the
Taramakau and over to the Deans at Riccarton, to whom

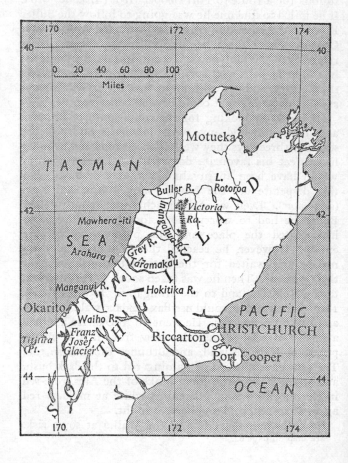

he carried a letter of introduction. When he did get to the Taramakau, no native would take him over the mountains.

Thus to return by a new route he had to go up the Grey river in January, 1848. He named it after the Governor and found a seam of excellent coal. The party, living mostly on eels and white-bait, went up the Mawhera-iti to an easy pass leading into the Inanga-hua. From the watershed he climbed a peak of the Victoria range and thought he saw in the distance the Canterbury plains. This was impossible and fortunately for him the hungry Maoris refused to return that way. They preferred the Inangahua, which led them to the Buller and to food. But even there game was scarce. The weather was bad and Brunner, constantly wet, lost the use of one side of his body. E Kehu and his wife were most loyal, but the other couple left and went ahead eating up the game. Brunner was in agony most of the way, and to fill his cup of sorrow his sketches, specimens, and curios were burnt. At last, on 15th June, 1848, he reached the sheep station in the Motueka, which he had left 560 days before. In all that time he had not heard one word of English save "the broken gibberish of E Kehu and the echo of my own voice."

Thus ended the greatest piece of exploration in the history of New Zealand. Brunner had explored a great part of Westland, found coal, and traced the course of the Grey river. The cost was £33 9s. 4d. He did not think that future exploration would be worth the expense, and did not encourage anyone to complete the unknown section between Tititira Point and Milford Sound.

W. G. McCLYMONT (b. 1905)
The Exploration of New Zealand

THE WAKAMARINA

On the banks of the Wakamarina,
From Nelson some thirty-two miles,
A splendid goldfield's been discovered
Where dozens are making their piles.
They work on the banks of the river,
And in many a crevice I'm told,
With their knives they can pick out the nuggets—
A nice easy way to get gold.

Chorus

I'm waiting for fresh information,
If the field is all there you will see,
I'm off to the golden location,
The Wakamarina for me.

It's affecting the city of Nelson,
Provisions are gone up in price,
And servants and tradesmen have started
To the goldfield, all scorning advice.
Milkmen give their customers warning,
They're leaving their usual walks,
And off to the Wakamarina
Old Skyblue is walking his chalks.

The crews all desert from the vessels,
The skipper on board vainly grieves,
And to help to discharge the ship's cargo,
He has to turn to in shirt sleeves.
Blacksmiths and Bakers get cheeky
When they think of the new golden ground,
And the Butchers are talking of raising
Pleuro to a shilling a pound.

AUCKLAND IN 1858

At the time when J. Bunney painted this impression of Auckland, it had a population of about 3,000 and was the capital and centre of government. In 1851, it had elected the first New Zealand mayor, and in 1852, the first Parliament met there.

MODERN AUCKLAND

his aerial view looks from the North Shore of the Waitemata Harbour the centre of the city and to the populous suburbs beyond. The Harour Bridge, opened in 1959, connects the two sides of the harbour. uckland is New Zealand's largest and fastest growing city.

PARLIAMENT BUILDINGS

The home of New Zealand's legislature, the Parliament Buildings in Wellington, houses the single-chamber parliament of 80 members, including 4 Maori members. Wellington has been the centre of government since 1865.

WELLINGTON

A view of the capital city from Mount Victoria looking towards the wharves and main business area, with the Tinakori Hills on the right. First settled in 1840, it now has a population of over 120,000. The head offices of all government departments and the consular representatives are located here.

The new chums start off for the diggings,
But some of them never get there,
When others arrive and look at it,
One glance sinks them into despair.
No comforts they get in that quarter,
For home again, oh, how they yearn,
They can't stomach working in water,
And they curse it and quickly return. . . .

This rush will soon clear out Otago,
For passenger ships advertise,
And each steamer will bring up a cargo
Of Victorian diggers, no flies;
They're the boys that can drop on the metal,
And when from Dunedin they come,
They'll get all the gold from the river,
And there'll be no chance for a new chum.

CHARLES ROBERT THATCHER (1831-82)

DISCOVERY OF THE MACKENZIE COUNTRY

From a distance the range beyond Fairlie blocks off
the plains with such an air of finality that the squatters
who began to arrive in South Canterbury in 1850
assumed that it was part of the main divide and that
the passes they could see led through to the West Coast.
Not for five years did they discover that beyond the
range lay a great basin some thirty miles long by
twenty broad where sheep could be pastured. The
story of the discovery has become a sort of folk-tale
in Canterbury. In 1855 the land in the Opihi Valley
from the sea inland to the neighbourhood of what
is now Fairlie comprised the great Levels Station, held
by the Rhodes brothers. In March of that year, J. H. C.
Sidebottom, manager of the station, was at the Cave

"paring a sheep's feet" when Seventeen, a Maori shepherd, came to tell him that a man named Mackenzie
had stolen the greater part of his flock. Taking with
him Seventeen and another Maori named Taiko,
Sidebottom set off in pursuit and picked up tracks along
a branch of the Tengawai River.

The rest of the story is told in a letter to his employers.
"Just before sundown we came to the pass to the West
Coast through the Snowy Mountains, and on looking
down a very abrupt hill we saw the sheep and one man
keeping them together. When I got to the flat below,
the man was preparing to turn in for the night. I rode
up and collared him and tied his hands. Being regularly
knocked up, I meant camping for the night, so I laid
down and took a feed of his damper, mutton, tea, and
sugar. Foolishly, I untied his hands, but took his boots
away, thinking three were surely enough for him.
After we had stopped about two hours, we heard some
suspicious calls, the dogs began growling and the
sheep broke camp." Sidebottom then decided to travel
back by night, but ran into mist almost immediately,
and his prisoner escaped. . . .

At the end of his letter to his employers, Sidebottom
noted that "there seemed to be a fine plain just at the
back of Snowy Range and a first-rate pass through
the mountains to it." A month later a Christchurch
paper reported the discovery of "a plain of immense
extent capable of depasturing sheep" beyond the mountains in which Mackenzie had been captured. The first
pastoral lease in the Mackenzie was taken up in the following year; four years later there were eight runs
pasturing 17,500 sheep.

Our Own Country (1948)

THE EARLY DAYS

Comforts were few in eighteen-fifty-five,
They got up at dawn and they had to strive
With element and enemy to keep alive
And were lucky if they lived to woo and wive
    In the early, early days.

O joy was a stubborn and costly boon
To those young lovers on their honeymoon:
They met a flooded river as night came on
And horses and riders were all swept down
    In the early, early days.

We're all sane, but there were madmen then
Like old Sir Thomas Tancred who fired his gun
Through a drawing-room window at a prowling
    man
That was only a sunflower looking in
    In the early, early days.

One captain at sea drank more than he ought
And set his course for the rocks, but they caught
And drugged him though he cursed and fought,
So the ship came safe to Lyttleton port
    In the early, early days.

I've read of a serving Australian black
Who ran from Mount Peel to Ashburton and back
And wanted no wages but a glass of sack.
Poor fellow, he died with a rope round his neck
    In the early, early days.

And where is the equal of Parson Gore
Who pausing once in his sermon swore
He heard a wild pig go past the door
And the whole congregation ran to hunt the boar
    In the early, early days.

The sun was fiercer then on plain and steep,
The rain fell heavier, the snow more deep,
And a house in the wind was a rocking ship.
Now the folk it buffeted are all asleep
        In the early, early days.

History tells us they were hard and bold;
They carved out forests and they dug for gold.
But many died young and some died old
And their passionate hearts are quiet and cold
        In the early, early days.

                                BASIL DOWLING (b. 1910)

MINING ON THE CLUTHA
1862

Meantime the rush had commenced, and the tide of
miners flowing towards Dunstan could not be stemmed.
. . . Work was commenced at once, but for some days
by no other means than the tin dish. Timber was not
to be had, and to illustrate its scarcity, I may mention
one anecdote well known to many who were amongst
the early arrivals there. At Shennan's Station the head
shepherd was a married man, and had then one little
child, a girl, of a few weeks old, and her cradle was
improvised out of a J D K Z gin case. This piece of
furniture took the eye of one of the miners who was
in the house making some purchase of food or what
not, and he immediately bid the sum of £5 for the
cradle. The little occupant was quickly hoisted out,
and the property changed hands at this unusual figure,
and I never heard that the lucky purchaser repented his
bargain. At any spot between Clyde and Cromwell that
winter, where the low waters of the river exposed any
sandy beach, gold could be obtained in considerable
quantities—even with a tin dish the men washed fairly

good returns, but with the aid of a cradle many ounces of gold were obtained for a day's work. The great difficulty was the want of timber to make the cradles, and many strange means were resorted to to supply this want. One adventurous miner, whose ideas of *meum* and *teum* were not in accordance with generally received opinions on the subject, abstracted the door from one of the out-buildings on the Mount Ida station, and carried it over the Raggedy Range on his back to Dunstan, followed by the irate manager, revolver in hand; but the chase had been determined on too late, and the thief and the stolen property were lost in the crowd by the time the proprietor arrived at the young township.

quoted by VINCENT PYKE (1827-94) in
History of the Early Gold Discoveries in Otago

BROWN BONE

Bone in the river bed,
Old bone like a honeycomb,
Brown bone, man bone,
Where do you come from?

I camped in a shingle flat
Beside the loud Rakaia,
And drove my tent pegs in
And built a fire of dry manuka.

I'd bread in the saddlebags
And tea in the black billy,
And enough tobacco to last me
All the way to Gabriel's Gully.

I stretched out like a log
Dreaming of girls and cider,

And Death came like a riding man
With proud hooves of mountain water.

Bone in the river bed,
Old bone cracked by the sun,
Brown bone like a honeycomb,
Don't take it hard, man.

JAMES K. BAXTER (b. 1926)

A TERRIBLE VOYAGE

They had not lived long at Mount Somers before Tripp decided on a visit to England to see his father at Silverton in Devon, and out of that trip sprang another adventure, their voyage back to New Zealand on the barque *Ivanhoe*, in 1864. When the time came for that, the Tripps had three young children, so arrangements were made to carry a live cow on board, and that, as it turned out, was extremely lucky because in no time the passengers found that the Captain was no more than a drunken lout and the ship in a shocking condition. As well as the cow, they carried pigs on board (a large number of them) and these were allowed to camp in the saloon every night. Soon typhoid was raging on board. Of good food there was none and what food there was, was doled out in starvation rations; twenty-eight passengers, for instance, attempted to dine off a sheep's head. Often the men, seeing how little there was at meals for the women and children, would walk away without eating anything—so you can see how lucky an investment that cow must have been. Even so, twenty-five people died on board from fever.

At last, nearly four months after leaving England, New Zealand was sighted, but to everyone's horror the drunken skipper declared Timaru was Lyttleton, and making for it, was going straight on the rocks.

Tripp, knowing the coast and its dangers so well, said that if the Captain wasn't put in irons he'd shoot him there and then. They compromised by drugging him, and as the First Mate was drunk too, the Second Mate took charge. Owing to a sickness on board, the ship was quarantined for three weeks and so terrible was the filth on board that when the Health Officer, Dr. Donald, boarded her at Lyttleton, he had to turn up his trouser cuffs; from stem to stern she was for all the world like an unclean stable. It hardly seems a surprising end to this adventure that the *Ivanhoe's* skipper, Captain Dunn, fell off the pier at Lyttleton while drunk and drowned himself.

DOUGLAS CRESSWELL
Early New Zealand Families

VOGEL'S VISION

The vision of a promised land, never long absent from Vogel's mind, was not exactly an exalted concept. It was a world of carefully planned financial enterprise, of guaranteed loans at cheap rates of interest, with careful provision for eventual amortization—a realist's Utopia where honest worship of cash and credit replace a false lip service to higher ideals. Yet the fiscal manoeuvres he continually contemplated were always the means to an end rather than the end itself. He was neither blind nor unsympathetic to the universal human suffering that cried for redress, but he believed that political reforms were mere palliatives, that to spend time and energy in enacting social legislation was tantamount to putting the cart before the horse. The better state of existence would come of itself through the increase of commerce, the demand for labour and the enhanced circulation of currency. The role of government was to organise prosperity, after which the people might be safely left to their own devices. To regulate the life of a community by rule and law was to inflict upon it superfluous and irritating restraints which might well be dispensed with in a state where ordered prosperity could be expected to produce the same results without coercion. With little confidence in the efficacy of acts of parliament to prevent the abuses of exploitation, he had a naïve faith in figures, an ingenuous belief that the millenium could be arrived at by simple arithmetical calculations, combined with a chronic weakness for overlooking the human factor or the unavoidable margin of error to be encountered in all financial enterprises. Thus he was continually evolving schemes for the welfare of his country which the wealth of his imagination and the magnitude of his vision inclined to render suspect in the eyes of his fellow citizens.

R. M. BURDON (1896-1965)
The Life and Times of Sir Julius Vogel[1]

NEW ZEALAND LIVING IN THE EIGHTIES

The necessities of life, with a few exceptions, are on the contrary dearer in New Zealand than at home, but the out-of-door pleasures of life are *infinitely cheaper*. Small properties of twenty or thirty acres planted, fenced, and laid out in paddocks, orchards, etc., with a good six or seven roomed house, and outbuildings, can be bought for four or five hundred pounds; decent hacks to ride at from seven to ten pounds a piece; and a good second hand five-ton sailing-boat for between twenty and thirty pounds. . . .

[1]Sir Julius Vogel "the first politician in New Zealand whose talents were at all remarkable" (Dr. Keith Sinclair) played a leading part in successive governments in the 1870's.

KAWERAU—A MODERN TIMBER TOWN

Begun in 1955 as a project shared by the N.Z. Government and over-seas capital, the Tasman Pulp and Paper Company, using wood from man-made pine forests, turns out up to 75,000 tons of newsprint annually. The factory is in the background; the township was constructed around the project.

WAIRAKEI POWER STATION

In the Wairakei geothermal region, a steam power station, the second of its kind in the world, was established in 1956 and began in 1958 to produce electric power from subterranean steam. Steam is carried in twenty steel mains having a total length of some 45,000 feet.

THE OCTAGON, DUNEDIN

Founded by Scottish settlers in 1848, Dunedin is the home of New Zealand's first university, established in 1869. Today the city has a population of 105,000. The Octagon is the heart of Dunedin,

In New Zealand it is not necessary to keep up the same style as in the old country—a man is not supposed to keep a wine cellar; he eschews top hats, kid gloves, etc; his dress suit is more likely to deteriorate by moths than by wear; he lives plainly, and dresses so; his clothes which are too shabby for town he can wear out in the country—no one will think him one whit less a gentleman if he appears in trousers patched at the knees. Set dinner parties are not fashionable, though pot luck invitations are. To gentlemen and ladies who cannot enjoy their meal unless it is served *à la Russe*, I say—Stay where you are!—but to those who can enjoy a good plain dinner plainly put on the table, and are contented to drink with it a glass of ale or a cup of tea, the usual colonial beverage, I emphatically cry— Come! this is the country for you. You can also have your town and country house—your horses and your sailing-boat, your fishing and your shooting—and can save money. Ay! and invest it profitably too, if you keep your eyes open.

P. W. BARLOW (1847-90)
Kaipara or Experiences of a Settler in North New Zealand (1889)

STATE CONTROL

In 1890 a new force came into the political field— organised labour. The growth of the cities and of factories in them, the decline of the alluvial and more easily worked gold-fields, and the occupation of the more fertile and accessible lands, all gradually tended to reproduce in the new country old-world industrial conditions. Even the sweating system could be found at work in holes and corners. There need be no surprise, therefore, that the labour problem, when engaging so much of the attention of the civilised world, demanded notice even in New Zealand. There was nothing novel in the notion of extending the functions of the State in the hope of benefiting the community of the less fortunate classes of it. Already in 1890, the State was the largest landowner and receiver of rents, and the largest employer of labour. It owned nearly all the railways and all the telegraphs just as it now owns and manages the cheap, popular and useful system of telephones. It entirely controlled and supported the hospitals and lunatic asylums, which it managed humanely and well. It also, by means of local boards and institutions, controlled the whole charitable aid of the country—a system of outdoor relief in some respects open to criticism. It was the largest trustee, managed the largest life insurance business, did nearly all the conveyancing, and educated more than nine-tenths of the children.

It will thus be seen that the large number of interesting experiments sanctioned by the New Zealand Parliament since 1890 involved few new departures or startling changes of principle. The constitution was democratic; it has simply been made more democratic. The functions of the State were wide; they have been made yet wider.

W. PEMBER REEVES (1857-1932)
The Long White Cloud

RICHARD JOHN SEDDON[1]

Few politicians have been so successful as he in applying the principles of democracy where others were concerned and simultaneously rejecting their application to his own actions. His egalitarian precepts, though never practised in the actual administration of government, were preached with enormous effect. In his day

[1]Prime minister of New Zealand, 1893-1906

New Zealand politics lost what resemblance they had ever had to being the preserve of a privileged class; nor since his death has wealth or social position been anything but a handicap in the political field. The same might also be said of outstanding intellectual attainments. It was neither right nor proper in his view—a view that has never since been wholly rejected—that the common man, whose destiny it was to inherit the earth, should be offended by displays of mental or cultural superiority.

Seddon's patriotism was fervid and genuine but tinged with arrogance, and the vanity of an infant nation fed upon the teaching of an archtype who personified smugness and self-satisfaction no less than energy and self-reliance. God's own country was, presumably, inhabited by people who enjoyed God's special favour. Seddon's statesmanship was guided and governed by a love of humanity. His conduct was dictated by a gregarious instinct which prompted him to mix with crowds on terms of good-fellowship. In the interests of equality and fraternity he abandoned the post of dignity held to be incumbent on a ruler, without loss of prestige or danger of earning popular contempt. The tradition of the commonplace in public life, to which he subscribed and gave countenance, was also a tradition of self-sacrifice, accessibility, and sympathy towards the helpless—a tradition which none of his successors have wished or dared to ignore.

R. M. BURDON (1896-1965)
King Dick

THE NINETIES

I rejoice in the greater freedom women have won, and the franker and friendlier relations that have developed between the sexes, at the removal of certain old conventions, prejudices and inhibitions in everyday life. However, there is always a debit side to progress. Life was pleasanter in some ways. It was quieter and slower. We had more time to stand and stare. Manners may have been too formal at times, but they counted for a great deal. Despite all the legislation since then to improve the lot of the masses, there was far less class feeling, class bitterness, than there was in later years. It was a younger world, which with a bright eye of wonder saw frontiers on every horizon, and believed in the law of progress. Science had got into its stride, but its application to daily life was so limited that I did not use a telephone until I was grown up. The next fifty years, with their motor-cars, their radio, their aeroplanes, and their wars, were to dull that sense of youth and wonder a great deal, even to destroy it and replace it in some minds with cynicism and despair.

So I beg of you not to pity the people of the nineties too much. It is a mistake we often make about the past. We are impressed by its hardships, or what we think of as hardships. Sometimes all that is involved is that people in those days lacked our comforts. Driving through the country with my wife one day, I remarked to her on the enormous convenience of the electricity service in New Zealand. What a change from the days of kerosene lamps and candles! "Yes," she replied, "it used to take one of the family an hour a day to trim and fill the lamps and look after the candles. But the curious thing is that with all the time saved through electricity, and other improvements, we don't seem to have any more leisure." Fifty years ago and farther back, people had resources which many of us lack to-day. Our grandparents did not go about bemoaning their lot; they did their daily jobs and enjoyed life. I think the people of the nineties were at least as happy as those of today, probably happier. They did not carry, visibly, the burden of their woes. In certain pictures that have come from the Left, of a people oppressed and unhappy, it is difficult to recognise one's country.

ALAN MULGAN (1881-1962)
The Making of a New Zealander

GALLIPOLI

The events of the Gallipoli campaign are deeply etched on the memories of an older generation of New Zealanders. These memories are renewed annually by the ceremonies of Anzac Day, which now commemorates also those who fell in other actions in the two world wars. In the desperate struggle to effect a lodgment on the peninsula under heavy artillery bombardment, the allied forces sustained very heavy losses. The landing at Anzac Cove of the Australians and New Zealanders resulted in casualties on a scale which shocked a country which had, with impulsive patriotism, almost eagerly committed itself to the war.

The whole campaign on Gallipoli was difficult. In early August the New Zealanders captured Chunuk Bair, the hill-top dominating the peninsula, in the face of desperate Turkish resistance. The position was held in the face of heavy counter-attack, when the men in the forward trench held out until they were annihilated. The main position had later to be given up. The failure of this supreme effort by the allied forces, in which New Zealand troops had greatly distinguished themselves, led to the abandonment of the whole costly attempt[1] to open a route by the Black Sea to Russia and to disrupt Turkish resistance. . . .

From Gallipoli to the Western Front, from the

[1] Of the 8,556 New Zealanders who served on Gallipoli, 7,447 became casualties.

North African desert to the towns of Palestine, New Zealand troops had proved themselves in the field to be as good as any fighting beside them or against them. It would, however, be wrong not to attribute part of this success to good training. New Zealanders have generally shown themselves to be well disciplined and vigorous. This has enabled them in the field to strike a balance between initiative and steadfastness which has been the foundation of whatever success they have gained.

This high reputation has not been won without cost. In the 1914-18 War, 98,850 New Zealanders served overseas in the expeditionary force; of these, 16,697 lost their lives. In addition, over 4,000 left New Zealand to join other Commonwealth forces. Of the 124,211 men enlisted (including 7,000 who served at home) nearly 100,000 had volunteered. New Zealand enrolled for service overseas more than forty per cent of the male population eligible to serve (twenty to forty-five). Thus the 1914-18 War made a deep impression on New Zealand. Nearly every family had its members in the forces; few were spared the toll of death or wounds. The event of the war stirred the public mind in a way no comparable event had done. While it enhanced the New Zealand sense of nationhood, it also, paradoxically, re-affirmed the ties with Great Britain.

W. P. MORRELL (b. 1899) and D. O. W. HALL
A History of New Zealand Life

UNEMPLOYED ON THE MARCH

On the night of April 14, 1932, a march of unemployed in Auckland, in protest against Government inaction during the depression, culminated in a serious riot and led to severe damage to property in the city's main street. The author of the novel from which the following extract is taken served as a special constable during the period of rioting in Auckland.

In the grimness and tenseness of that mass of men a
new spirit came over them. It was a very silent procession that marched, without bands or songs or
shouting. Johnson going with them felt this change.
He lost the sense of waste and frustration that had been
with him. Instead he felt that he had a part in something. What it was he could not have said, but only
that he was with men who shared his lack of fortune,
who were the same as he was and had the same purpose;
that they were going forward together, where, he
could not say, but only that they were going somewhere
and would be together.

The onlookers who filled the pavements were silent,
too, while they went by. At street corners, and here
and there along the route, there seemed to be a great
many policemen, occasionally mounted, their horses
turning restlessly. When the marchers came to the
open space by the town hall, the advance guard of post
and telegraph workers had gone inside. The unemployed
who followed them were being held up at the door. As
more and more marching men pressed up behind them,
the square became packed, and the silence that had
been with them seemed to break ominously. There
was a kind of murmured shouting and excitement that
ran down the street and through the watching crowds
as if they felt, not that anything was happening, but
that something must. After the march, which had been
a beginning, to be held in check like this made men
angry: they shared between them an anger that was
overwhelming.

Johnson fighting for a place in this press saw a
mounted policeman on a great white horse trying to
hold his ground at the head of the street. Not far from
him, in the centre of the crowd where the street lamps
were shining, he could see a man addressing the unemployed marchers, held up on their shoulders, his cap
pulled up and waving in the air, the light shining on

his sweating face. The tide moved round and round him like a broken tide-rip. . . .

Some men were still going into the hall, but the police were holding the unemployed back and the little man held up on their shoulders was still talking. Then two policemen went in towards him to try and stop him and there was a surge just as if the wave had spilled over and was rolling up the shore. Johnson saw a baton go up and an arm raised and the little man go down with a blow on the side of the head, and then at once men seemed to know where they were going. . . . It was a wild business, like a dream in which no one seemed real any longer. Across the road men were stripping palings from the fence of a church to fight with and from the side streets they were gathering stones. The white horse of the mounted policeman reared up as it was struck, unseating him so that he fell into the mob and was lost to sight. Johnson saw the police go back or down; two that were near him were driven back and one fell against a shop wall, hit with a stone that drew blood. . . .

After that the shop-windows began to go, first with the stones and then with a long rake of the fence palings. The fight turned from the hall, no longer a fight, and the men who led it went back down the main street with their palings. They had tried to enter the hall and had been stopped. Now they no longer wanted to go inside. They were outside in the streets and had won their fight and were free from restraint. They were the swift runners and the leaders who went first and broke everything they saw without caring. To them it was the release of accumulated desire, a payment for the long weeks and months of monotony and weariness and poverty and anxiety that could be satisfied like this in a few moments of freedom and destruction.

JOHN MULGAN (1911-45)
Man Alone

AT ALAMEIN

The barrage still shattered the night. The assault troops had moved forward long since. Support Group were given the order to move. The long slow crawl forward—nose to tail—losing the vehicle ahead in the dust—the gap in the minefield, cleared by New Zealand sappers—the wrecked Scorpion blocking the cleared track. The long hours—barrage still thundered—D.A.K. (*Deutsch Afrika Korps*) and Italians spat back fitfully. The sky lightening as dawn broke, and just as it became light the sudden activity as Support Group were diverted to the right and through the gap cleared for 51st Highland Division.

Trucks and carriers trailed through the dust of the gap, swung left again, and raced across the front in daylight. Jerry threw everything at them, they should have been a perfect target—a gunner's dream. Then into the comparative shelter of a ridge. "No. 1 gun here." "No. 2 there." and so on. Our long training stood us in good stead as ramps were flung into position—guns eased into the ramp—wheels locked into position—ramps stowed away—ammunition off—and away went the parties.

"Dig in", "Just a minute, we'll have to change your position", "Pack up again", "Can't they ever make up their . . . minds?" A jeep draws up—the gun is hooked on—a few boxes of ammunition flung aboard—shovels and picks—and away goes the gun and two men. Two more walk across carrying rifles and bren—the fifth man stacks up the gear left behind and makes his own way. The shells still scream over, odd ones coming close.

The new position is about 20—30 yards back from the ridge facing a break—just a shallow depression

breaking the line of the ridge. By no means a good
anti-tank site, but our tanks haven't come up (they
never do) and that gap must be covered. It's a one shot
position—either you get him in the belly as he breasts
the rise or—you've had it. Hope he doesn't set hull
down and stick his gun through, but he couldn't do
that—on a slope the other side—couldn't depress his
gun sufficiently—we hope. Dig, dig, dig.

No. 4 plods back and forth. A box of ammunition and a pick—another box of ammunition and the
cleaning rod—and so it goes on.

"Here come the tanks."

Looking back they can see clouds of dust and occasional
glimpses of tanks through the dust. One or two draw
up close and sit hull down behind the ridge. Someone
yells, "Hell, look at that!" A long line of tanks breaks
through the gloom. One, two, three—no use trying
to count them as they appear and vanish in the gathering
dust.

"They can't be ours. Too many of them." To old
desert digs who have waited so often in vain for our
tanks to arrive it seemed too good to be true. But it
is true, and they are ours—an endless stream pulling
in to form a wall of steel along the ridge where a short
time before a lone two-pounder crew weighed up their
chances of a lucky belly shot as the first German tank
came over the ridge and then—curtains.

B. A. COX
reported in *Twenty-Second Battalion* by
JIM HENDERSON (b. 1918)

Places

NEW ZEALAND

The great Pacific salt so steeps our air
That noon-tide burns it to a driftwood blue
Such skies are passion to a lark upflown,
As if a hemisphere of harebells caught,
Clapper to clapper running silver fire.
The lovely conflagration dies in dew,
Such dew as only rivered lands beget
Where air lies long with heavy, crystal streams
As clear as are the firths of Paradise.
Our midnight stretches a tremendous targe,
Transfixed with planets, each a golden boss,
Among the lesser nail-heads of the stars.
Within the northern island here and there
Are burning hills that smoulder, sulk and brood,
Great fireseeds furious for shoots of flame;
But farther down an alp-line, calm and cold,
Looks southward to the mountains of the pole
That lean like gods with comets in their slings
Lancing auroras in the whistling air.
And we have birds, Atlantic birds and ours,
So that at once from out the self-same tree
Can come an anthem and a karakia;
And birds that think in oceans come and go,
Their chart behind their eyes that scarcely sleep
To find the Southern Cross beyond the Bear.
Our flowers are pale, the mock of pander bees,
Save those red trees that put forth such a blaze
The very Tasman could not put it out
When summer strikes the tinder of their boughs.
We call this country ours—but who can hold
Such youth transcendent, unassailable,

Like a great moment or a flashing glance?
Go free, my land, we are content to be
The commoners of such a valiancy.

                                        EILEEN DUGGAN

IN THE COTSWOLDS

Yes, it is beautiful, this old, old land:
These houses root their being in the earth,
These walls, these stones, share in a larger birth
With strong-set trees and painted blades that
        stand
About the slopes, the russet furrows, and
Join in the deep impulse that through the girth
Of hill and valley's limits, moulds its worth—
So meet for love, to hold within the hand!

I tread these roads, and know once more the race
Of blood, the tissue's balance with the bones;
A wind strikes—and my opened eyes are blind
With gazing on an unseen distant place;
My deaf ears hear Orongo-rongo's stones—
Bloom bursts on wind-swept hills within my
        mind.

                              J. C. BEAGLEHOLE (b. 1901)

A LAND OF FATNESS

It is a land of unusual beauty; unusual because in a
little compass it may show pastoral grace and mountain
grandeur, rivers winding through deep woods, and
long white beaches—and because the general aspect
has so little to spoil it. There are no large scenes of

industrial squalor, no excess of human ugliness, and the rural view is hardly ever less than pleasing. There is, in the North Island, a sterile heath which is called, ostentatiously, a desert, and about Rotorua are upland moors which under rain-clouds wear a sombre hue; but they lend a difference to the scene, they please by contrast, and make the incredible green pastures under their myriad sheep seem all the brighter. Much of the rural scene is hand-made, smoothed and coloured by hand, for the native bush that covered it a hundred years ago was rough and dark. And the houses of the inhabitants are small and trim and tidy, surrounded by careful gardens; evidence, beyond doubting, of prosperity, of a thoroughly domesticated way of life, of respectability. . . .

The tawny uplands of the south, rising tumultuously under miles of tussock-grass to a desolate grandeur like the third act of *King Lear*: and the deep black water of Lake Manapouri under mountains freaked with snow. A public garden, clouded with cherry-trees in bloom through which the grass-clear Avon meandered, and somewhere, beyond a hedge of wild lilies, a flotilla of black swans sailing. Black swans again, an elegant great fleet of them, on a windy lake where I caught a good trout. The rushing, tumultuous little Otopiri River, and a cliff near Dunedin where a dozen most exquisitely groomed and sublimely solemn penguins clowned on slippery paths. The placid small towns of Hamilton and Cambridge and the majestic sides of Ruapehu. Alpine heights with frosty lances impaled the sky, and wild horses bolted across a moor. Cowmen, roughly mounted, gathered their herds on steep hillsides, and in snug houses—the domestic theme insistently occurs—women vied with their neighbours to whip a stiffer, richer cream. It is a land of fatness, and in white silks and muslins fatness decorates, in every town, the photographers' shop-windows. Wedding groups

abound, and, oh, what brides and bridesmaids broadly
smile beyond the glass.

ERIC LINKLATER (b. 1899)
A Year of Space

SPRING FIRES

The running rings of fire on the Canterbury hills,
    Running, ringing, dying at the border of the snow!
Mad, young, seeking, as a young thing wills,
    The ever, ever-living, ever-buried Long Ago!

The slow running fire on the Canterbury hills,
    Swinging low the censer of a tender heathenesse
To the dim Earth goddesses that quicken all the thrills,
    When the heart's wine of August is dripping from the
       press!

The quiet bloom of haze on the Canterbury hills!
    The fire, it is the moth that is winging to the snow,
Oh, pure red moth, but the sweet white kills.
    And we thrill again to watch you, but we know, but
       we know!

The long yellow spurs on the Canterbury hills
    To a moon of maiden promise waken once in all the
       year,
When the fires come again and the little tui trills,
    And who will name or think upon a January sere?

The lone, large flower of the Canterbury hills
    On the slender ti-tree will hang her honeyed head
When the moon of fire has called her to the spurs and
       the rills,
    Dim and strong and typical of tintless river-bed.

The scent of burning tussock on the Canterbury hills,
  The richness and the mystery that waken like a lyre
With the dearness of a dreaming that never yet fulfils!—
  And we know it, and we know it, but we love the
    moon of fire!

JESSIE MACKAY (1864-1938)

EARLY AUCKLAND

In the dim misty greyness of early morn we crept past
the towering bulk of Rangitoto, the giant sentinel that
guards Auckland harbour, and all hands hurried on
deck to get the first glimpse of the far-famed panorama
of beauty that lay stretched before us. This renowned
harbour ranks in order and loveliness among the "most
excellent of the earth." "See Naples and die," is an oft
quoted saying. Rio has its worshippers. Peerless
Sydney has her liege votaries, whose ardent homage
none can quench—and yet, in many respects, Auckland
harbour has a beauty of its own, which in some measure
exceeds that of any other spot of earth I have yet seen.

Its charm seems to me to lie in its wide diversity, the
vastness of its extended embrace. Every charm of
landscape blends together into one magnificent whole.
Open sea, land-locked bay, deep firth, rocky islet, placid
expanse of unruffled deep blue, cloud-capped mountain,
wooded height, bosky dell, villa-crowned ridges, and
terrace on terrace of massive buildings, all can be seen
by a single roving glance from whatever coign of
vantage the beholder may command. For league upon
league the eye may run down the ever-varying con-
figurations of a beautiful coast, the promontories
reflected in the lapping waters of magnificent bays, till
far out to seaward the Coromandel headlands lie
shimmering in the sun, crowned with fleecy clouds,
and almost hidden in the misty haze of distance.

Out towards the open sea, the watery void is broken
up and relieved by lovely mountainous islands, round
whose wooded summits the quick changing clouds chase
each other in bewildering rapidity; and ever and anon
white sails flash across the ken of vision, or trailing
lines of black smoke from some swift steamer mar for
a moment the clear brilliancy of the azure sky. The
cloudless blue of the Australian sky has here given
place to the exquisite variety of ever changing hue and
form.

HON. JAMES INGLIS
Our New Zealand Cousins (1887)

AUCKLAND—ANOTHER VIEW

This city is the most populous (in its suburbs) and the
most northerly in New Zealand. It lies on a narrow
isthmus, and is so surrounded by inlets and islands it
is rather part of an archipelago, with an ocean climate,
than part of the mainland. Its situation is remarkable
from the craters of many small extinct volcanoes which
project above parts of the city like grassy acropoli. Its
people are grasping in business, destructive and wanton
in Nature, dishonest in dealing, and dissolute in their
lives, but delightful to know, lavish and open with
strangers, loving indulgence and pleasure, and more
acclimatized than the New Zealanders elsewhere, with
whom they have little in common except a long line
of railway and a wrangling assembly. But who they
are or what they intend they have never made known.

WALTER D'ARCY CRESSWELL (1896-1960)
Present Without Leave

THE FOX GLACIER

The Fox Glacier in the Southern Alps is a river of ice nine miles long, which falls some 9,000 feet and moves several feet a day. The terminal of the glacier is only 670 feet above sea level, the lowest outside the polar regions.

JERUSALEM

The Wanganui River, "the Rhine of New Zealand," is one of the most picturesque in the land and was an ancient area of Maori settlement. The picture shows Jerusalem, an early Catholic mission centre on the banks of the river.

THE AVON RIVER, CHRISTCHURCH

Named nostalgically by the English settlers of the Canterbury province of the South Island in 1850, the River Avon is one of the attractions of the Garden City of Christchurch. Here canoes busily ply the river while nurses and patients from the nearby City Hospital relax on the bank.

THE LONG HARBOUR
AKAROA

There are three valleys where the warm sun lingers,
gathered to a green hill girt-about anchorage,
and gently, gently, at the cobbled margin
of fire-formed, time-smoothed, ocean-moulded curvature
a spent tide fingers the graven boulders,
the black, sea-bevelled stones.

The fugitive hours, in those sun-loved valleys,
implacable hours, their golden-wheeled chariots'
inaudible passage check, and slacken
their restless teams' perpetual galloping;
and browsing, peaceable sheep and cattle
gaze as they pause by the way.

Grass springs sweet where once thick forest
gripped vales by fire and axe freed to pasturage;
but flame and blade have spared the folding gullies,
and there, still, the shade-flitting, honey-sipping
    lutanists
copy the dropping of tree-cool waters
dripping from stone to stone.

White hawthorn hedge from old, remembered England,
and orchard white, and whiter bridal clematis
the bush-bequeathed, conspire to strew the valleys
in tender spring, and blackbird, happy colonist,
and blacker, sweeter-fluted tui echo
either the other's song.

From far, palm-feathery, ocean-spattered islands
there rowed hither dark and daring voyagers;
and Norseman, Gaul, the Briton and the German
sailed hither singing; all these hardy venturers
they desired a home, and have taken their rest there,
and their songs are lost on the wind.

I have walked here with my love in the early spring-
        time,
and under the summer-dark walnut-avenues,
and played with the children, and waited with the aged
by the quayside, and listened alone where the manukas
sighing, windswept, and sea-answering pine-groves
garrison the burial-ground.

It should be very easy to lie down and sleep there
in that sequestered hillside ossuary,
beneath a billowy, sun-caressed grass-knoll,
beside those dauntless, tempest-braving ancestresses
who pillowed there so gladly, gnarled hands folded,
their tired, afore-translated bones.

It would not be a hard thing to wake up one morning
to the sound of bird-song in scarce-stirring willow-trees,
waves lapping, oars plashing, chains running slowly,
and faint voices calling across the harbour;
to embark at dawn, following the old forefathers,
to put forth at daybreak for some lovelier,
still undiscovered shore.

                              MARY URSULA BETHELL (1874-1945)

THE NEW ZEALAND FOREST

The luxuriant beauty of the New Zealand forests almost
equals that of the tropics, indeed the presence of the
graceful fern-trees, and elegant nikau palms, gives them

quite a tropical aspect. There is scarcely a bare stem to
be seen, even the tallest are embraced by a variety of
twining plants, parasites and creepers, amongst which
the *kia-kia*, decked at every joint with bunches of iris-
shaped leaves, and the *mangamanga*, a creeping fern,
are the most conspicuous; the *kareo*, also, forming a
network of cane-like stems, hangs its bunches of glossy
leaves pendant from every bough, and many others
of equal beauty join to form a verdant arch, midway
between the spreading branches of the noble trees to
which they cling. Each decaying trunk is covered with
mosses and lichens of the richest hues, while a perfect
shrubbery of lesser trees, among which the beautiful
laurel-shaped *karaka* is prominent, fills up every otherwise
vacant space, and an endless variety of the most delicate
forms cover the ground. This constant succession of
beautiful objects repays the toil of progress, which is
both slow and painful, for the roots of the trees being
chiefly horizontal, form a hard and slippery network,
over which it requires the utmost patience and caution
to pass without falling, and is certainly the most
inconvenient road I ever travelled. Besides, the trunks
of fallen trees continually cross the road, over which,
if low enough, it is necessary to clamber, and under
which, if too high, to creep, while the pointed branches
and tough stems of the creepers, unless a sharp eye is
kept on these obstacles, bring one up, as sailors say,
"all standing", with a jerk that is far from being
pleasant.

DR. JOHN JOHNSON[1] (1794-1848)
Journal of a Journey to the Central Lakes, 1846-7

[1] Dr. John Johnson was New Zealand's first colonial-surgeon,
appointed to assist Lieutenant-Governor Hobson in 1840.

THE PASSING OF THE FOREST

All glory cannot vanish from the hills,
  Their strength remains, their stature of command,
Their flush of colour when calm evening stills
  Day's clamour, and the sea-breeze cools the land.
Refreshed when rain-clouds swell a thousand rills,
  Ancient of days in green old age they stand
In grandeur that can never know decay,
Though from their flanks men strip the woods away.

But thin their vesture now—the restless grass,
  Bending and dancing as the breeze goes by,
Catching quick gleams and cloudy shapes that pass,
  As shallow seas reflect a wind-stirred sky.
Ah! nobler far their forest raiment was
  From crown to feet that clothed them royally,
Shielding their mysteries from the glare of day,
Ere the dark woods were reft and torn away.

Well may these plundered and insulted kings,
  Stripped of their robes, despoiled, uncloaked, dis-
    crowned,
Draw down the clouds with white enfolding wings,
  And soft aerial fleece to wrap them round,
To hide the scars that every season brings,
  The fire's black smirch, the landscape's gaping wound;
Well may they shroud their heads in mantle grey,
Since from their brows the leaves were plucked away.

Gone is the forest world, its wealth of life,
  Its jostling, crowding, thrusting, struggling race,
Creeper with creeper, bush with bush at strife
  Warring and wrestling for a breathing space;

Below, a realm with tangled rankness rife,
    Aloft, tree columns, shafts of stateliest grace.
Gone is the forest nation. None might stay;
Giant and dwarf alike have passed away.

Gone are the forest birds, arboreal things,
    Eaters of honey, honey-sweet of song,
The tui and the bell-bird—he who sings
    That brief, rich music we would fain prolong.
Gone the wood-pigeon's sudden whirr of wings;
    The daring robin, all unused to wrong.
Wild, harmless, hamadryad creatures, they
Lived with their trees, and died, and passed away.

And with the birds the flowers, too, are gone
    That bloomed aloft, ethereal, stars of light,
The clematis, the kowhai like ripe corn,
    Russet, though all the hills in green were dight;
The rata, draining from its tree forlorn
    Rich life-blood for its crimson blossoms bright,
Red glory of the gorges—well-a-day!
Fled is that splendour, dead and passed away.

Lost is the scent of resinous, sharp pines;
    Of wood fresh cut, clean-smelling, for the hearth;
Of smoke from burning logs, in wavering lines
    Softening the air with blue; of cool, damp earth
And dead trunks fallen among coiling vines,
    Brown, mouldering, moss-coated. Round the girth
Of the green land the winds brought hill and bay
Fragrance far-borne, now faded all away.

Lost is the scene of noiseless, sweet escape
    From dust of stony plains, from sun and gale,
When the feet tread where shade and silence drape
    The stems with peace beneath the leafy veil,

Or where a pleasant rustling stirs each shape
   Creeping with whisperings that rise and fail
Through labyrinths half-lit by chequered play
Of light on golden moss now burned away.

Gone are the forest tracks, where oft we rode
   Under the silver fern-fronds climbing slow,
In cool, green tunnels, though fierce noontide glowed
   And glittered on the tree-tops far below.
There, 'mid the stillness of the mountain road,
   We just could hear the valley river flow,
Whose voice through many a windless summer day
Haunted the silent woods, now passed away.

Drinking fresh odours, spicy wafts that blew,
   We watched the glassy, quivering air asleep,
Midway between tall cliffs that taller grew
   Above the unseen torrent calling deep;
Till, like a sword, cleaving the foliage through,
   The waterfall flashed foaming down the steep,
White, living water, cooling with its spray
Dense plumes of fragile fern, now scorched away.

Keen is the axe, the rushing fire streams bright,
   Clear, beautiful, and fierce it speeds for Man,
The Master, set to change and stern to smite,
   Bronzed pioneer of nations. Ay, but scan
The ruined beauty wasted in a night,
   The blackened wonder God alone could plan,
And builds not twice! A bitter price to pay
Is this for progress—beauty swept away.

                    WILLIAM PEMBER REEVES (1857-1932)

THE LIMESTONE CAVE

The portal was some ten feet in width at the base,
narrowing as it extended upwards until, at twenty
feet above the ledge, it became a mere crack. A yard or
so above this was an opening, more or less in outline,
over which no creepers grew. It was plainly visible
inside, resembling the rose window of a cathedral and
illuminating the cavern, which must else, owing to the
thick curtain of greenery, have remained in total
darkness. Though I have often, from various points
on the river and its banks, endeavoured to catch a view
of the window in the cliff, I never succeeded, and I
doubt if, in fact, it would be possible to do so.

Had Nature intended at once to reveal and conceal
the wondrous work with which she had amused herself
for thousands and even tens of thousands of years, she
could not have selected a better spot than that in which
she had placed the opening, whereby the glories of the
cavern were displayed to our awed and enchanted
vision. From the impenetrable obscurity of the roof,
far overhead, huge stalactites flashed into the light,
while beneath them, like sheeted ghosts, the stalagmites
rose from the cavern floor. Of all sizes and the most
fantastic shapes, they gleamed around us, as though the
spirits of the dead, summoned from their long sleep,
were bursting the chrysalis of the tomb. Here the curve
of an arm seemed to develop and thrust aside its covering
through some distorting veil. The suggestion of something human in the figures was everywhere. The
spacious cavern might have been the workroom of a
sculptor who had dimly conceived humanity and sought
to fashion from a knowledge of human history the
physical characteristics of a being his eyes had never
seen. Pain and passion and adoration, sin that writhed

and horror that transfixed, the tragedy—yes, and the comedy of humanity struggled for expression in the glittering stone. Nor did the perception of this aspect of the cavern make a heavy call on the imagination. Vanishing on minute examination of the isolated growths, it blazed forth in astonishing strength as the eye swept the scene and took in the solitary figures, the singular groups, gaining in force as they receded into the distance where the light failed.

It was, then, to me, no matter for surprise when Rangiora, after taking a few steps forward, stood rooted to the floor, looking around him with perplexed and fearful eyes. "*Kehua* (ghosts)", he muttered under his breath.

Puhi-Huia, in whom use had inspired confidence, was moving calmly forward, when the young chief caught her by the arm. "Wait, Curly One", he whispered. "These are things of evil. It is well that we disarm them by an offering of cooked food. Stay you behind, and the Little Finger and I will undertake the matter."

"They are but stones," said I doubtfully, for his air of confident knowledge, and the distrust he showed, impressed me in spite of the better information I possessed. "Water drips from the roof and builds up the stone."

"How shall water build up stone, foolish one?" he replied. "Rather will it wear it away till the rock becomes but sand. These are *kehua*, though of a form unknown to our wizards. Let us, then, offer them cooked food, and they will disappear."

WILLIAM SATCHELL (1860-1942)
The Greenstone Door

FOX GLACIER ICE

Climbers on the Fox Glacier pause to investigate one of the numerous crevasses that mark this mighty torrent of ice.

THE WAR MEMORIAL MUSEUM, AUCKLAND

Built in classic style, the War Memorial Museum was originally erected to commemorate the fallen of World War I, and was extended after World War II by public subscription. It contains one of the finest Polynesian collections and relics of the various wars in which New Zealanders have fought.

MILFORD SOUND IN THE WINTER

An outstanding scenic attraction, Milford Sound is located on the West coast of the South Island. On the left is Mitre Peak (5,560 feet). The South Island sounds vary in length from ten to thirty miles, and near their heads are as deep as 300 fathoms.

ANGLING AT MISSION POINT, LAKE TAUPO

Lake Taupo ranks among the best trout-fishing centres in the world. Some 500 tons of trout are fished here each year. Regulations demand that all under fourteen inches be thrown back; brown trout up to thirty pounds and rainbow up to twenty-five pounds have been caught.

THE RIVER AVON

Fies nobilium tu quoque fontium—HORACE

I love thee, Avon! though thy banks have known
　No deed of note, thy wand'ring course along
　No bard of Avon hath poured forth in song
Thy tuneful praise; thy modest tide hath flown
For ages on, unheeded and alone.
　I love thee for thy English name, but more
　Because my countrymen along thy shore
Have made new homes. Therefore not all unknown
　Henceforth thy streams shall flow. A little while
Shall see thy wastes grow lovely. Not in vain
　Shall England's sons dwell by thee many a mile.
With verdant meads and fields of waving grain
　Thy rough, uncultured banks ere long shall smile;
Heaven-pointing spires shall beautify thy plain.

HENRY JACOBS (1824-1901)

OTAGO IN THE 1860's

The reader who is unable to draw upon memory and
personal experience cannot possibly conceive more than
a very faint idea of the absolute solitariness which in
those days pervaded and enveloped the Interior of
Otago—the solemn loneliness of its mountains; the
ineffable sadness of its valleys; the utter dreariness of
its plains. The weary traveller pursued his lonely way
from point to point, always viewing around him a
continuous and apparently interminable expanse of
lofty hills—range succeeding range in monotonous
uniformity, everywhere clothed in a sober livery of pale
brown vegetation, relieved only by grim, grey rocks

B.N.Z.   D

of fantastic form, sharing the desolation to which they contributed—backed by distant mountain peaks, which bounded and encompassed the horizon in every direction, piercing the blue ether, and clad in dazzling snows— an expanse diversified by no pleasant forests; devoid of animal as of human life; where the profound stillness was painful in its prolonged intensity; and the only sound that greeted the ear from dawn to dusk was the melancholy wailing of the wind among the tussocks.

VINCENT PYKE (1827-94)
History of the Early Gold Discoveries in Otago

THERE'S NAE PLACE
LIKE OUR AIN FIRESIDE

There's nae place like ane's ain fireside,
    In humble cot or ha';
There's nae thing like ane's ain fireside
    When frosty winds do blaw.
Nae place can warm the heart sae weel,
    If peace and love preside;
It's there a man feels like a man,
    Wi' a' a father's pride.

When heavy toil our body racks,
    And weary banes are sair,
What better place to seek solace
    Than in his ain arm-chair?
The youngsters playing roun' about,
    His wife sae kind and braw,
Compared wi' this I ken nae scene
    Can be compared ava.

'Tis worthy of the poet's pen,
    As well's the painter's brush,
The humble cot, the curling smoke
    Within the fragrant bush;

The burnie wimpling by the door,
    Its pebbly bed sae clear,
The feathered throng wi' mony a song,
    Gies music to the ear.

Otago boasts her valleys green,
    Her hills and fertile plains,
Where scenes like this are often seen,
    Spread o'er her wide domains;
Where happy hearts make happy homes,
    Where plenty reigns supreme,
'Tis worthy of the painter's eye,
    And of the poet's theme.

JOHN BARR (1809-1889)
Poems and Songs, Descriptive and Satirical

THE PINK AND WHITE TERRACES

The Pink and White Terraces, of silica formation, were destroyed by
the eruption of Mount Tarawera in 1886.

The eye is at once turned on the terraces, that on the
left, and the nearest, Te Tarata, being the chief object
of admiration, as Otu Kapurangi, the pink terrace, is
scarcely visible from this spot. Imagine a shelving
slope descending gradually to the margin of the lake
in an uneven series of steps for some hundred and
fifty feet, bounded on each side by low scrub-bush, and
culminating at the top in an open crater, whence rolls
out cloud after cloud of white steam. The steps appear
from the height to be now white and now purple,
contrasting strongly with the azure hues of the basins,
and glistening under the hot sun whose rays dance on
the thin films of water constantly trickling down. At
irregular intervals on the grades are pools;—pools!
the word is a profanation; they are alabaster basins

filled with molten silver, blue as the vault of heaven, over whose gracefully-recurved lips pours down with a gentle murmur a never ceasing flow derived from the boiling contents of the crater above. The more we gazed upon the scene, the more difficult it was to realise it, till at length one bold attempt was made at comparison, and H— exclaimed that this must be the abode of the Queen of the Naiads as it would be depicted by Grieve and Telbin in a transformation scene. To reach the Tarata we had to wade across the stream and then we found ourselves on a ripple-marked surface which crunched under every footstep just as if we were walking on so much sugar, and which on the margin of the pools lost its roughness and became as smooth as marble. These reservoirs, situated for the most part at the edge of the steps of this gigantic staircase, and resembling in the recurved shape of their rims the basins of the flower-vases in the transept of the Crystal Palace, contained luke-warm water; but each successive upward step as the terraces rose tier above tier increased the temperature as the distance decreased from the parent fountain. About halfway up we reached the first really comfortable bathing place, and after undressing, we began to have a dim idea of the comforts of a pilgrimage with peas—unboiled—in one's boots. The spiculae played the very mischief with our feet as we gingerly took the few paces intervening between our clothes and the bath, but then came such a header! Down we went into the liquid blue mirror, piercing, as it were, through different strata of warmth, the water getting cooler and cooler the nearer we sank to the bottom, and then we rose and swam round and round, each bather's limbs looking through the intervening medium blue as Marryatt's chalcedony statues in *The Pacha of Many Tales;* then we sat in turns on a convenient ledge sticking out some two feet under water, and smoked; but the sitting down part of the business had to be done with

caution, for, if any hurry was displayed, the cuticle
was bound to suffer. The pipe finished, came another
header and swim; then the water was voted cold, and
all very gingerly and tiptoedly made their way to a
higher terrace, and yet to a higher, till we ended by
standing in a row beneath the projecting lip of a basin,
and receiving a shower bath at a temperature which,
if indulged in at first, would have been simply scalding.
It was glorious, but slightly enervating; so we dressed
and went on to the crater itself.

LIEUT. J. H. H. ST. JOHN (1836-76)
Pakeha Rambles Through Maori Lands

SETTLEMENT

Remembering the general store, post-office above
And match-box church below, the bridged stream
Speaking the sun's mood in supercilious whispers,
Or the moon's incandescence when eels click,
I wonder at fascination preserved in memory.

In this image returning to mind the wind whispers
To pine-belts, whistles in the wires of time above,
Or plays with smoke where cattle-trains clatter and click
On the track, and passengers, each carrying a memory,
Turn the blank walls of their eyes to the laughing stream.

Here a past stopping-place where I drank at the stream,
And the present is cleansed by the cool draught of
    memory.
The roads in brief embrace of dust, above
The field where a long-distant past whispers
Among the stumps in the remembered echoing click

Of the axe, are the cross of more recent memory
That the old farmer speaks of, though his teeth click
In his head, and his words are a difficult stream
In a youthful land, under storm-clouds of age above.
How much of this scene has changed?—Its pattern
       whispers

As if preserved from time and the machine's click
It is to remain for ever, hearing grasses whisper
And milk cans clatter, so that all memory
In each generation shall include the symbol stream,
The bush on distant hills, and the warm sun above.

                                        C. K. STEAD (b. 1932)

MILFORD SOUND

There is nothing on the North Sea half so magnificent.
For more than an hour you see a deep blue band on the
horizon, exactly ahead; this band grows wider and
wider, and at last you make out its serrated upper edge,
and see that it is a lofty chain of mountains. The vessel
approaches at full speed; gradually the lower portion
of the band becomes brown and green instead of blue,
and the rugged outlines grow more distinct. While
some of the mountains are bare, and seem to fall verti-
cally into the sea, others are only a trifle less steep, and
clothed to the height of many thousand feet with the
most luxuriant vegetation. Soon the steamer appears
to be close under the cliffs; but she still holds her
course, though no inlet appears, no opening by which
that great wall will admit her. At last, when the more
timid of the passengers fancy she must be touching the
rocks, a gap appears on the starboard bow—a gap so
narrow that it might only suffice for a mountain
torrent. But the height of the mountains is so great
that the steamer seems to be much nearer to their foot

than she really is. The helm is ported slightly, and the *Mararoa* enters an opening, of which you may form some idea if you remember the narrows of Dartmouth Harbour, and multiply the height of the hills on either side by twenty, leaving the width of the waterway as it is. The vegetation of South Devon is luxuriant, but the black birches, silver pines, and splendid tree-ferns, which seem to hang on the sides of the Milford Sound Mountains rather than to grow on them, far surpass even the vegetation of Mount Edgecumbe. One huge rock, of which the summit towers right over our foremast, falls sheer into the sea, offering no foothold even to the bold trees of New Zealand. This is Mitre Peak. It is nearly 8,000 feet high—no great height perhaps when compared to the giants which Alpine Club-men conquer, but truly formidable when seen, as this is, from the sea-level to its spire. As we steam past it, a white speck—a mere dot—appears on the narrow beach behind its huge shoulders. This is a house, the only one in the Sound, and it enables us to apply some sort of scale to the huge mountains round us. A speck only is it in the mass of rock, forest, and glacier. For on the port side, opposite the Mitre, and apparently a few yards only from the ship's side, a mountain torrent falls into the creek, descending in a succession of steps. When we look up the wild, weird ravine down which flows this silver thread, we see far above us the deep blue of glacier ice, and above this, snow-covered peaks rearing their summits against the blue sky. Then, again, in a few minutes we round a projecting cape; the rocky valley and the glaciers are shut out, and the mountains are again covered with trees and grass of the brightest green.

E. H. D'AVIGDOR
Antipodean Notes (1888)

A VIEW OF RANGITOTO

Harshness of gorse darkens the yellow cliff-edge,
And scarlet-flowered trees lean out to drop
Their shadows on the bay below, searching

The water for an image always broken
Between the inward and returning swells.
Farther, beyond the rocks, cuffed by pert waves

Launches tug at their moorings; and in the channel
Yachts that sprint elegantly down the breeze
And earnest liners driving for the north.

Finally, holding all eyes, the long-limbed mountain
Dark on the waves, sunk in a stone composure;
From each far cape the easy flanks lift

In slow unison, purposeful all their rising length,
To meet and lock together faultlessly
Clasping the notched worn crater-cone between them.

That cup of fire, drooped like an ageing head,
Is fed with dew now and a paler brightness;
For the rushing anger sank down ages past,

Sank far beneath the sea-bed, leaving only
A useless throat that time gradually stopped
And sealed at last with smoky lichen-skin.

The mountain still lives out that fiercer life
Beneath its husk of darkness; blind to the age
Scuttling by it over shiftless waters,

And the cold beams that wake upon its headlands
To usher night-dazed ships. For it belongs to
A world of fire before the rocks and waters.

CHARLES BRASCH (b. 1909)

GEYSER AT ROTORUA

Rotorua is advertised not only as a spa, but as a spectacle.
They took us out to Whakarewarewa, where the Arawa
Maoris dwell, to see the sights and smell the smells.
They showed us the geyser valley, and "Look" they said
proudly, and we looked; and lo, it was like hell. Steam
issued from the earth in all directions; beside the path
were bubbling pools of water, deep, blue, bottomless
and boiling; hot sulphur oozed among the bushes;
steam vents, mud cones, blow-holes, fumeroles, sulphur
wells and I know not what, they were everywhere at
work. The whole valley, and indeed the whole country,
has been built over a hot bath. Not far away, in 1886,
the mountain Tarawera blew up and buried a village;
there was an earthquake and electric storms; the
beautiful silica terraces of Rotomahana were destroyed;
a lake was made and a new island and so forth. New
Zealand is intensely proud of this eruption and bitterly
resents the small notice that is taken of it. Had more
lives been lost, the pamphlets say, the country would
have got more credit for the thing. Could they have
staged a new eruption for us I know they would have
done, for they are nothing if not kind. As it is, they
speak with regret of those old days, and of the Waimunga
Geyser, which used to shoot sixteen hundred feet high,
and blow up rocks the size of houses, sometimes playing
with them, I believe, in the manner of pingpong balls
which are balanced on fountains at penny rifle ranges.
Indeed one lady told me that this great geyser spouted

four thousand feet high. "Two thirds of a mile?" I said politely, "Is that a fact? You amaze me."

"Oh well," she replied, "it was something like that, I know."

As it was we saw Pohutu make a "shoot" which was not an inch less than sixty feet. Pohutu spouts by spasms and capriciously. He did not play for the Prince of Wales, neither did he spout for the Admiral of the American Fleet a day or two before us, but we had not been in the valley twenty minutes before up he went, a beautiful Prince of Wales's feathers hot water fountain; and very fine he was! Our Maori guides (all ladies and very charming) remarked that our Mission was exceptionally favoured by fortune; and so we thought till someone whispered that they are able at will to provoke the marvellous natural forces of Pohutu to artificial activity by the application of common yellow soap.

A. P. HERBERT (b. 1890)
"Mr. Punch Goes A-Roving: Rotorua"
Punch, October 28, 1925

COUNTRY ROAD

The wind brings no sad tales across the grass
That shines like soft gold hair and moves like water,
Only tales of sun on earth and rock,
And a cold smell that might be rain, or ferns.

If there were veins once in this roadside dust
That clings like snow to every blade and bough,
They were the veins of birds, the veins of leaves.

There will be coins and trinkets buried here,
Hewn and hollowed stones, there will be legends
In the rocks and sandy hills; but then
How sad will seem the singing of this wind,
How different the dust upon the leaves.

Over the grass and over, moves the wind;
This moment will not come again, white dust
Upon green leaves as innocent as snow,
A wind that sings of nothing in the grass.

                                    RUTH DALLAS (b. 1919)

A DESERTED MINING TOWN

Narrator: Look and listen. A star falls from the roof
of the sky. A wind is beginning in the thick bush of
the night. It blows in Abelstown, quiet as a miner's
ghost, shifting the shingle of the long-dry dusty pubs
where only the dark drinks now. It dances like a high-
heeled whisky Jane on the gapped floor of a shanty,
puffing and smiling in a whalebone and a feathered hat,
while the hot dead whistle for more. It shuffles in flat
slippers among graves and pines on the island of earth
left by the glassy shovels and the swivel gunning hoses.
And the Chinamen in exile there, lying down light and
lank under a clay quilt, hear it ruffle above them, like
a swaggering bandit, waves between them and China.
They hug hard their wives of gold to their bony chests.
Under the sailing moon Abelstown is full of the empty
dead. But no blood runs, except in the willow veins,
and the cold water race that sighs all night like a naked
girl under the old moon's eye, twisting and turning
on a mattress of wet stones and needles.

What did you hear then? The morepork, with blood
on its claw, hooting? A rabbit screeching, with blood
on its fur, as the weasel slashes and sucks? No. Stoat
and owl run to their holes. The dead hide under God's
hand. A man is climbing the hill of the night, out of
dry Abelstown.

                                    JAMES K. BAXTER (b. 1926)
                                    Jack Winter's Dream
                                    A Play for Radio (1959)

AT THE FISHING SETTLEMENT

October, and a rain-blurred face
Walking, walking into the sea. The place
Was a bare sea-battered town
With its single street leading down
Onto a gravel beach. Sea-winds
Had long picked the hills clean
Of everything but tussock and stones,
And pines that dropped small brittle cones
Onto a soured soil. And old houses flanking
The street hung poised like driftwood planking
Blown together and could not outlast
The next window-shuddering blast
From the storm-whitened sea.
It was bitterly cold; I could see
Where muffled against gusty spray
She walked the clinking shingle; a stray
Dog whimpered, and pushed its small
Wet nose into my hand;—that is all.
Yet I am haunted by that face,
That dog, and that bare bitter place.

ALISTAIR CAMPBELL (b. 1926)

DESIGN IN THE MOUNTAINS

One morning, many years after he had ceased to work
on farms, Ashley stood among tussocks on the lower
flanks of Ben Lomond, in view of a little beech forest
that struggled up a gully down which there came a
stream so hidden beneath the trees, and so musical in
its passage over boulders and shingle, that the trees
themselves seemed to be singing. A turn of the head
showed massive ridges on the opposite shore of Wakatipu,

and the light of morning was revealing more than he
had seen before in the shapes of mountains. Why was
it that the hills had each their special character, their
unique features that could be brought by the imagination into a total impression which became purely
aesthetic, a bloom of the senses, and perhaps an imprint
of the mind, on the work of natural forces through
unknown reaches of time? There is nothing beautiful
in the fact of erosion, whether it be caused by wind and
frost, by the slow denudation of timber, or by glacial
action. Indeed, the word has become in New Zealand
a warning and a reproach. Nor can it be said that an
aesthetic design exists in contours that have been shaped
fortuitously, taking a chance addition of pattern from
every rain-cloud which bursts upon the peaks. Yet the
results of what could be described as disorder in nature
are seldom without dignity and beauty, although the
range of beauty may extend from tranquillity to a
black frown of anger. There is even a hint of laughter,
an air of the unexpected and eccentric which, in the
fluid movement of human relations, could be ridiculous.
But the mountains are sublime where man would be
awkward; their massive foundations and inorganic
composition give them the dignity that comes with
stillness. Nevertheless, there is something in that
tremendous variety of form and structure, breaking
everywhere into a clear individuality, which belongs
also to human experience. And later, as Ashley stood
on the saddle of Ben Lomond, and looked at the corru-
gations of an inner range, and across the lake to a
chaos of peaks and ridges, sliding towards the central
vertebrae of the island, he saw that the word he wanted
was "emotion." The idea behind it was gone as quickly
as it had come: he could not hold it against the dis-
tractions of the scene. For several years it came and
went, widening sometimes towards clarity, and contracting into darkness as he tried to draw it up into

consciousness. In all this concentration upon an idea he might have been following a thought or fancy which came to him as a tourist; but the substance of the thought upon which it fed and grew had been supplied from memories that could be traced back to years when he had worked on the land. These memories were not merely impressions of scenes with which he had become familiar; they were also the integrated feelings, the interest and half-awakened delight, the mystery and constant attraction, which accompanied his discoveries.

M. H. HOLCROFT (b. 1902)
Dance of the Seasons

THE MOUNTAINS

In this scarred country, this cold threshold land
The mountains crouch like tigers. By the sea
Folk talk of them hid vaguely out of sight;
But here they stand in massed solidity
To seize upon the day and night horizon.

Men shut within a whelming bowl of hills
Grow strange, say little when they leave their high
Yet buried homesteads; return there silently
When thunder of night-rivers fills the sky
And giant wings brood over loftily and near.

The mountains crouch like tigers—or await
As women wait. The mountains have no age.
But O the heart leaps to behold them loom:
A sense as of vast fate rings in the blood; no refuge,
No refuge is there from the flame that reaches
Across familiar things and makes them seem
Trivial, vain. O spirit walks on the peaks;
Eye glances across a gorge to further crags.

There is no desire; but the stream, but the avalanche
    speaks
And their word is louder than freedom, the mountain
    embrace
Were a death dearer than freedom or freedom's flags.

I will go to the coast-line and mingle with men.
These mountain-buttresses build beyond the horizon;
They call: but he whom they lay their spell upon
Leaves home, leaves kindred. The range of the telescope's
    eye
Is well—if the brain follows not to the outermost fields
    of vision.
I shall drown myself in humanity: better to lie
Dumb in the city than under the mountainous wavering
    sky.

The mountains crouch like tigers.
They are but stone yet the seeking eyes grow blind.

                      JAMES K. BAXTER (b. 1926)

HYDRO WORKS

    First the valley where the houses
    Are cherished by hedges and trees,
    The pastures flowing green
    To the river, the willows
    Frail against a face of rock.
    Nothing to threaten the eye,
    Sheep penned in the peace of summer,
    Larks with the song of certitude.

    Emerging from the valley the mind
    Encounters like an enemy, itself,
    Rock-like in the cowering wilderness:

The idling spirit
Recoils from the resolute wall,
The squat citadel spraying power.

And the hills stand in submission
And the dumb, disciplined waters;
For harder than driven stone or defiant rock
The hard core of the purpose and will of man.

J. R. HERVEY (1889-1958)

THE RANGIPO DESERT

As he went on in the early morning, fearful of losing
all direction, but trying to judge the slope of the land
as it ran down to the plain, he came to a strange and
desolate country. What he saw was a waste of scarred
and pitted desert, bare of all growth for long stretches,
loose scoria and pumice powdered to sand by years of
weathering, and lifting now, as the gale came violently,
so that it rose in swirling clouds that wrapped him
round and blinded him. Here and there stunted shrubs
clung desperately in the shelter of breaks and hummocks
in the sand, and the ground was strewn with charred
fragments of old forests wasted by volcanic fire. He
had heard men speak of this, too, of the Rangipo desert,
the waste area where, long before, the volcanoes of the
mountain had burned and embedded the forests, and
the loose volcanic sand, played on by years of driving
winds, had given no home for anything to grow. It
was a legend-haunted country, dreaded by the Maoris.
He could remember them telling him how long ago
the first natives of the country had been driven down
here by invaders to die and after that there were stories
of Maori tribes caught by snow and starved to death
in these same deserts. There had been times when the
desert held packs of savage and wandering dogs until

they, too, died away in that lifeless area, and it was
left as barren and desolate as ever. As he went blindly
forward, going doggedly, his head down, barely seeing
the ground beneath his feet, he came at length to what
he knew must be the heart of it all, Onetapu, the place
of the shivering sands. And there he seemed to be
caught in something that was wild and furious and
stronger than himself. The wind came no longer
directly against him, but eddying and whirling in
gusts of sand and storm so that he could hardly stand
or go forward in any direction. The quiet and silence
of the mountain-side was gone and in its place came a
sighing and moaning of the wind and sand as it stirred
in the corridors of the desert, more mournful and more
frightening than anything human that he had known.
He fought this for a long time, both the feeling of
terror and the force of the storm, baffled and angry,
going sometimes forward or being swayed to left and
right, stumbling and falling, going on his hands and
knees until at last he caught the shelter of a pumice
bank and stayed there, burrowed into it, with his back
against the shelter and the rain and sand blowing over
him. He was exhausted and if snow came, he told
himself, ready to die.

JOHN MULGAN (1911-1945)
Man Alone

ARROWTOWN

Gold in the hills, gold in the rocks,
Gold in the river gravel,
Gold as yellow as Chinamen
In the bottom of the shovel.

Gold built the bank its sham façade;
Behind that studded door

Gold dribbled over the counter
Into the cracks of the floor.

Gold pollinated the whole town;
But the golden bees are gone—
Now round a country butcher's shop
The sullen blowflies drone.

Now paved with common clay
Are the roads of Arrowtown;
And the silt of the river is grey
In the golden sun.

DENIS GLOVER (b. 1912)

RIVER BED

This was the river's course.
Its fields of stone remain,
Pathways and sprawling mounds
Dry from the troubled foam,

Where a great broken tree
Rolled once, green foliaged,
Grounding, entering again
Its wild path to the sea.
Between these stones and the rain
Beating from vanished skies
How strange that voyage, that flood
Of shadows through the past.

HUBERT WITHEFORD (b. 1921)

THE OTIRA GORGE COACH

In 1918, the Otira Tunnel was opened, linking the West Coast with
Canterbury through the Southern Alps. The tunnel is five miles,
25 chains long.

I have made my last coach-journey over that twisted
road, and, to use Lamb's beautiful sentence, "I reluct
at the inevitable course of destiny." I am not comforted
by metaphors of the East and West joining hands, of
the island's iron girdle. Now, when I have lost them,
I am in love with those grey heights, those mountain
solitudes. Once yet, I plead, a sight of crowded platforms,
red coaches and brown horses, high-piled luggage,
passengers buccaneering for seats. For all the curses
I have expended on drivers, vehicles, and horses, on
luggage that must be hoisted and stowed and paid for
at excess rates, on shrill, bone-chilling winds and icy
rain, on the endless hill to be toiled up in summer's
dust and heat, on perilous seats and hairless rugs forlorn,
on tedious delays, on Hall, Cassidy, Beale, Yde and
Lam-something, I stretch out my hands to them all,
and would hold them back a little while from the
darkness of things past, would endure them all again,
were they never so distressful.

At Otira they heaved your stuff cheerfully forth from
the van; you sorted it out and, if you were lucky, saw
it packed away. Otherwise, you trusted in Providence.
Your old friend, the driver, gave you a decent seat if
he could and you climbed up and smoked placidly in
contemplation of the swarming tourists, commercials,
and waifs and strays of travel, beseiging other coaches.
You were careful not to knock your head on the shelter-
roof as your coach pulled out. You stopped a little
further on to pick up a dribble of passengers from the

hotel. You bowled along, past the public works cottages with their dejected gardens, the hospital, the yellow school, the stony slip marked with a wooden cross; you rattled across the bridge, so narrow that the swingle-trees almost caught the rails, past another hotel, very populous, where dogs yapped furiously, and a rooster crowed from a glorious manure-heap. You thundered on by the cramped cricket-pitch, with its pitch of concrete sloping absurdly, and so up the first rise. To the right was the line from the tunnel, perched upon a ridge of spoil blasted out of the mountain. (It would never be finished. The moss would grow and creep over that clean, fresh stone.) You crawled along the hillside, brushing the scrub-faced rock on the left and peeping over the edge into the brawling torrent or blue-green pools of the Otira. You showed your ticket, hopped down, looked down back with rather envious contempt at the grossly fat man whose gross fat anchored him safely to the coach, and plugged off up the hill.

Mostly it rained, and you faced driving sheets of water which the wind flung into your eyes and drove down your neck. Playful streams flowed about your boots. Or else it was grilling hot, with the dust clouding the air. If you looked ahead you saw the heat-swirls dancing, so that the air rippled like water. A century or two dragged you to the top, and you waited for the crawling coaches. Then off down the other side, by the little lakes, through the stream with a profuse splashing of diamond spray, and on and on, and on until the brown paint of Arthur's Pass and the black line of the train came into sight.

Who can forget the air, fresh from heaven, the huge slide, the jagged peaks towering above, Rolleston Glacier, the long razor-back ridge, the bluff, stout hills, so densely bushed? Above all, who can forget the Pass under snow? The stunted trees near Arthur's Pass touched to dazzling beauty, and the road, the rocks,

and bushes by its side all a white loveliness? Two red
bridges to be dashed over, falling water, cheering brats
by the roadside, two or three bent and weather-beaten
roadmen straightening up to gaze critically and nod
or wave a hand, mailbags and crates tumbled mountainous on the platform, boxes of fowls (alive) and
lettuces and cabbages (dead)—these I have forgotten
to mention in their place; and, now, shall we ever
see them again?

J. H. E. SCHRODER (b. 1895)
Remembering Things and Other Essays

THE OLD COACH ROAD

On blackberry, on fern falls the pale dust
Milled up by cattle shambling to the gate;
The weathered road's satirical reply
Should time and chance seek to obliterate
That legend on the milking shed:
Muldoon's Coaches—Livery and Bait.

Old Muldoon died of wheels in his head,
Rims and horseshoes muttering to clay
Of his lost high seat and feather-footed teams
Racing the wind. To his angry life's last day
He'd crack a whip at the smooth-as-silver
Highway through pasture land two miles away.

He and the old coach road were deviations
But his turn-off was far and far to seek;
The time his dapples went at a flying trot
From Dead Man's Gully down to Firewood Creek;
The time his eyes danced with forests
In a music of bells rung in the tui's beak.

That highway took the farm's snowy rillets
To swell vast torrents of Waikato cream,
Back to the younger Muldoons flowed the riches.
Bright with the century's neoteric dream.
The old man's wheel lurched into silence—
His death dried up in it like a summer stream.

The legend fades, the road will not give in;
Cream lorry, cattle, the fluttering return
Of pipits to their dust-bowls, all evoke
Wry clouds of gritty unconcern
Settling pale as rime over the verges
Where long days blacken the berry and gild the fern.

GLORIA RAWLINSON (b. 1918)

THE CITY FROM THE HILLS

There lies our city folded in the mist,
Like a great meadow in an early morn
Flinging her spears of grass up through white films,
Each with its thousand thousand-tinted globes.
Above us such an air as poets dream,
The clean and vast wing-winnowed clime of Heaven.

Each of her streets is closed with shining Alps,
Like Heaven at the end of long plain lives.

ARNOLD WALL (1869-1966)

A CONSTRUCTION CAMP

In Tangahano the river is made to be snared. It drops
to a valley—part of the thousand feet it drops in less
than a hundred and twenty miles. Geological exploration has analysed its rock structure and formation and
geophysical survey has sounded its continuity and

steadiness for the impounded waters of the artificial lake that will rise, spread out and drown the ancient keeps of wild bird and beast, that now in the night raise sensitive heads of alarm and eyes of panic at every new thunder of the intruders.

It is pig and deer country and land of shy bird. But they stay, for nest and lair is there. Not yet can danger be smelt and clarioned through the forests with hoof, caw and cry. Not yet, for the river still glides playfully against their muzzles when they come out to drink, and skimming wing feathers scatter its crystal beadlets.

Already the land is defaced, for there can be no anaesthesia in blueprints. It is a series of plateaus and gulches; acres of chaos and buckled rock veins and excavations; pushed-back forests; flattened contours and stockpiles of volcanic boulders, streaked, pebbled, glazed, marbled, some large as barrels, like collapsed pagan temples.

Raw roads, rock strewn and scoured, stretch, loop and twist on it at different levels. They seem to lose themselves in scrub or at cliff face, or cross themselves as if looking for a way out. This is illusion. . . . They all lead someplace. And the vehicles that lurch, shudder, bounce and skid over them are all going someplace.

Supply stores, workshops and crib huts perch where they can out of the range of blast percussion. But they do not escape entirely. Large holes disfigure their walls and windows, and rocks of all sizes lie on their roofs as if holding them in place.

Bulldozer and euclid, grab and grader, truck and jeep amble, waddle, scurry and scoot all over the place like disturbed insects. And vehicles with wheels as high as a man rumble through stretches of blasted clay country lying like breaking yellow ice-packs.

Below it all the deflected river rushes like fury into the trap set for it—the diversion tunnel—and thunders under the hill to crash out the other side fuming white, and crawling up on to itself to get ahead, to spread out

and settle down into being a river again. It is a force
of water that could pound a man to death even before
he swallows it, unless he goes down with it as a companion and waits his one chance as he is swept under
Spaghetti Bridge with its dangling ropes, frequent as
the teeth of a comb.

It is a project that dwarfs men and machines. But
the men know what they are doing. And machines do
what they are told.

FRANCES KEINZLY (b. 1922)
Tangahano

THESE ISLANDS

These islands;
the remnant peaks of a lost continent,
roof of an old world, molten droppings
from earth's bowels, gone cold;
ribbed with rock, resisting the sea's corrosion
for an age, and an age to come. Of three races
the home; two passing in conquest
or sitting under the leaves or on shady doorsteps
with quiet hands, in old age, childless.
And we, the latest; their blood on our hands; scions
of men who scaled ambition's
tottering slopes, whose desires
encompassed earth and heaven: we have prospered
          greatly,
we, the destined race, rulers of conquered isles,
sprouting like bulbs in warm darkness, putting out
white shoots under the wet sack of Empire.

A. R. D. FAIRBURN (1904-1957)
from *Dominion*

WHERE THE SOLDIERS HAD BEEN

After the rear party had moved out, the Italians moved in to search the ditches and rubbish pits. They found little of value, and after a while they went away. Only the children stayed, twittering like birds and recalling where this cookhouse had stood and that vehicle had been parked. They threw sticks and stones into the tall walnut tree that had sheltered Headquarters' orderly-room lorry and the ripe walnuts pattered down, bouncing on the naked earth. When evening came there were still children in the area.

The shadows from the oak trees flowed down the hillside, bridging the creek and poking long fingers across the football ground. When it was quite dark and the goalposts could be seen no longer, the children went home—to dream, perhaps, of the strange, friendly soldiers, the *Neo Zelandesi*, who had come, had stayed for a little while, and had moved on. And after a few months, after the weather had removed all traces of the camp and the last biscuit had been eaten, the last tin of marmalade had vanished from Mamma's shelves, and the small cut foot had healed, and the bandage provided by the New Zealanders had been washed and washed until it was of no further use, they forgot. For the world was full of soldiers and they stayed for a little while and they went away.

The children forgot, yes, but not at once and not completely. Between them and the migrant soldiers there was a bridge, a bond, some fragments of a common language. They sensed, it may be, that soldiers were no different from themselves in some ways, that they, too, had a kind of innocence, and were not, in a world abounding in meanness, mean. Careless, perhaps, destructive certainly, but not—not in the last resort—

meriting hate and terror from children, even from burnt children in London, Naples, Rotterdam, Berlin, Hiroshima.

So the children came back for a night, two nights, three nights, to the place that remembered the soldiers and their lorries and their gear, and played until the walnut tree was deep blue in the sweet, heavy evening and the hills were purple and the stream flashed under the stars like dark silver.

S. P. LLEWELLYN (b. 1913)
Journey Towards Christmas

The Land

THE PLOUGH

To sing of the plough, and the joys thence arising,
  With labour made easy, how welcome, I trow;
For long I've been sharing hard labour, preparing
  My lands, for the pleasure of using the plough.
      Of using the plough, of using the plough,
        My lands for the pleasure of using the plough.

My grub-hoe has long had hard active employment,
  In clearing the roots from the old forest ground;
But now, at its leisure, it may rest with pleasure,
  Its work is completed, which once did abound.
      Which once did abound, etc.

How hard, in the outset, to clear off a forest,
  With back often aching, and sweat bedew'd brow;
Such labours got over, I now can discover
  How pleasing indeed 'tis to follow the plough.
      To follow the plough, etc.

My spade did its duty when only small patches
  I tilled; but uniting them all as one now,
My oxen all ready, so active and steady,
  Must give now their labour to till with the plough.
      To till with the plough, etc.

How many the trials, privations and sorrows,
  I've often endured from beginning till now;
But since my endeavours are crown'd with high favours,
  I'll smile o'er the past, and sing speed to the plough!
      Sing speed to the plough, etc.

Let thoughtless goldhunters make haste for the diggings,
  Beguiled by false visions 'mid dangers enow;
But I'll seek my treasure with comfort and pleasure,
  In reaping rich harvests by guiding the plough.
    By guiding the plough, etc.

WILLIAM GOLDER (1810-76)
New Zealand Minstrelsy

BURNING OFF

Towards noon, then, the fateful match is struck, the smoke curls upwards blue and thin, the clear flame, steady at first but soon lengthening and stretching itself, arises like a snake from its cold coils. Then, as often seems to happen, the draught of the fire summons at once the waiting wind; out of the hot calm bursts forth the new-born storm; the circle of flame lengthens into a streak which, widening at every edge, is pounced upon, flattened to the ground, and furiously fanned this way and that, as if in attempted extinction. A few minutes later a line of commingled flame and smoke, moving ahead with steady roar, sweeps the hillsides.

Few sights are more engrossing, more enthralling, than the play of wind and flame. Wind in the hills, like water in its course, never for an instant remains even in its force, but ceaselessly swells and fails, waxes and wanes. In the very height of a gale the rushing charge of fire will in an instant check, the flames previously pinned down will erect their forked tongues like a crop, or lift as if drawn upwards from earth in the very consummation of their burning embrace; the smoke, a moment previously flattened into the suffocated fern, will rise then like steam through the winged fronds. Upon slopes exposed to greater weight of wind the pace of the conflagration quickens, forked sheets of flame that singe and scorch the shrivelling upper growth reach far ahead; forward the conflagration rolls—sometimes grey, sometimes glowing, sometimes incandescent, according to the changeful gusts. As a lover wraps his mistress in his arms, so the flames wrap the stately cabbage-trees, stripping them naked of their matted mantles of brown, devouring their tall stems with kisses of fire, crackling like musketry amongst the spluttering flax, hissing and spitting in the tutu groves, pouring in black smoke from thickets of scrub. On the tops pressed forward by the full force of the gale the roaring conflagration passes upwards and over in low-blown whirlwinds of smoke darkened with dust of flying charcoal and lit with showers of fiery sparks and airy handfuls of incandescent and blazing brake. To leeward fire is no less wonderful to watch as it slowly recedes downhill, devouring in leisurely fashion first the driest material, then sapping the stems of the later, greener, still upright fronds, so that they too bow like Dagon and fall to earth, perpetually replenishing the flames. A fire thus fed, burning against the wind or downhill, presents at night-time a peculiar twinkling, winking appearance from the perpetually recurring fall of the grass fronds into the blaze, and the consequent alternation of darkness and light.

In windless hollows yet another mood may be noted: there the flames, burning slowly, stretch and dip and curtsey and sway to the draw of the gale above; in the mazes of a magic dance they take their time and measure from the wind, veering now to one point of the compass, now to another, sliding and gliding in accompaniment to the unheard harps of the air. So, on that afternoon of March, like the waters of Lodore, the fire passed over Stuart's paddock, roaring and pouring, and howling and growling, and flashing and dashing and crashing, and fuming and consuming not only the block so named, but hundreds of acres besides of the Rocky Range—then included in the Moeangiangi run—the whole of the Black Stag, and nearly the whole of the Tutu Faces.

At nightfall, over every acre unswept by the wind lay a delicate grey veil—a light ash of shrivelled fronds still retaining their shape. A tang of salt, as from the ocean, scented the air, whilst here and there on the driest flat rose thin lines of blue from smouldering totara logs. Everywhere the contours of the countryside lay dim; the sard sun, low in the dun horizon, glowed a burning, blood-red ball; like the fog of a great city, a pall of smoke hung over the land. Oh! the ride home, salt with dry sweat and black with dust, not a hair left unsinged on hands and arms, but rejoicing, triumphant. Oh! the dive into the cool lake, the slow swim in limpid water past the snag Karawaitahi, over the shoal Tarata; alas! that the run cannot once more be broken in: alas! indeed, that the past years cannot be relived; a fire on a dry day in a dry season was worth a ride of a thousand miles.

W. H. GUTHRIE-SMITH (1861-1940)
Tutira: The Story of a New Zealand Sheep Station

WATCHING THE MILKING

1

In the ashen evening a bird's song spouts in silver
That swirls to the shed where an engine spits and chugs.
The yard is muddy. Sunk to the knees the cows
Await the sucking cup, the hand that tugs,
Content and chewing, and not afraid of man
Or the weird machine that robs their swollen dugs.

2

As torchlight stabs a pool and splits the stillness
The madness of motherhood tore those gentle eyes;
And the fawn cows that stand so quietly in the yard
Felt tides of ancient passion in them rise,

And knew great tenderness, were wild and savage,
And bawled in torment to the lost calf's cries.

3

"They soon forget . . . This happens every year."
The light fades, and the thrush no longer sings.
"And every year, and every year, and always."
A match glows. The odour of warm milk brings
Remembrance of hay, and woodsmoke, and horses;
    and then
Of pine-trees and scented hair, and magical things.

4

The hills grow dark, are monstrous upon the earth—
Where leads the trail beyond their sprawling weight?
Day is a broken dream, and night fantastic;
Ghost in a ghostly world alone and late,
I might have been watching the cold craters of the
    moon,
Or Pithecanthrope gesturing to his mate.

DOUGLAS STEWART (b. 1913)

A BUSH DELICACY

Let not those who are unacquainted with the bush
imagine that explorers are not, in their way, epicures.
True, they must occasionally content themselves with
but a slender meal, and that may be of sowthistle or a
zoophyte, and *miko* or fern-root they must substitute
for bread; but more frequently they dine off pigeon,
off grey and blue duck, off eel and crayfish, or, queen of
wild fowl, woodhen. When can blue duck taste savoury
as when served on the top of an oilskin cap? Or how
else can an eel be cooked to equal its flavour when
roasted on a supplejack? And weka, uncared for in the
settlements! Catch it, as Mrs. Glass would say, at

Rotoiti or Cape Foulwind; stuff it with sage and onion (for even these condiments accompany the epicurean explorer), roast it on a stick, watch it for half an hour at daybreak, spattering and hissing between you and the fire as you make the damper or pancake, while your companions are snoring under their blankets around you, and then serve it upon the saucepan lid. No dish at Very's was ever more *recherché*; no Christmas dinner ever gave more satisfaction.

Hail to thee, weka!—tender as chicken, gamey as pheasant, gelatinous as roaster. Elia, when he wrote his essay on sucking pig, knew not of thee. Charles Lamb had need but to have partaken of thee to have been inspired; but he, unfortunately, knew nothing of the bush. In the settlements they skin thee, and the cook is wrathful at the difficulty of plucking thee. Cast pearls before swine, but let them not desecrate thy crackling!

Observe a gourmand when he visits his poulterer at Michaelmas, notice the admiration of the epicure at the Christmas prize beef, or the alderman before his venison, and discover, if you can, the same interest, all-engrossing if not passionate, as is evinced by the explorer as he watches his weka, the capture of which is yet doubtful.

CHARLES HEAPHY[1] (1820-1881)
Expedition to Kawatiri and Aruara

WHY DON'T YOU MEND THE ROADS?

" Why don't they mend these dreadful roads?"
    I heard a stranger ask,
" For that blessed lazy old Town Board,
    It can't be such a task.

[1]Charles Heaphy, official artist and draughtsman to the New Zealand Company, and later Chief Surveyor at Auckland, won New Zealand's first V.C., in 1863 during the Maori Wars.

MTS. TONGARIRO AND NGAURUHOE

Mt. Ngauruhoe (7,515 feet), in the background, an active volcano, and Mt. Tongariro (6,517 feet), with active thermal vents, constitute with a third mountain Ruapehu (9,715 feet), the Tongariro National Park, an area of 150,000 acres in the North Island.

ARROWTOWN

A famous gold-mining town in central Otago, Arrowtown boomed in the 1860's. The Arrowtown Museum preserves the history of the many gold-mining activities of the district. Much of Arrowtown today remains as it was a century ago, when miners planted the trees that line its main street.

QUEEN STREET, AUCKLAND

A modern view looking up the main street of Auckland. Trolley-buses have replaced trams, and all the traffic problems of a modern city beset the rapidly expanding Queen City.

A WEST COAST BEACH

A view of Piha Beach near Auckland, and of the breakers of the Tasman Sea, from a cliff-top track. Plumes of the toi-toi ("Prince of Wales Feather") flax are in the foreground. New Zealand has hundreds of miles of beaches, those on the West Coast being mainly of black iron-sand.

They've splendid quarries close at hand,
Of stone they might get loads,
Oh Doctor Hulme what are you at,
Why don't you mend the roads?"

Chorus
You don't, you won't, mend the roads.

"Why don't they mend these blessed roads?"
A Manse Street merchant cries,
"That thoroughfare's a sea of mud,
All traffic it defies.
Deep holes engulf pedestrians,
And pent up wrath explodes
And they d——n that lazy Town Board,
'Cause they won't repair the roads."

"Why don't they mend the roads?"
A lady did enquire,
As crossing to Kirkpatrick's shop,
She sank down in the mire.
"My feet are wet, my nice new dress
It sadly incommodes,
You naughty Mr. Cargill,
Why don't you mend the roads?"

"Why the devil don't they mend the roads?"
I heard the carter say,
As starting for the diggings,
He stuck fast with his dray.
In vain with curses loud and deep,
Poor Strawberry he loads,
His axle breaks and all because
They won't repair the roads?

Why the dickens don't you mend the roads?
You'd better now look out,
Sir George Grey's certain to get bogged,
If here he walks about.
Kilgour and Cargill, unto you
No good this song forbodes.
I'll give you such a warming soon,
If you don't mend the roads.

CHARLES R. THATCHER (1841-1873)

THE ROAD BUILDERS

Rolling along far roads on holiday wheels
now wonder at their construction, the infinite skill
that balanced the road to the gradient of the hill,
the precision, the planning, the labour it all reveals.

An unremembered legion of labourers did this,
scarring the stubborn clay, fighting the tangled bush,
blasting the adamant, stemming the unbridled rush
of the torrent in flood, bridging each dark abyss.

Their tools were pitiful beside the obdurate strength of
    the land:
crosswire of the theodolite, pick-point, curved shovel,
small tremor of a touched-off charge; but above all
the skill and strength, admirable in patience, of the hand.

These men we should honour above the managers of
    banks.
They pitted their flesh and their cunning against odds
unimagined by those who turn wordily the first sods.
And on the payroll their labour stands unadorned by
    thanks.

Who they are, or where, we do not know. Anonymous
    they die
or drift away; some start the job again; some in a
    country pub
recount old epic deeds amid that unheeding hubbub,
telling of pitiless hills, wet mountain roads where
    rusting barrows lie.

                          DENIS GLOVER (b. 1912)

THE GREAT SNOW-STORM OF 1867

When I awoke the next morning, I was not much
surprised to see the snow falling thick and fast: no
sheep were now visible, there was a great silence, and
the oppression in the atmosphere had if possible increased. We had a very poor breakfast—no porridge,
very little mutton . . . and *very* weak tea; coffee and
cocoa all finished, and about an ounce of tea in the
chest. I don't know how the gentlemen amused themselves that day; I believe they smoked a good deal.
I could only afford a small fire in the drawing-room,
over which I shivered. The snow continued to fall in
dense fine clouds, quite unlike any snow I ever saw
before, and towards night I fancied the garden fence
was becoming much dwarfed. Still the consolation
was, "Oh, it won't last; New Zealand snow never
does." However, on Wednesday morning things began
to look very serious indeed; the snow covered the ground
to a depth of four feet in the shallowest places, and still
continued to fall steadily; the cows we knew must be
in the paddock were not to be seen anywhere; the
fowl-house and pig-styes which stood towards the
weather quarter had entirely disappeared; every scrap
of wood (and several logs were lying about at the back)
was quite covered up; both the verandahs were impas-

sable; in one the snow was six feet deep, and the only
door which could be opened was the back-kitchen door,
as that opened inwards; but here the snow was halfway
over the roof, so it took a good deal of work with the
kitchen-shovel, for no spades could be found, to dig out
a passage. Indoors, we were approaching our last
mouthful very rapidly, the tea at breakfast was merely
coloured hot water, and we had some picnic biscuits
with it. . . .

It was wonderful to see how completely the whole
aspect of the surrounding scenery was changed; the
gullies were all filled up, and nearly level with the
downs; sharp-pointed cliffs were now round bluffs;
there was no vestige of a fence or gate or shrub to be
seen, and still the snow came down as if it had only
just began to fall; out of doors the silence was like
death, I was told, for I could only peep down the tunnel
dug every few hours at the back-kitchen door. My two
maids now gave way, and sat clasped in each other's
arms all day, crying piteously, and bewailing their
fate, asking me whenever I came into the kitchen,
which was about every half-hour, for there was no
fire elsewhere, "And oh, when do you think we'll
be found, mum?" Of course this only referred to
the ultimate discovery of our bodies. There was
a great search today for the cows, but it was
useless, the gentlemen sank up to their shoulders in
snow. . . .

(*A week later, it becomes possible to examine the effects of
the storm*). . . . The gentlemen wanted me to go home
before they attempted to see the extent of the disaster,
which we all felt must be very great, but I found it
impossible to do anything but accompany them. I
am half glad and half sorry now that I was obstinate;
glad because I helped a little at a time when the least
help was precious, and sorry because it was really such
a horrible sight. Even the first glance showed us that,

as soon as we got near the spot we had observed, we were walking on frozen sheep embedded in the snow one over the other; but at all events their misery had been over some time. It was more horrible to see the drowning, or just drowned, huddled-up "mob" . . . which had made the dusky patch we had noticed from the hill.

No one can ever tell how many hundred ewes and lambs had taken refuge under the high terrace which forms the bank of the creek. The snow had soon covered them up, but they probably were quite warm and dry at first. The terrible mischief was caused by the creek rising so rapidly, and, filtering through the snow which it gradually dissolved, drowned them as they stood huddled together. . . .

We forgot all our personal sufferings in anxiety about the surviving sheep, and when the long-expected dray arrived it seemed a small boon compared to the discovery of a nice little "mob" feeding tranquilly on a sunny spur. It is impossible to estimate our loss until the grand muster at shearing, but we may set it down at half our flock, and *all* our lambs, or at least 90 per cent of them. Our neighbours are all as busy as we are, so no accurate accounts of their sufferings or losses have reached us; but, to judge by appearances, the distant "back-country" ranges must have felt the storm more severely that we have. . . . Not only were sheep, but cattle, found dead in hundreds along the fences on the plains. The newspapers give half a million as a rough estimate of the loss among the flocks in this province alone. We have no reliable news from other parts of the island, only vague rumours of the storm having been still more severe in the Province of Otago, which lies to the south, and would be right in its track; the only thing which all are agreed in saying is, that there never has been such a storm before, for the Maoris are strong in weather traditions, and though they

prophesied this one, it is said they have no legend of
anything like it ever having happened.

LADY MARY ANNE BARKER[1] (1831-1911)
Station Life in New Zealand

GRUB AWAY, TUG AWAY

The birds gang to rest when tir'd wi' their warblin',
  But rest I get nane frae the mornin' sae early;
For either I'm mawin', or thrashin', or sawin',
  Or grubbin' the hills wi' the ferns covered fairly.
    Grub away, tug away, toil till you're weary,
      Haul oot the toot roots and everything near ye;
    Grub away, tug away, toil till you're weary,
      Then take a bit dram, it will help for to cheer ye.

It's no very pleasant this rough way o' livin',
  Sic tuggin', sic ruggin', it makes my banes crazy;
And aye when I rest me the wife's tongue besets me,
  Wi' "Gang to your wark, man, and dinna turn lazy."
    Grub away, etc.

Bricht was my brow in life's early dawnin',
  Licht was my heart as the blush of the mornin';
Noo I am dull and wae, like a dark winter's day,
  Deep in some glen where nae sun is adornin'.
    Grub away, etc.

O for the wings o' the swift flyin' eaglet,
  Quick ower the sea I would hurry me early,
To the land o' the heather bell, mountain, and foggy dell,
  Land of the brave that my heart lo'es sae dearly.
    Grub away, etc.

[1]Lady Barker, the widow of Sir George Barker, married again in
1865, her second husband being Frederick Napier Broome. With
Broome she came to New Zealand to live on the Canterbury sheep
run of Broomielaw, a station of 9,700 acres near Christchurch, in
the South Island.

Haste away, fly away, home to my fatherland,
  Land of the thistle, and mountain, and river,
Haste away, fly away, home to my fatherland,
  There on her bosom, I'd rest me for ever.
      Grub away, etc.

JOHN BARR (1809-89)
Poems and Songs, Descriptive and Satirical

BULLOCK LANGUAGE

If the English sailors have acquired a not undeserved reputation for their curses, surely the New Zealand bullock-drivers must be reckoned superior to them in this accomplishment, for such an assortment of fantastic oaths from all kingdoms of Nature, Heaven and Hell I have never heard before from mortal lips. Astounded I listened to this blue-eyed son of Albion and was at last impelled to ask him why he cursed so horribly; it could serve no purpose and only made the beast more stubborn. "You don't understand, Sir," the young man answered. "I'm only speaking the bullock language. The animal certainly wouldn't understand or obey me if I spoke to him as I would to my horse. The bullock has been brought up to carry in this way, and if I want to get on fast, I've got to talk to him like this."

To this argument advanced by the driver with a good-natured smile I naturally could find no reply. I refer it to the linguists to enrol this new language in the appropriate family of dialects.

SIR JULIUS VON HAAST (1822-87)
quoted in *The Life and Times of Sir Julius von Haast*
by H. F. VON HAAST

A SHEARING SHED

Then began a busy time, but one which had for Gilbert the charm of novelty. He had seen sheep shorn at home, but he had never beheld such a scene as the shed at Waitaruna. The shed, a large building of corrugated iron, was surrounded outside by innumerable pens, most of them crowded with sheep packed as close as they could stand. Inside, the woolshed was also filled with penned sheep, except at the end where the wool-press stood, and along each side, where space was left for the shearers. In these vacant spaces stood seven shearers at each side, most of them having already started to work. It was indeed work, hard work. Each shearer caught a sheep, dragged it struggling from the pen, turning it on its hindquarters, and propping it against his own legs, he stooped over it, and began to clip away its wealth of wool, turning it gradually round as he removed the fleecy covering. Occasionally a little more than the wool would be cut away, and the poor sheep would bear a red scar where the skin had been wounded. If the cut was a bad one, the shearer would "sing out" for tar, which would be brought and a little applied as an ointment to the wound, while Mr. Ramshorn, who was continually passing up and down the shed and seemed to be everywhere at once, would growl at the offending shearer and make use of some vague threat of "knocking him off."

Meanwhile the "pickers up" were busy gathering up the fleeces as they fell from the bereft sheep and carrying them to the sorting table, where they were stripped of the "pieces", which were thrown aside, while the best of the fleece was quickly classified, rolled together, and deposited in a kind of bin, according to its quality, whether "clothing" or "combing." No time was lost

by any one; the shearers were paid by the number of
sheep shorn, and as they hoped to get other sheds when
the Waitaruna shearing was finished, they hurried on.
Besides, there was a rivalry among them as to who
would have the biggest tally. There were two at least
among the number who were able to put through over
a hundred sheep a day each, and the others strove to
come near their numbers. . . .

During the morning, when there was a cessation of
work for a few minutes for "smoke oh", a large bucket
filled with tea and a number of pannikins were brought
up to the shed, and with draughts of this beverage the
shearers refreshed themselves, the bucket being replenish-
ed as occasion required. Gilbert was kept busy assisting
to bale the wool, which was removed from the bins to
the wool-press, where it was carefully packed and
tightly pressed into the compact bales which might be
adopted as emblematic of the wealth of the Australian
colonies, as the woolsack was that of Britain. Since the
days of Abel, the first shepherd, sheep seem always to
have formed a very material part of this world's wealth,
and they have undoubtedly formed a most important
factor in the growth of these Southern settlements.

ALEXANDER BATHGATE (1845-1930)
Waitaruna, A Story of New Zealand Life

SHEARING

"All aboard! All aboard!" is the cry.
They're a ripping lot of shearers in the shed;
Big Mick the Speewah ringer, must make skin and
    trimmings fly
This season if he means to keep ahead;
For Barcoo Ben will run him and half a dozen more
Of the lank Australian crush upon the board,
And it ain't no use to tell us of the tallies that he shore,
There'll be records broke this year, you take my word.

"Wool away! Wool away!" is the cry,
And the merry game of busting is begun!
They're going sheep and sheep, for Big Mick will do or
    die,
And the fleecy boys are kept upon the run.
It ain't no kind of joking, it's a game of killing men—
Up the neck and down the shoulder in a flash,
And the scruffing and the rattle on the battens of the pen
As to gain a catch the ringer makes a dash.

"Sling 'em out! Sling 'em out!" is the word.
You can hear the grinding pinions of the press,
Snipping shears and flying brooms upon the board,
And the sheep are growing wonderfully less.
The shepherds' dogs are barking in the yard,
And the penner-up is cursing at the back,
And the boss is looking savage at a long Australian card
With a look that means it's odds he'll get the sack.

"Clear the board! Clear the board!" is the shout,
And Barcoo Ben is caught upon the tail!
Big Mick is smiling grimly as he takes the cobbler out,
With a lead of two at breakfast he can sail.
The shearers laugh like schoolboys as they hurry from
    the shed,
There's a clinking of the pannikins and knives,
There's the "barrack" at the table and the clever things
    are said,
Yet all those blokes are shearing for their lives.

DAVID McKEE WRIGHT (1867-1928)
Station Ballads

SHEEP-DRIVING

Even where no large rivers had to be crossed, sheep
driving in the earliest days was not without its difficulties and hardships. There were no convenient fences

or friendly paddocks where sheep could be secured, and no homesteads or even sheds where you could obtain a night's shelter; the weather had to be faced, whatever it was; wild dogs were occasional visitors, so that somebody had often to watch all night; and if a sou'-wester came tearing across the plains all hands would have to stand out in it to prevent the mob from breaking away and going miles before it could be got together again. Even when settled on your own run this latter risk was on the plains a serious one. The old-fashioned sou'-wester was a very different thing from its present degenerate namesake; it generally brought torrents of rain, and lasted three days. Wire fences were then unknown, and one of these good old sou'-westers coming on in the night would send your sheep off to perhaps a scabby neighbour under your lee, or until they were brought up by the next river many miles away, which in that case was a welcome ally. Sheep driving in those days, like travelling, was apt to make strange bed-fellows; some of the best helpers to be obtained were the rough characters who, as whalers or runaway sailors, had been long in New Zealand. They were not choice in their language, but they had great local knowledge, took hardships without grumbling, and were honest workers if grog was not too handy.

SIR JOHN HALL (1824-1907)
Canterbury . . . Old and New

FARMING IN THE 1870's

The first home I knew, the first trees and flowers, were on the soil that had less than ten years before been a battlefield. The place had originally been a grant to a Waikato Militia officer, who sold it. The farm lay with a gentle tilt to the north. Wheat was much grown and gave large yields. Memory lingers on the many peach groves and cherry groves, Maori planted, laden with the largest and sweetest fruit ever grown.

There were tongues of raupo and flax swamp thrust into the land from the broad belt of forest that covered the main swamp on the north—rich pasture land now, with scarcely a white pine or a rimu left. A small swampy stream flowed through the deep valley on the west of the knoll on which our home stood. Harry, the North of Ireland man who worked on the farm, made a toy water-wheel for us; it clacked merrily at a tiny water-fall. Lower down there had been a small Maori flour-mill, in the wheat-growing days before the war. The old mill-dam, fed by the little creek and large springs, was now used for watering the farmer's cattle and sheep. Where the stream crooked its way past a large grove of acacia trees and a peach grove, there were ruins of Maori houses, relics of the peaceful missionary days when there were several villages of Ngati-Raukawa here.

The farm life was comfortable and happy, however primitive in some ways. There were farm and household utensils never seen now. Peaches fattened the pigs; even the horses and cattle munched those peaches. We had everything we needed; to the youthful mind, that knew no other life, it was endless comfort. I came to know later how short cash often was, and how settler and storekeeper often had to resort to the barter system in which no money passed. Later on I carried to the township every Saturday on the saddle in front of me a box of home-churned butter, that surpassed in excellence of flavour any factory butter of today. We got fourpence a pound for it, not in cash, but took it out in groceries—tea, and sugar. . . .

The farming then was mixed; root and grain crops of many kinds were grown, and there were sheep as well as cattle on every farm of any size. Candles were made by the farmer's wife from tallow; I remember the tin moulds used. Smelly candles they were, but better than nothing, expecially when kerosene was hard to get. We had orchards of generous size. There were no orchard pests; but caterpillars once destroyed a wheat crop.

The flax-bush was all important. No farmer could have done without it, for a score of purposes. The down or pollen (*hunehune*) of the raupo flowerhead was a substitute for feathers or kapok in filling pillows and cushions. Harness was made, in the early farming days, from green cowhide, cured with salt and alum. Plough and bridle reins and stirrup leathers were manufactured in that way. Floor mats and carpets were made by Maori neighbours, and on these were often laid dressed and dyed sheepskins. The old-fashioned flail was used for threshing grain before the first steam thresher arrived.

The housewives made much use of the abundant fruit. The big honey peaches were cut in slices, which were strung with darning needle and thread or string, and hung out in the wind and sun to dry, then they were laid out on boards, or on sheets of corrugated iron, thoroughly dried in the hot mid-summer sun, and finally hung up in festoons in the rafters of the kitchen for future use in pies. This practice seems to have become a lost art in the country. . . .

There was no factory-cured bacon in the pioneer days, for there were no factories. We dealt with our pigs on the farm, and we had a hand in every stage of the process from sty to kitchen. After the killing the meat was well rubbed in with salt, a business several times repeated, and then was transferred to the smoke-house, a small slab whare without a window and entered by a low door. Here the dissected pig was hung in the smoke of a sawdust fire which was kept steadily burning, or rather smouldering, on the earth floor for many days. When thoroughly smoke-cured the rolls and sides of bacon, now a fine golden colour, were suspended on wire hooks in the high-roofed kitchen. How often I think now at breakfast-time or thereabouts, of that airy old kitchen with its rafters all hung with our hoard of home-cured bacon! Never has there been any like it to me since those days on the farm.

JAMES COWAN (1870-1943)
Settlers and Pioneers

FARMHAND

You will see him light a cigarette
At the hall door careless, leaning his back
Against the wall, or telling some new joke
To a friend, or looking out into the secret night.

But always his eyes turn
To the dance floor and the girls drifting like flowers
Before the music that tears
Slowly in his mind an old wound open.

His red sunburnt face and hairy hands
Were not made for dancing or love making
But rather the earth-wave breaking
To the plough, and crops slow-growing as his mind.

He has no girl to run her fingers through
His sandy hair, and giggle at his side
When Sunday couples walk. Instead
He has his awkward hopes, his envious dreams to yarn to.

But ah in harvest watch him
Forking stooks, effortless and strong—
Or listening like a lover to the song
Clear, without fault, of a new tractor engine.

JAMES K. BAXTER (b.1926)

THE TUI

The houses in the valleys often had what we called
"a bit of native bush", with tall ferns above and stream
and leaf mould underfoot, and above a singing tui.
The tui was not an impassioned songster, he was more
a perfectionist. You could see him in a kowhai tree,
among the yellow beak-shaped blossoms, and above
him the bright pupil of the sun in the great iris of the
sky. In the stillness he would sing one note, usually
three times, and then one more note a tone or two
lower. There would be silence again, as if he were
listening and reflecting on the quality of the notes. Had
he got them perfect that time, should he not try again?
He would try them again, exquisitely, roundly, fluting
them out into the sky, this feathered composer who
never got beyond the opening bars of his symphony
because he must get them perfect, quite perfect. If
only he had let himself go, just once in a rhapsody,
but he never did, he was too self-conscious an artist.
He would try his four lovely notes, listen as if holding
his breath, and then chuckle and fly off.

JOHN GUTHRIE (JOHN BRODIE) (1905-1958)
Paradise Bay

NORFOLK PINES

These tall pines are the pines
Of an Oriental print
At close quarters real
But further off stark
As old calligraphy.

Echoes of Eastern shrines
Their laterals curve out
And upwards; they conceal
The white terns' mottled eggs
Frail and solitary.

On mid-blue nights they stain
The grass with shafts of shade,
Their boughs draw down the dream
The lunar light bestows
On ordinary sights.

Nurtured by the rain
The luminiscent eyes
Of white fungi gleam
Underneath the pines
On dim unquiet nights.

MERVAL CONNELLY (b. 1914)

THE RABBIT

While I was walking round the sheep this morning I
saw a rabbit throwing great quantities of earth out of
a burrow in a bank 50 or 60 yards away. I stood still
for a minute or two and watched, but at that distance
noticed chiefly the speed and efficiency with which the
work was being done. So far the rabbit had not seen
me, and I therefore moved forward to within 30 yards,
and then saw that it was a doe opening a burrow that
had already been made and sealed. I saw, too, that she
was holding a big bunch of tussock in her mouth, and
it was this, I suppose, that still prevented her from seeing
me, though I was now so close and standing upright.
For about half a minute she went on with her work
with her head turned away from me, and then stopped
for a moment and listened. I don't think she heard

me, or heard anything, but she apparently sensed something that gave her a moment's uneasiness. She resumed her scraping, however, throwing the earth vigorously back through her hind legs, and then, without stopping her feet, turned her head in my direction like a pianist who looks round at someone entering a room but does not stop playing. The tussock was still in her mouth, and this for some reason made shooting her more of an outrage. I knew that her family would not have been born, and that death in the womb is more merciful than death by starvation in a burrow. I remembered, too, that bullets are kinder than traps, and kinder than myxomatosis. But I felt a little ashamed when I picked her up still holding her babies' bed in her mouth.

OLIVER DUFF (1883-1967)
A Shepherd's Calendar

SCYTHING

All day I swing my level scythe,
　Slow-marching on the severed sward;
Content to know myself alone
　With grass, and leaves, and gusty sun.

The random handle that I hold,
　A strong lopped bough, bone-dry and curled,
Is emblem of an ancient time
　When wandering man first dreamed of home.

Scared by my near blade's foreign hiss
　A lizard flickers where I pass
Like Adam stooping to the ground
　With a lost Eden in his mind.

BASIL DOWLING (b. 1910)

HIGH COUNTRY SHEEP DOG

Away ahead a cloud of dust rolled down a spur and Brownie growled a savage curse. That cloud of dust told of a mob of sheep breaking for the saddle; it was Brownie's job to catch them and from where he was, perhaps a mile back, it would be a long and difficult run. Sidling to a handy shoulder, he scanned the basin ahead and at a low command one of his dogs shot away downhill and swung round above the bush line. Fortunately there were no sheep low down in the basin and urged by Brownie's shrill whistles, the little dog was soon streaking over the far spur and out of sight.

The dog was "running on the blind" and Brownie could now only trust to luck that it would cross the track of the escaping sheep and follow their scent. Anxious to gain a position from where he could get a view down into the saddle, Brownie dropped into the basin and commenced the long sidle out on to the far spur. Twenty minutes later, through in the next face, he cut the track of the sheep as it zig-zagged down through the tall snow-grass. Judging by the way the country was torn up there might have been anything up to fifty sheep in the mob—and they had not been lingering. They had had a full mile start on the dog, and Merino wethers all, they would take some catching. With his dogs streaming behind him, Brownie raced down a strip of loose shingle, his objective a jutting prominency a few hundred yards below.

From this vantage point he was able to get an unbroken view, and squatting on a snowgrass clump, he searched the country for signs of dog or sheep. Immediately below was a half-mile gap in the bush through which the saddle linked the country beyond. In years gone by, a fence had been erected across the saddle, but heavy snows had made its maintenance such a problem that it had eventually been abandoned and was now only a tangle of half-buried wire and broken standards. Beyond the saddle, the country consisted of a chain of easy shingle tops and open bush-bound faces, and from where he sat, Brownie had a clear view of the face straight opposite. Of the dog and the missing sheep, there was no sign, but half a dozen woollies which were zig-zagging their way slowly up from down near the bush line, told the watcher all he wanted to know— the missing sheep had gone through the face above them and the dog, following on their track, had passed these few and wheeled them back. His confidence in his dog unlimited, Brownie sprawled in the sun and puffed contentedly at a cigarette. That confidence was justified, for a few minutes later, the mob, a smudge of grey in the distance, came into sight round a far spur. Behind them was the little dog. Quietly and kindly, with a sagacity which was almost uncanny, he was piloting them back towards his master. As they sidled out above the other half dozen sheep, a shrill command had the dog recasting to gather them in also. In another few minutes, the mob, sixty-odd, were stringing back through the saddle and out above the bush.

Nothing gives the high country musterer greater satisfaction than to have one of his dogs put up a meritorious run and, old hand though he was, Brownie felt a glow of pride as he called the little dog back to heel. He glanced surreptitiously up the spur. Sure enough, young Wallace was sitting on a shoulder far above; he would have seen the whole run and it was a safe bet that the head shepherd from his vantage point on the high ridge had also been a witness.

Nowhere in the world is the sheepdog seen to such advantage as in the high country of New Zealand and this had been a fine example of their work. It had been at least a two mile head run on the "blind" and for the greater part the little dog had been out of sight of his master. Withal it had been performed on "hard" country, where courage must rank high in the many qualities essential for such work.

PETER NEWTON (b. 1906)
High Country Days

COMING OF SPRING

Already a brittle light chills
And hardens the wind-bent trees.
A post away a morepork shrills
In sudden short alarm. Cows on knees

Deep-buried in the grass turn
Ceremoniously their steaming heads
As we walk past. How strangely burn
The daffodils in your arms! So we tread

The long valley home with no word
Spoken, and into deeper night
Where cold air rushes like a bird
Released into our faces, and the light

Cast by the daffodils illumines
Your brow and eyes so dark
In their anguish, and past the pines
Where the leaping farm-dogs bark.

ALISTAIR CAMPBELL (b. 1926)

A MARAUDING PACK

He rose and went to the clearer space where the animals lay. One glance and he was back.

"Make haste! Make haste! There's wolves at the sheep!"

"Wolves? You're dreaming, man!" exclaimed Duncan, but sprang up immediately. Hamish called out to his brother, "Let off the dogs." He paused to pick up his crook, then instead chose a stout branch of manuka which had been cut down to make place for their bed.

The sheep dogs, already straining at their chains, needed no urging when they were let loose. They flew to attack the marauding pack which had been cunning enough to make sure the collies were not free before they disturbed the sheep. They fled now before the onslaught of the larger, heavier animals, and could be heard yapping as they retreated up the side of the hill whence they had come. Only one remained; its teeth were sunk in the flank of a sheep and it was determined not to let it go. The dogs in triumphant excitement were careering after their routed foes; it was left to the shepherds to attack the loiterer. Hamish belaboured it with his manuka club, while Dugald, grasping the sheep, attempted to pull it from its tormentor. Just as Duncan, carrying his heavy boots which he had not waited to put on, came up to them, the dog relinquished its hold of the sheep, but sprang at Dugald, and would have seized him by the throat had not Duncan, swinging one of his boots by its thick laces, aimed a blow which struck the creature on the side of the head so that it fell stunned. Hamish finished it off with his thick stick, and all three stood back breathless.

"You saved my life, Duncan," said Dugald at last in a hushed tone.

"Och, man, you're havering," said Duncan lightly. "I've heard of men being sair pit to it by wild pigs, but in a' the farfetched yarns they've telt me there's ne'er been a man brocht doon by a wild dog. For that's what your wolf is, Dugald. A wild dog, merely."

"Dog or wolf, if it had got at his throat, Dugald would have been done. We owe you more than we can repay, Duncan," said Hamish.

"It a' come of having larger feet than most men," claimed Duncan.

GEORGINA McDONALD (1905-1959)
Grand Hills for Sheep

THE MOREPORK

A quiet night, and over the hills fog
After a day of late December heat.
I listen to the stillness; then of a sudden the sharp
Clear double shout of a shepherd calling his dog
On the hill, but no answering bark or bleat:
Then the call again and again, as the driven silence goes.
No shepherd it is but an owl
As old as Europe and as full of woes
Hooting from under his cowl
Of bush on the lonely height;
A native of no country but the night
Of whose wide city he is sentinel
Going his noiseless rounds to cry the hours
To the somnambulist moon and watching stars.
"Twelve of the clock, and all's well"
Might be his words now as I go indoors,
And yet I cannot sleep
For that most melancholy voice up on the hill
Monotonously calling, mustering the midnight sheep.

BASIL DOWLING (b. 1910)

DISCOVERIES

Solitariness never bothered me. The more I was left
to myself, the greater the throng of people and incidents
in my day-dreams. The absence of matter-of-fact people
who saw only what existed liberated my mind. A
thousand new impressions crowded upon me as barriers
fell down, and made me unaware of Douglas's absence.
He must have gone in the springtime, for I remember
the earth coming to life as I played around alone. I
found little spiders that burrowed and tunnelled into
soft banks, and I found that if I inserted a straw or a
piece of grass into their tunnels and waited until the
grass or straw commenced to move and then gave the
straw or grass rod a sharp tug, I could draw out the
clinging spider. I found black earth on white clay
where I could delve for fat earthworms that glowed at
night and that were appreciated when my uncles went
trout fishing. I discovered Pukeko, the New Zealand
swamp hen, strutting in a nearby swamp. And in the
swamp I found tall spikes of a swamp flower to gather
in armfuls. There were millions of buttercups and
long-stemmed white daisies. Bees came to drink honey
from the heavy yellow gorse. A tall weed, ragwort I
think, harboured thousands of black and hundreds of
crimson butterflies. And butterflies in their drunken
moments of life are easy for children to catch. I decorated the wallpaper with beauties impaled upon cruel
pins until butterflies played as important a part in the
pattern on the walls as the brown tea spots. I hung
festoons of birds' eggs around the edges of pictures.
And my uncle found me a market for fledglings' heads.
County Councils, in their efforts to reduce the quantity
of wheat- and oat-eaters, paid a penny a dozen for

the heads of sparrows. I must have made a few pence
a week.

JOHN A. LEE (b. 1891)
Children of the Poor

THE PAINTER'S EYE

There were also those autumn mornings, foggy and
silent, the time of slackening yield before the winter
drying-off. The cows would come in reluctantly from
their lying down places. The green hillside looming
faintly over against the front of the cowshed would be
traced with darker tracks where their feet had knocked
the dew from the grass. Sometimes three-quarters of
the way through milking it would be discovered that
such-and-such a cow had not yet come down. The dog
would be sent out of sight to find her, and, when he
failed, one of us would be sent to the top of the hill to
look for her. I used to beg for this duty; and many a
time my reward was to find myself above the fog in a
luminous, uninhabited world. Before me at the other
side of a continuous sea of whitish mist the Mountain
swept upward from the right and left horizons, tenderly
sunlit blue and only streaked at the summit with
summer-surviving snow. Behind me rose the dark
islands of crested hills neighbouring ours. The sound
of the only rapids in the Mangaehu River collaborated
with the silence, and the glare of recent sunrise burned
white above the region of hidden Ruapehu. I would
remain and gaze as long as I dared; then dislodge the
truant cow from her warm nest in the bracken and
drive her down into the mist.

M. T. WOOLLASTON (b. 1910)
The Far-Away Hills

FARMYARD

He made a place in his dream for the pines to grow,
He saw their shadows lengthening, as now
In the slanting sun they lengthen, the house absorbing
This still coolness; he saw the dogs asleep
Each in the shade of his kennel; weathered shafts
Resting on the ground, and big wheels resting.

This giant trees he saw spring from his hand,
And made a place in the air for them to grow,
A place for the low white house in their deep shelter;
But now if he could enter as once he entered
This cool yard, the dogs would suddenly rise,
Their barking shatter the dream and the sleepy stillness.

Nobody remembers him, the woman
Swinging her pail as she walks beneath great branches,
Going down through shade to the cool swept cowshed,
The man on the dusty roadside bringing the cows;
They do not know they follow the paths he made
In a dream once for a man and a woman to follow.

This is the resting centre, leaf and flower
Have budded from the dream, the roots have grown,
The earth has accepted the roots and the burden of
    wheels,
All is fulfilled; only the man who saw
In seedlings in his hand this quiet hour,
Has passed from the dream, passed from the trees' long
    shadows.

RUTH DALLAS (b. 1919)

WHEN ALL THE LAND'S DARK FORESTS

When all the land's dark forests
Are felled—I tell thee then,
Dark growth will still need felling
Within the minds of men.

When all the fields are cleared
And ploughed—I tell thee then,
Still shall fields need ploughing
Within the souls of men.

When every field is harrowed
And sown—I tell thee then,
Seeds shall still need sowing
Within the hearts of men.

DONALD McDONALD (1912-1942)

People, Great and Small

GOVERNOR HOBSON

Governor Hobson died at Auckland after ruling New Zealand for a little less than three years. His best monument is the city he founded, and the most memorable verdict on his life is written in a letter addressed by a Maori chief to the Queen. "Let not," said this petition, "the new Governor be a boy or one puffed up. Let not a troubler come amongst us. Let him be a good man like this Governor who has just died." When these words were written, the judgment of the English in New Zealand would have been very different. But time has vindicated Hobson's honesty and courage, and in some important respects even his discernment. He anticipated the French, baffled the land-sharks, kept the peace, was generous to the Maori, and founded Auckland. No bad record this for the harassed, dying sailor, sent to stand between his own countrymen and savages at the very end of the earth, and left almost without men or money! If under him the colonists found their life unbearable, the fault was chiefly that of his masters. Most of his impolicy came from Downing Street; most of his good deeds were his own. It must be remembered that he was sent to New Zealand not to push on settlement, but to protect the natives and assert the Queen's authority. These duties he never forgot.

W. PEMBER REEVES (1857-1932)
The Long White Cloud

LOWERING THE FLAG

It was rumoured that Captain Pearson had reported us at the Bay of Islands as "a turbulent set of rebels, who were establishing a republic at Port Nicholson" and that the thirty soldiers had been sent to quell the rebellion! . . . Some hours' amusement was derived from this ludicrous mistake of the Government as to our hostility and the overwhelming force which they had sent to exterminate us.

The first measure of the Royalist forces was to send a man on shore the next morning to pull down all the New Zealand flags which he might find hoisted. This was probably an experimental measure only; as a single constable performed the task very early, before anybody was up. The man who performed this bold deed at Petone assumed, while he did it, the most ridiculous appearance of authority. He had been one of our early immigrants, brought out, I think, in the *Aurora*. He was usually styled "Captain" Cole. He had succeeded in getting appointed Chief Constable for Port Nicholson, and had accompanied Lieutenant Shortland, not a little elated with his official dignity. Although I have often since observed the remarkable pomposity which a Government official assumes in a colony, I never saw a more complete instance than Constable Cole.

As he strode up to the flag-staff near Colonel Wakefield's house, on which a rather ragged New Zealand flag was hung, he threw disdainful and yet cautious glances around him. When he saw that there were only two or three people in their night-caps peeping from their doors and windows to know who had been boating so early on such a cold morning, he plucked up spirits, and seemed to reflect that he had to represent the dignity of the British Crown. His funny little head arranged itself quite straight in a most appropriate military stock; his ungainly figure and gait became almost martial; he frowned sternly, as though to awe the rebels; and advanced straight upon the flag-staff with as much resolution as though he had been taking Ciudad Rodrigo by storm. He had some little trouble in undoing the string, and it would not run very freely through the hole at the top of the staff; but at length he accomplished his gallant undertaking, and proceeded with a flourish to extend the sovereignty of England over the flags which adorned the snoring grog-shops along the beach.

E. JERNINGHAM WAKEFIELD (1820-1879)
Adventures in New Zealand

A PIONEERING COURTSHIP

Sarah Higgins, who married in 1849 in the Nelson district, did not learn to write until she was over seventy years old, when she set down a simple account of her early life for her grand-children.

When I was going away from home, my boy, for I did have one that came sometimes (he was the same boy that helped the men to make the mud oven to bake the bread, and he was with the men making the road round the beach when I came ashore—I did not notice him but he did me) went home and told his mother that he had seen the prettiest (girl) he had ever seen in his life and he would have her if he could get her for a wife, so he never lost sight of me long together. He said he would come and see me, but I told him not to come for I did not want the lady to think I had a boy to see me, so I said, "If you can be true to me I can be true to you." Well, he thought he would try me and see if I could be true. So he was in Nelson one day and

he saw————"Well John, have you found a wife yet?"
He said "No." He said, "Could you tell me where to
find one?" My boy said "Yes, there is one at Mr. Otter-
son's if you can get her." So John came to see me. I
did not know him. He said "Good-day" and I said the
same. He said he wanted to talk to me a little. I told
him I had too much work to do to talk to him, so he
said "Are you engaged?" I said "Yes, to Mrs. and
Master————" but that is not what I meant. I said
I could not be engaged to anyone else. Well, the master
was just outside and when I went out he laughed at
me. He said I was a witty girl. I said "I did not know
the man. What did he want?" "The master said "Oh,
he wanted a wife." I said he would not get me. I was
there 14 months and only went home four times and
that is all we saw of each other, my boy and me, until
I left and went home. We had a crying match when I
left to go home. My brother came for me. He had to
carry me through the Wairau River and go back for
my things to bring them over. Well I got home once
more with my father and the hard times were getting
better. My father had bought a cow while I was away,
so then when I went home (there was) a cow to milk.
I took in sewing and got a lot to do. My brother got
a dog and ammunition and he used to get a wild pig
occasionally. Our vegetables grew and we had a nice
lot, so when I had been home about a year my boy
wanted to be married, but I said "No"! I wanted to wait
until I was 21 years, but he said he could not save anything for a home while he had to pay for his board
when he could only get 2/6 a day, so he got my father's
consent by promising he would not take me away from
him. Well, I gave my consent, then he and Mr. Jeffries
got to cut the timber for our room and he got Mr.
Wratt to build a nice room next to my father's, so we
were to be married when that was done. There was no
furniture in those days, we had to make our own.

I wanted a nice bed-stead so he cut the timber and made it and when we got a better one I had that made into a wash-hand-stand. It took Mr. Wratt about five or six weeks to build the room and we were to be married on the Monday, as he finished on the Saturday. When we got up in the morning we had to scrape the snow away from the door and the whole place was white. There was not a green tree nor a house that was not covered with snow. We had never seen it before nor since. It was a time to be remembered. We all thought the minister could not get up. He came up on a mule. There were no horses in the place, we all had to go about in bullock carts. Well, we did not have any party, but the neighbours, and they all gave and made, cooked and brought all that was wanted. I found two pairs of ducks; my father (gave) me a little sucking pig. He bought a big one and she had little ones. My brother had some goats and he killed a nice fat one; and I had a bottle of brandy sent me and that made sauce for the plum puddings. There were about 60 set down to dinner. They had a great game of snow-balling, they could not have any other game. Mr. Ironside (the Minister) said he had not seen so much snow since he had left "Old England". He came and shook hands with us and said God meant us to be angels. There were four of us in white. My boy was a favourite with the neighbours and so was I, so that is why they were so kind. . . . When we had paid the Minister we had just 10/- to begin our life's journey.

SARAH HIGGINS
from *Married and Gone to New Zealand*
ed. ALISON DRUMMOND (1960)

TO SIR GEORGE GREY

Within a forest stood a grand old tree,
  Whose head above the other plants rose high;
  He was the forest's first-born. Sun and sky
Had known him, and had smiled on him ere he
  Had kinsfolk near, or leafy brethren nigh;
The wild birds brought to him their minstrelsy;
  The singers knew that when the scene was rude,
He grew and gave a shelter to their race.
  By him the wandering melodists were wooed
To trill and warble in that lonely place;
  A sanctuary in the solitude
He gave to them. In him the birds could trace
  The forest's king, and so from hills and plains
  They flew to him, and sang their sweetest strain

THOMAS BRACKEN (1843-98)

BARON CHARLES DE THIERRY

Baron de Thierry bought a private Kingdom in the North Island
of New Zealand, and arrived in 1836 to proclaim himself "Sovereign
Chief of New Zealand," a claim nullified when Britain assumed
sovereignty over the country in 1840.

He is forty now. The mould has set; the last mould
but one. Nature, you know, experiments on our features
with a number of moulds. First there is that button-
nosed, hairless, toothless effect, not much to brag about.
Then suddenly there is individuality; a face has taken
shape. The child may be quite ridiculously like its
father or mother, and yet, in its own right, the little
face is so clear, so unspoiled by wrinkles and sly disguises,

NEW ZEALAND BUSH
Bush typical of the kind from which early farms were won, is shown here.
Fern, supplejack and nikau palms combine with kiekie, a trailing and
climbing vine sprouting many heads of long razor-sharp leaves.

THE TAURANGA-TAUPO RIVER

A scene at the mouth of the Tauranga-Taupo river, Lake Taupo. This lake is the largest in the country, twenty-five miles long, seventeen miles wide and discharging 5,000 cubic feet of water per second. Tauranga-Taupo is one of the many fishing settlements around the lake's southern shores.

AERIAL TOP-DRESSING

Because of the hilly nature of many New Zealand farms, top-dressing of the soil with fertiliser has long been carried out from the air. Crop-spraying is also done by helicopter. This scene shows top-dressing in the district around Mt. Wellington, Auckland.

so clean, with its soft, downy skin, that it exists in a world apart. We understand, looking at it, why poor Ponce de Leon dragged himself about looking for a Fountain of Youth.

Then that perfection is marred. The legs are too long, there are hairs on the boyish chin; or the little girl's flat chest—to her tearful embarrassment—produces overnight the elements of a bosom. What a pity! We avert our eyes. Behold, when we look back, the shining new mould, perfect again, so bright that it hurts our tired eyes. Youth stands before us, swaggering a little, kicking up the winged sandals. "Oh, God . . . Oh, God," cries that unreasoning, thwarted voice in our heart, "I was like that, too. . . . It isn't fair."

A peal of thunder, and the beautiful silver-gilt mould, which looked as though it would last for ever, has fallen in pieces to the ground. Now the face emerges as it is going to look for a long time . . . for Nature, growing impatient, has constructed the mask to last. It still retains a little of youth, even a little of childhood. But, with deft, sardonic touch, the fine details have been added, wrinkle, spot and scar.

Portrait of a gentleman in broadcloth. His face is long, shield-shaped, his fringes of chestnut whiskers are turning iron-grey. Otherwise, he is clean-shaven, revealing the fact that his mouth is long, sensitive, obstinate as a mule's. He has a long nose with a bump at the end. His eyebrows are bushy, and beneath them the hazel eyes look out with a glance at once fierce and appealing. He is not—for which one may be grateful—in the least bald. His hands are beautiful—long-fingered, slender, determined.

Yes, it is a scarred face. That twitch of the mouth, that rather too arrogant stare of the eyes, followed by the humble, appealing glance. The face of a sensitive man who has quarrelled frequently with his inferiors, and thought too much, in the subsequent hours, of

what he has said, and what an immortal, ineffaceable
fool he was to say anything at all.

He would stay like this for a long while, until there
is that strange little chiming stroke of the gong, not
hard at all, this time merely as if the gilt clock had
sounded the hour. Then the mould will split in halves,
and out of it will emerge the incredibly fragile figure
of old age.

ROBIN HYDE (IRIS WILKINSON) (1906-39)
Check to Your King

THE REMITTANCE-MAN

Once I was riding with my husband up a lovely gully,
when we heard the crack of a stockwhip sounding
strangely through the deep eternal silence of a New
Zealand valley, and a turn of the track showed us a
heavy timber-laden bullock-wagon labouring slowly
along. At the head of the long team sauntered the
driver, in the usual rough-and-ready costume, with his
soft plush hat pulled low over his face, and pulling
vigorously at a clay pipe. In spite of all the outer
surroundings, something in the man's walk and dejected
attitude struck my imagination, and I made some
remark to my companion. The sound of my voice
reached the bullock-driver's ears; he looked up and on
seeing a lady, took his pipe out of his mouth, his hat
off his head, and, forcing his beasts a little aside, stood
at their head to let us pass. I smiled and nodded, receiving
in return a perfect and profound bow and the most
melancholy glance I have ever seen in human eyes.
"Good gracious, F———," I cried when we had passed,
"who is that man?" "That is Sir So-and-so's third
son," he replied: "they sent him out here without a
shilling, five years ago, and that is what he has come
to: a working man living with working men. He

looks heart-broken, poor fellow, doesn't he?" I, acting
upon impulse, as any woman would have done, turned
back and rode up to him, finding it very difficult to
frame my pity and sympathy in coherent words. "No,
thank you, ma'am," was all the answer I could get,
in the most refined, gentlemanly tone of voice: "I'm
very well as I am. I should only have to struggle all
over again if I made any change now. It is the truest
kindness to leave me alone." He would not even shake
hands with me; so I rode back, discomfited, to hear
from F——— that he had made many attempts to
befriend him, but without success. "In fact," concluded
F——— with some embarrassment, "he drinks dread-
fully, poor fellow. Of course that is the secret of all
his wretchedness, but I believe despair drove him to it
in the first instance."

LADY MARY ANNE BARKER (1831-1911)
Station Amusements in New Zealand

CONVERSATION PIECE

Where are you off to, Bill?
Surely the river's too full.

Me and my billy don't worry:
We take the track for the sea,
And there's no hurry.

But why are you leaving, Bill
When you've just fetched up?
Stay for a bite and a sup
Or a few square meals.

I've tea and sugar and flour,
And inside the hour
I'm heading into the hills.

Bill, have you struck it rich?

No,—but you never saw such
Promise of colour, not a doubt
Of it—till the cloudburst
Drove me out of it.

*Bill, what will you do
When you strike it?*

Me, I might go to town
—I don't like it—
But I'd cut a bit of a dash,
Buy a billycock hat and maybe
Go on the bash.

But I really need
Some tough new boots
And a stout pair of breeks
For crossing the rivers
When the weather breaks.

DENIS GLOVER (b. 1912)

THE COLONIAL SURVEYOR

The Indian Survey officer is clothed in snow white from "sola topi" down to canvas pipe-clayed shoes. He smokes his perfumed "hooka" or the fragrant "manilla" with an air of listless satisfaction. When he walks on duty he is followed by a "Piada" carrying an umbrella to shield him from the sun, and should a gutter cross his path, two lusty "bearers" are ready to lift him over. Two or three hours of out-door exposure of his precious self suffices for the day, which done he sits at the door of his capacious tent enjoying his "otium cum dignitate" and his brandy "pance". . . .

The Colonial Surveyor in these regions is clothed in fustian trousers and blue shirt, Panama hat, and stout hobnailed shoes. He is not known from his chainman. If he smokes, it is foetid negrohead through a "cutty" pipe, and he puffs at that energetically. He has a hundred things about him; knives, needles, telescopes, matches, paper, ink, thread and buttons; these are stowed away in all corners of his dress; and then his "swag" contains his tent-blankets, and change of clothes. These with his theodolite he carries on his back, and walks away through bogs, "creeks", and scrubs, at the rate of three miles an hour. He cleans his shoes once a month with mutton dripping, and he lives on "damper", salt junk and oceans of tea. His fare is homely, but it is refreshing to see his voracity. His bed is on the ground, and he considers himself lucky if he gets into a bush where he can luxuriate in the warmth of a blazing fire. In this land of equality he shares bed and board with his men, but they are not of the common sort, for "the service" is popular amongst the enterprising colonists, and he has to pick. They are men that know their place and duty.

Having partaken of the bitters and sweets of both services pretty freely, I must state that upon the whole, as surveyors are made to be killed, I prefer "dum vivimus" cold air and stout appetite, to a hot air and general prostration. I prefer the homely enjoyments of a colonial life.

JOHN TURNBULL THOMSON[1] (1821-1884)
Reconnaissance Survey of the
Southern Districts of Otago

[1]J. T. Thomson, after being Chief Surveyor of Otago, became Surveyor-General of the Colony in 1876.

A COUNTRY M.P.

The member for the district, eyes for all,
Moves in the crowd, at duty's pleasant call;
A sturdy brown-faced man, with kindly hand,
And head well-stored with facts of men and land.
The Burke of precedence he slightly knows,
But not the Burke of England's throes.
From year to year he never reads a book;
At State reports he gives a casual look.
But nothing in the "game" escapes his eye;
The turns and twists, what's fit to sell or buy;
A weakness here that can be deftly touched;
Advantage there that can be quickly clutched.
Himself his true magnetic north, his star
His mounting vote in each triennial war;
But next what he can lever for his clan,
Who like and treat him as the farmer's man.
First principles are air, but money grants
Are solid food for hungry voters' wants.
He knows the turns of every off-shoot road;
What every holding bears in mortgage load;
The names of man and boy, who married whom;
Kinship of portraits in the stiff front room;
The favourite cow, the housewife's champion cake
(Many a one his gossip's helped to make).
The district's dotted with his victories,
Fruits of his tireless importunities:
Bridges and schools and metal strewn on mud,
A groyne to stop the ravening of a flood;
Buildings and wharves and comfortable jobs—
Billets for Jane and Harry, where the only mobs
Are men, not cattle, and the servant hours
Exact no tax beyond their written powers.

"A road and bridges member," so some sneer,
He takes it as a flower of pride to wear.

ALAN MULGAN (1881-1962)
Golden Wedding

AT THE DINNER TABLE

"For what we are about to receive," said Mr. Garnett,
"may the Lord make us truly thankful."

"Amen," murmured his wife. Miss Muriel did not
speak.

Walter sat himself down opposite to Mrs. Garnett,
feeling the cold white table-cloth slide against his
knees. The first time he had heard grace spoken in the
Garnett household he had not understood what was
expected of him—his own parents invoked no such
blessing—and had not even stood up for the ceremony.
Only a stiff reminder from old Mrs. Garnett had brought
him to his feet. "We always stand, young man." Walter
had blushed and had not since forgotten the hint.

Now there was a silence as Mr. Garnett, his napkin
already tucked into his waistcoat, carved the mutton.
The lamp threw a creamy bubble of light against the
ceiling.

"Walter," said Miss Muriel presently, "will you pour
the water, please?"

It was his dinner-time task. He went round the table,
clasping the curly glass handle of the jug against him.
Unless he poured the water boldly the lip of the jug
dribbled on to the cloth and down the side of the
tumblers. With Mrs. Garnett's glass he was especially
careful. When he had finished, she took a small box
from her lap and dropped a pinkish pill into the water,
a pill that misted the surface with bubbles. Walter
thought the pills might be sherbert.

"Knife sharp enough, father?" Miss Muriel watched

the old man as he carved. "I did run the steel over it."

"This colonial mutton . . . not like the English Southdown . . . it wants consistency." He grunted, breathing heavily, his beard trembling a little. "One would think, in this land of sheep, the farmers might breed meat of a closer texture." He passed a plate to his wife, then handed Walter a helping. "Do you know what the words 'consistency' and 'texture' mean?" he asked the boy absently, without looking at him.

Walter hesitated. This was a test because he had failed with the word "expediency." "Do they mean a sort of thickness?" he ventured. "Do they, sir?"

"He hasn't the least idea." From across the table Mrs. Garnett drawled her comment. "He's only a colonial." She took a sip of the misted, pinky water before her. "Besides, he never remembers anythin'."

"I do," Walter protested. "I remember nearly everything." He looked morosely down at his plate. "I do remember things."

Mr. Garnett smiled at the boy's bent head. "Well, you make a good guess at 'consistency.' Almost an alpha for that."

Miss Muriel interrupted. "Let him alone, father. He's hungry; he's been at school all day."

"I questioned him only from academic interest, my dear." The old man, ruffled, attacked his mutton. "And the son of a farmer, even here in New Zealand, might be expected to show some knowledge of the classical rudiments of his own language, after all."

"Yes, but not now. Let him eat."

JAMES COURAGE (1903-1963)
The Young Have Secrets

LORD RUTHERFORD

One evening, in 1880, a violent storm broke over the hamlet of Foxhill, near Brightwater in Nelson. In their house in Foxhill the family of James Rutherford were unable to sleep, so after Mrs. Martha Rutherford had looked after the customary shrouding of mirrors, silverware and windows against the lightning, both parents and children trooped out on the veranda of the house to watch and listen to the storm. There James Rutherford ran a spirited commentary on the scene in the sky, describing for his children what was sheet, what was fork, what was ball lightning, showing how, if they counted the interval between flash and thunderclap, they could tell whether the storm was approaching or moving away.

Great damage was done in the Brightwater area that night, but after the dead stock—both the beasts that had gone wild and galloped into fences, and those struck by lightning—had been replaced, the storm became for most people a fading memory. But not for one of the Rutherford boys, whose nine-year-old mind was given its direction for all time by the elemental fury he had witnessed. Naturally of a quiet disposition, he became even more withdrawn and thoughtful, and sometimes at the table he would lay down his knife and fork and stare into vacancy, so that his family would chaff him, saying: "Look at Ern! Look at Ern!" So started, over a storm in Nelson, the chain of thoughts and actions that irrevocably led to the man-made storm that broke over Hiroshima some sixty-five years later with incalculable significance for mankind.

RAYMOND ANTHONY KNOX (b. 1926)
New Zealand Listener

THE RABBITER

You say that killing rabbits is not a manly game;
It's honest work, it seems to me—there's little in a name.
Your hands are whiter far than mine, your clothes are
    better, too.
In the store, behind the counter, is the place for chaps
    like you.
But sure as summer's coming and nor-wester winds will
    blow,
The people working in the towns have something still
    to know.

To measure yards of calico may be a noble thing—
I'd rather face the mountain side and hear the skylark
    sing.
If tailors' shops are far away it's little odds to me,
When blood and fur are flying round you can't lick
    dungaree.
It isn't heavy boots that make a fellow mean and low—
The people working in the towns have plenty still to
    know.

If you could come along with me some morning when
    I start,
You'd feel the brightness of the air go stealing to your
    heart;
You'd reckon you were twice the man, and be so too
    perhaps,
While dew beads hang on all the grass along the line of
    traps.
You'd tell your mates when you went home that work
    in town was slow—
There's something up the country that some other
    fellows know.

There's pleasure working in the sun and frost and wind
    and rain,
There's glory on the mountain top and on the shining
    plain,
There's fragrance in the spear-grass fire, there's music
    in the creek,
And duff on Sunday in the hut that's eaten once a week;
Good healthy work for simple men, an honest wage to
    earn—
The people living in the towns have something still to
    learn.

And you who say that rabbitting is not a manly game—
There's better men than you and I who do it all the same.
The fishermen on Galilee were pretty lowly chaps
(There isn't such a mighty odds in fishing nets and
    traps);
The Pharisees were better dressed and did the talk and
    blow,
But there was something after all they didn't get to
    know.

So you can do the talk and sneer—"a dirty, savage life"—
There's clean-lived chaps among the men who wield the
    rabbit knife;
It isn't sun and mountain air that lead to sin and crime;
There's blackness in the city night, but not in morning
    rime;
And if you take them as a class the rabbiters will show
There's better feeling on the hills than in the town below.

DAVID McKEE WRIGHT (1867-1928)
Station Ballads

A COUNTRY MAYOR

The mayoralty of Rangitira was not a position that
was keenly sought after. Frequently the election was
not even contested. On one occasion it seemed doubtful
whether anyone at all would offer his services to the
community until some scheming fellows whose public
spirit was dominated by their sense of humour enticed
Wilkins into the Rangitira hotel. There they flattered
him and bought him drinks until a new realisation
was borne in on him—that he was by nature a leader
of men. The next morning he felt that perhaps he was
mistaken but as his faith in himself was beginning to
falter a deputation of the same men who had paid for
the drinks the night before arrived in his shop and
asked him to stand for the mayoralty.

In the early days of his reign there were difficulties
he had not foreseen. When asked questions at meetings
of the Borough Council or on other occasions he found
that he was expected to give answers and make decisions.
Ashamed to explain that he was unused to making any
decision without first consulting his wife, he was often
at a loss for a reply. At civic functions, however, when
he was expected to make a speech, he acquitted himself
with great credit. No one else in the town had a greater
facility for stringing together a series of clichés into
what bore some resemblance to a connected discourse.
He soon found that he liked making speeches. The
beauty of his borrowed diction touched a responsive
chord in his own emotions and frequently brought
tears to his eyes. As a dipsomaniac takes to alcohol
so Wilkins took to speech-making. Very soon he found
that when asked to make a decision he could avoid the
point at issue by making a speech on the subject. It
was quite impossible to keep him to the point. Away

he would soar on the wings of oratory and in consequence
very little business was done. His intoxicating rhetoric
had the effect of arousing in his bosom a longing for
self-sacrifice. He was always offering to lay down his
life in some municipal cause. To mention only a few,
he had professed himself ready to die in order to obtain
(1) a macadamised road leading from the coast to
Rangitira (2) an additional wing to the Post Office
(3) a proper town drainage system. In this way he had
earned the nickname of Ready-to-Die Wilkins.

R. M. BURDON (1896-1965)
Outlaw's Progress

KATHERINE MANSFIELD

In her best short stories, Katherine Mansfield holds a
place unique in English literature. It is, I think, a
two-fold achievement that gives her this place. First,
she enlarged the potentialities of language, of the
English language. She made something out of words
quite new and unthought-of. She wrought a new
texture in prose. Second, she explored a realm of
emotional experience, she communicated a quality of
emotional experience found nowhere else in literature.
It is not merely that no one else has taken the New
Zealand sea-side as subject-matter for story-telling. It
is not merely that no one else has conveyed, for example,
the salty, sandy, gritty memory of a summer day on
the beach. What Katherine Mansfied wrote about
only partly explains this quality in her stories. It has
something to do with her people, too, her old maids
and her children. It is a kind of tremulous quality, as
when experience is a little uncertain in its lights and
shadows and we don't know whether to laugh—no,
to smile, or cry. . . .

Her art was the form of the short story; at its best

the "lyric" form of narrative prose, for it catches the nature and meaning of some quality in human personality or human relationships, not much extended in time, volatile, perhaps, but not necessarily slight, static or else at the very crisis of change. Katherine Mansfield was a great short-story writer, because she had the supreme gift of perceiving and communicating the totality of such a fragment of emotional experience. It may be the disappointed hope of a child: she catches it, still quivering like a bird caught in flight. It may be the timid excitement of a girl at her first ball: when "the lights, the azaleas, the dresses, the pink faces, the velvet chairs, all became one beautiful wheel." It may be the last, faint shadow of hurt that a man feels at the death of a son, killed in the war, a shadow just dark enough to leave him preoccupied, so that he teases a fly drowning in a pool of ink spilt on the table, teases it abstractedly but wholly absorbed in its heroism, giving a new meaning to Gloucester's words in *King Lear:*

> As flies to wanton boys are we to the gods;
> They kill us for their sport.

Or else it may be a moment in human relationships that is caught—little eddies of love and hate that disturb the stream of intimacy, the odd loneliness of an old man in the house he has built and amongst the daughters he has fathered. Or else it may be the very texture of life as it is lived by a group of people in a certain place, at a certain time—the sunlit, sandy quality of life by the sea, boisterous with the noise of children's play, criss-crossed with tiny tensions between family and family, and in the heart of the family, too.

ARTHUR SEWELL (b. 1903)
Katherine Mansfield: A Critical Essay

GRANDMOTHER AND GRANDCHILD

Kezia and her grandmother were taking their siesta together. The little girl, wearing only her short drawers and her underbodice, her arms and legs bare, lay on one of the puffed-up pillows of her grandma's bed, and the old woman, in a white ruffled dressing-gown, sat in a rocker at the window, with a long piece of pink knitting in her lap. This room that they shared, like the other rooms of the bungalow, was of light varnished wood and the floor was bare. The furniture was of the shabbiest, the simplest. The dressing-table, for instance, was a packing-case in a sprigged muslin petticoat, and the mirror above was very strange; it was as though a little piece of forked lightning was imprisoned in it. On the table there stood a jar of seapinks, pressed so tightly together they looked more like a velvet pincushion, and a special shell which Kezia had given her grandma for a pin-tray, and another even more special which she had thought would make a very nice place for a watch to curl up in.

"Tell me, grandma," said Kezia.

The old woman sighed, whipped the wool twice round her thumb and drew the bone needle through. She was casting on.

"I was thinking of your Uncle William, darling," she said quietly.

"My Australian Uncle William?" said Kezia. She had another.

"Yes, of course."

"The one I never saw?"

"That was the one."

"Well, what happened to him?" Kezia knew perfectly well, but she wanted to be told again.

"He went to the mines, and he got a sunstroke there, and died," said old Mrs. Fairfield.

Kezia blinked and considered the picture again. . . . A little man fallen over like a tin soldier by the side of a big black hole.

"Does it make you sad to think about him, grandma?" She hated her grandma to be sad.

It was the old woman's turn to consider. Did it make her sad? To look back, back. To stare down the years, as Kezia had seen her doing. To look after *them*, as a woman does, long after *they* were out of sight. Did it make her sad? No, life was like that.

"No, Kezia."

"But why?" asked Kezia. She lifted one bare arm and began to draw things in the air. "Why did Uncle William have to die? He wasn't old."

Mrs. Fairfield began counting the stitches in threes. "It just happened," she said in an absorbed voice.

"Does everybody have to die?" asked Kezia.

"Everybody!"

"*Me*?" Kezia sounded fearfully incredulous.

"Some day, my darling."

"But, grandma," Kezia waved her left leg and wiggled the toes. They felt sandy, "what if I just won't?"

The old woman sighed again and drew a long thread from the ball.

"We're not asked, Kezia," she said sadly. "It happens to all of us sooner or later."

Kezia lay still, thinking this over. She didn't want to die. It meant that she would have to leave here, leave everywhere, for ever, leave—leave her grandma. She rolled over quickly.

"Grandma," she said in a startled voice.

"What, my pet!"

"*You're* not to die," Kezia was very decided.

"Ah, Kezia"—her grandma looked up and smiled and shook her head—"don't let's talk about it."

"But you're not to. You couldn't leave me. You couldn't not be there." This was awful. "Promise me you won't ever do it, grandma," pleaded Kezia.

The old woman went on knitting.

"Promise me! Say never!"

But still her grandma was silent.

Kezia rolled off the bed; she couldn't bear it any longer, and lightly she leapt on to her grandma's knees, clasped her hands round the old woman's throat and began kissing her, under the chin, behind the ear, and blowing down her neck.

"Say never . . . say never . . . say never—" she gasped between the kisses. And then she began, very softly and lightly, to tickle her grandma.

"Kezia!" The old woman dropped her knitting. She swung back in the rocker. She began to tickle Kezia. "Say never, say never, say never," gurgled Kezia, while they lay there laughing in each other's arms. "Come, that's enough, my squirrel! That's enough, my wild pony!" said old Mrs. Fairfield, setting her cap straight. "Pick up my knitting."

Both of them had forgotten what the "never" was about.

KATHERINE MANSFIELD (KATHLEEN BEAUCHAMP) (1888-1923)
At the Bay

A GENTLEMAN OF THE ROADS

Six feet and a fraction of an inch tall. Strong. Broad-shouldered. Restless. He wore a straw boater tied to the lapel of his coat with a bootlace. Round his neck was a clean celluloid collar. His dark tie showed signs of weather and as was the way of blue and black fabrics in those days, was bleached green. His swag was a normal swag, blankets, a towel maybe, a few odds and ends somewhere inside, maybe a tin plate and a pair of scissors to trim his moustache and beard. Around all was rolled a calico tent and the roll was held by two straps and these were connected by a third from which the swag was slung on the shoulder. The tin billy which hung down from the end of the swag had the blackness of a thousand fires.

The straw boater, the celluloid collar and tie, all these were worn until the hat grew dark brown and its band greasy with sweat, until the collar grew yellow and the tie green. They were portion of the stock in trade of gentility, of eccentricity.

"A swagger in a boater." "A swagger wearing a collar and tie."

There was one other article of eccentricity long before that article became the emblem of international appeasement. From the top end of the swag protruded the bent handle of an umbrella. If he was of the open road he had many years ago decided to take precautions against the rain. His moustache and greying whiskers were poorly trimmed but the face was clean, if weather-beaten. His coat was made of a peppery brown, big-checked, rough-spun tweed with large buttons and had been given to him by a squatter. It fitted. If it had been too loud for the squatter, it suited the Shiner nicely.

His waistcoat was like his tie, weather bleached. It had been blue serge but was greenish, and as with all waistcoats at that time and day was cut high, so that the state of the shirt did not much matter. The trousers were of a dark material, and were almost skin tight and were too short. They, too, had been a gift and he had swapped at once for a stick of tobacco a comfortable full-fitting pair of dungarees. He could not start with a boater and a collar and end with dungarees. Nevertheless the trousers were tight enough to seem ridiculous, to make his pose of debased gentility merge into the farcical.

But when a tramp came off a road on a rainy day

wearing an umbrella over a summer boater and a collar
and a tie, and with a swag and a black billy, many
people, instead of shutting the door, felt almost apolo-
getic at the poor fare they could offer the presence. And
when they knew it was the Shiner they were still
inclined to say, "Come in." . . .

Most swaggers were ashamed to be swaggers and
were looking for work, but the Shiner glorified the
vagabond profession and boasted about how he dodged
work, and in consequence in most places his plate was
very well filled. If many a man on the road had a
measure of shame as he asked for a meal—the Shiner
only blanched with shame when someone offered him
a poor handout or a job. . . .

Work? What was work? Any fool could work.
Ditch? He could ditch with the best of them if he was
of the mind. Fork sheaves off the stack? Never in the
world was there a forker his equal when he willed.
Dig potatoes? His big shoulders could lift more earth
on a fork than two men and he would scatter the potatoes
clean along the surface with any man. But that sort
of thing had to appeal to a man and it did not appeal
to him. For fifteen minutes, yes. He could give the
greatest exhibition of work of any man living provided
it stopped at being an exhibition, but when he was
expected to go on and make it a habit that was too
much. This was a free country or should be. It took
health and strength to get up and go to work. It took
moral courage as well as strength to be in bed when
the sun was shining on the tent. Any fool could get
sunburnt at work. To get sunburnt in bed was different.

JOHN A. LEE (b. 1891)
Shining with the Shiner

OLD WOMAN

The years have stolen
all her loveliness,
her days are fallen
in the long wet grass
like petals broken
from the lilac blossom,
when the winds have shaken
its tangled bosom.

Her youth like a dim
cathedral lies
under the seas
of her life's long dream,
yet she hears still
in her heart, sometimes,
the far, sweet chimes
of a sunken bell.

A. R. D. FAIRBURN (1904-1957)

BOY WANTED

The settlers farming the lush lands between the fifty
little rivers running off the eastern and southern slopes
of Mount Egmont greeted the first woman doctor to
enter their province with a primitive curiosity and an
inarticulate gratitude.

Within four days of my arrival there was an 8 p.m.
peal at the door bell. It was a recent immigrant farmer
from Switzerland who pressed a bottlish parcel into
my hands.

"I give you this. You give me boy."

My mind worked briskly. This would be the husband of the woman we had confined a few hours earlier. She knew so little English that when we bade her lie down she would promptly sit up, but by telling her to do exactly the opposite of what we wanted we contrived to get along pretty well. She already had a son and wanted a girl this time. But another boy had arrived. I had been sorry for the mother's disappointment, and said, "But your wife wanted a girl. I am sorry I did not get her a girl."

"She not to have girl," vehemently. "Boy more use to me."

I presented the champagne to Mrs. Paget and sent the gold top seal to Bill in France, with the comment that where bush had to be felled and bogs drained, girl babies seemed about as popular as they were in China.

DORIS GORDON (1890-1956)
Backblocks Baby-Doctor: An Autobiography

SIR TRUBY KING

In 1907, Truby King founded the Plunket Society, for the care of the health of mothers and children, pioneering ante-natal methods which have spread throughout the world.

At the time the Society was founded, King, in his forty-ninth year, was no longer the frail-looking young man whose boyish appearance had once deceived his enemies at Seacliff into believing he might easily be crushed. The maturity of middle age had begun to overtake him; still slim and slight of frame, he had begun to stoop a little from the shoulders. In repose his features had an air of melancholy which disappeared at once when his interest was aroused. His head was massive, his hair dark and abundant. A strong, prominent chin, full but firmly closed lips and a clipped military moustache, suggested a soldier or administrator, but the large, sad, sombre eyes were those of a visionary looking out through time and space at things not yet apparent to the men of his generation.

He was inclined to pay rather less than the necessary attention to all those details of everyday life not immediately connected with his work. His absent-mindedness took the form of being extremely careless as to how his clothes were put on. If not carefully watched by Mrs. King he was quite capable of going out with his boots unlaced, dressed in whatever garments lay ready to hand, however unsuitable or ill-assorted. He seldom recognised his own hat or overcoat and would often come home wearing those of other people. . . . A story is told of how, after leaving a certain house where he had been staying, he found that his pyjamas were missing. Thinking they had been left behind he sent a wire asking for them to be forwarded on to him, but they could not be found. When he undressed the following night, he discovered that he had still got them on under his trousers.

He was as careless about money as he was about clothes. For him it was nothing more than a means to an end. He could never see why the lack of it should be allowed to hinder the accomplishment of anything requiring to be done. Meanness and avarice were things altogether outside the range of his comprehension. . . . But if he was careless about such things as clothes and money he gave undivided attention to the minutest details of child welfare. His absent-mindedness in everyday affairs was the result of an extraordinary concentration on his work. Every method of nursing and feeding had to be proved and checked over and over again before being adopted by the Plunket Society. Every contrivance used for the upbringing of children, prams, feeding bottles, etc., had to be tested and re-tested

till no shadow of doubt remained as to which kind were
the most suitable.

R. M. BURDON (1896-1965)
New Zealand Notables: Series Two

LAST STEPS TO EVEREST

I lay on the little rock ledge panting furiously. Gradually
it dawned on me that I was up the step, and I felt a
glow of pride and determination that completely
subdued my temporary feeling of weakness. For the
first time on the whole expedition I really knew I was
going to get to the top. "It will have to be pretty tough
to stop us now" was my thought. But I couldn't entirely
ignore the feeling of astonishment and wonder that
I'd been able to get up such a difficulty at 29,000 feet
even with oxygen.

When I was breathing more evenly I stood up and,
leaning over the edge, waved to Tenzing to come up.
He moved into the crack, and I gathered in the rope
and took some of his weight. Then he, in turn, commenced to struggle and jam and force his way up until I
was able to pull him to safety—gasping for breath. We
rested for a moment. Above us the ridge continued on
as before—enormous overhanging cornices on the right
and steep snow slopes on the left running down to the
rock bluffs. But the angle of the snow slopes was
easing off. I went on chipping a line of steps, but
thought it safe enough for us to move together in order
to save time. The ridge rose up in a great series of
snakelike undulations which bore away to the right,
each one concealing the next. I had no idea where the
top was. I'd cut a line of steps around the side of one
undulation and another would come into view. We
were getting desperately tired now and Tenzing was
going very slowly. I'd been cutting steps for almost

two hours, and my back and arms were starting to tire. I tried cramponing along the slope without cutting steps, but my feet slipped uncomfortably down the slope. I went on cutting. We seemed to have been going for a very long time and my confidence was fast evaporating. Bump followed bump with maddening regularity. A patch of shingle barred our way, and I climbed dully up it and started cutting steps around another bump. And then I realised that this was the last bump, for ahead of me the ridge dropped steeply away in a great corniced curve, and out in the distance I could see the pastel shades and fleecy clouds of the highlands of Tibet.

To my right a slender snow ridge climbed up to a snowy dome about forty feet above our heads. But all the way along the ridge the thought had haunted me that the summit might be the crest of a cornice. It was too late to take risks now. I asked Tenzing to belay me strongly, and I started cutting a cautious line of steps up the ridge. Peering from side to side and thrusting with my ice-axe, I tried to discover a possible cornice, but everything seemed solid and firm. I waved Tenzing up to me. A few more whacks of the ice-axe, a few very weary steps and we were on the summit of Everest.

SIR EDMUND HILLARY (b. 1919)
High Adventure

TEDDY BOY

Juke-box jungle, and flood of neon light
Fire the unspoken boredom in his eyes;
He leans at corners, gestured in defeat,
Ignoring the sly-eyed girls whose look speaks lies.

Both pimp and prophet of our prosperous time,
He flaunts indifference, an all-superior style,
To public eyes the image and the fact of crime:
They do not like a man who cannot smile.

His song is one with a juke-box by the bar
Whose anguish speaks for his and other tongues;
He is the man of a moment not his own,
Shifting beneath his feet, an unmapped mire—
The scapegoat reason for a public wrong
Who begging bread, received instead a stone.

JOHN BOYD (b. 1933)

MUM

You had only to watch her about the kitchen to know she was good at it. I seem to remember one of her friends telling her she had the cleanest cupboards in the whole of Raggleton.

Even Dad told me once that she was a wonderful housekeeper.

It got so that I used to just watch her, knowing she was something of a champion at it. I actually told her she was a champion. I suppose a kid likes to think his mother and father are champions in some respect. There was a kid at school once who skited that his mother had really big legs, though I don't see that it was much to skite about. It shows you, though.

So I didn't mind her not talking, and I watched her getting my tea, and all we said was pass this and pass that please, and excuse me, with her adding a few more words like more of this or more of that, and me saying thanks.

She was big, as I have probably said, and strong-looking, and her hair was straight and shiny, and she had a face some people would say was too long—in fact, when I was a tiny kid I seem to remember her saying that people said just that—and big brown eyes. But now I am getting her mixed up.

I suppose it's because I can think of three of her. As she was long, long ago; she was full of beans then, tossing me into the air, and laughing so loud, with big bright eyes, shining black hair, and a face that had a lot of love in it. Some faces are soft and fleshy and you would never guess that there was any bone there, but in her face you could see the bone under the smooth skin, around her cheeks, and on her forehead, and around her jaw, which I daresay was somewhat larger than most. Once, there I saw a picture of the Duke of Wellington, and he reminded me a little of my mother in the face. Whether it was before or after the Battle of Waterloo in 1815 I can't say. Long ago her skin was smooth, and she was bright-eyed, and when her arms lifted me I felt very weak and comfortable indeed.

The second picture I have of her is at the time I'm talking about. I said her hair was straight and shiny, and that was wrong—it used to shine, I meant. Now it was just straight hair, and I would think about what a pity she didn't wash and comb it more often to make it the way it used to be. And the skin puckered up a little somehow, and her face seemed thinner, and her eyes were still nice eyes, yet they made me a little scared sometimes, looking very hot and bothered, or staring away, and not blinking and not looking.

The third picture is my business. I'm not sure that I remember it, anyway, because more and more I see her as she was at first. Why isn't everybody and everything the way they were at first? I wonder.

IAN CROSS (b. 1925)
The God Boy

The Maori

MAUI SNARES THE SUN

The young hero, Maui, had not been long at home with his brothers when he began to think that it was too soon after the rising of the sun that it became night again, and that the sun again sank down below the horizon, every day, every day; in the same manner the days appeared too short to him. So at last, one day he said to his brothers: "Let us catch the sun in a noose, so that we may compel him to move more slowly, in order that mankind may have long days to labour in to procure subsistence for themselves"; but they answered him: "Why, no man could approach it on account of its warmth, and the fierceness of its heat"; but the young hero said to them: "Have you not seen the multitude of things I have already achieved? Did not you see me change myself into the likeness of every bird of the forest; you and I equally had the aspect and appearance of men, yet I by my enchantments changed suddenly from the appearance of a man and became a bird, and then, continuing to change my form, I resembled this bird or that bird, one after the other, until I had by degrees transformed myself into every bird in the world, small or great; and did I not after all this again assume the form of a man? Therefore, as for that feat, oh, my brothers, the changing myself into birds, I accomplished it by enchantments, and I will by the same means accomplish also this other thing which I have in mind." When his brothers heard this, they consented on his persuasions to aid him in the conquest of the sun.

Then they began to spin and twist ropes to form a noose to catch the sun in, and in doing this they discovered the mode of plaiting flax into stout square-shaped ropes, *tuamaka*; and the manner of plaiting flat ropes, *paharahara*; and of spinning round ropes; at last, they finished making all the ropes which they required. Then Maui took up his enchanted weapon, and he took his brothers with him, and they carried their provisions, ropes, and other things with them, in their hands. They travelled all night, and as soon as day broke, they halted in the desert, and hid themselves that they might not be seen by the sun; and at night they renewed their journey, and before dawn they halted, and hid themselves again; at length they got very far, very far, to the eastward, and came to the very edge of the place out of which the sun rises.

Then they set to work and built on each side of this place a long high wall of clay, with huts of boughs of trees at each end to hide themselves in; when these were finished, they made the loops of the noose, and the brothers of Maui then lay in wait on one side of the place out of which the sun rises, and Maui himself lay in wait upon the other side.

The young hero held in his hand his enchanted weapon, the jawbone of his ancestress—of Muri-rangi-whenua, and said to his brothers: "Mind now, keep yourselves hid, and do not go showing yourselves foolishly to the sun; if you do, you will frighten him; but wait patiently until his head and fore-legs have got well into the snare, then I will shout out; haul away as hard as you can on the ropes on both sides, and then I will rush out and attack him, but do you keep your ropes tight for a good long time, while I attack him, until he is nearly dead, when we will let him go; but mind, now, my brothers, do not let him move you to pity with his shrieks and screams."

At last the sun came rising up out of his place, like a fire spreading far and wide over the mountains and forests; he rises up, his head passes through the noose,

and it takes in more and more of his body, until his
fore-paws pass through; then were pulled tight the
ropes, and the monster began to struggle and roll
himself about, whilst the snare jerked backwards and
forwards as he struggled. Ah! was he not held fast in
the ropes of his enemies!

Then forth rushed that bold hero, Mau-tikitiki-o-
Taranga, with his enchanted weapon. Alas! the sun
screams aloud; he roars; Maui strikes him fiercely
with many blows; they hold him for a long time,
at last they let him go, and weak from wounds the sun
crept along its course. Then was learnt by men the
second name of the sun, for in its agony the sun screamed
out: "Why am I thus smitten by you! oh, man! do
you know what you are doing? Why should you wish
to kill Tama-nui-te-Ra?" Thus was learnt his second
name. At last they let him go. Oh, then, Tama-nui-
te-Ra went very slowly and feebly on his course.

SIR GEORGE GREY (1812-1898)
Polynesian Mythology

THE HAKA

Tena i whiua!
> With motion majestic, their arms now wide
> sweeping,
> Now circles describing, then to heav'n uplifted,
> Their bodies set firmly, yet limbs in mid-air!

Tena i takahia!
> With knee joints set loose,
> With frenzy in gesture, with eyebrows contracting,
> With eyes fiercely glowing, with bounding and
> leaping
> But mark, mild Apollo the War-god is soothing.

Powhiritia atu! Haere mai! Haere mai!
    Ha! Warriors are leaping! the ranks they are
        surging:
    The War-god has conquered; the war-cry is raised!
    'Tis sounding, 'tis swelling, 'tis roaring, 'tis
        thundering!
    Ha! Frenzy, thou workest: 'tis blood now they
        smell.
    "The battle, the battle; our taiahas and meres!"
    They shout as they leap: a madness has seized them.
    "Tako ki to kai rangatira! Tako!"

SIR APIRANA NGATA (1874-1950)
A Scene from the Past

A MAORI CHIEF

We found him and his party; his slaves were preparing
their morning repast. The scene altogether was highly
interesting. In a beautiful bay, surrounded by high
rocks and overhanging trees, the chiefs sat in mute
contemplation, their arms piled up in regular order
on the beach. Shunghie, not only from his high rank
(but in consequence of his wound being taboo'd, or
rendered holy) sat apart from the rest. Their richly
ornamented war canoes were drawn up on the strand;
some of the slaves were unloading stores, others were
kindling fires. To me it almost seemed to realise some
of the passages of Homer, where he describes the
wanderer Ulysses and his gallant band of warriors.
We approached the chief and paid our respects to him.
He received us kindly, and with a dignified composure,
as one accustomed to receive homage. His look was
emaciated; but so mild was the expression of his
features, that he would have been the last man I should
have imagined accustomed to scenes of bloodshed and
cruelty. But I soon remarked, that when he became
animated in conversation, his eyes sparkled with fire,

and their expression changed, demonstrating that it
only required his passions to be aroused, to exhibit
him under a very different aspect. His wife and daughter
were permitted to sit close to him, to administer to his
wants; no others being allowed to do so, on account
of his taboo.

He was arrayed in a new blanket, which completely
enveloped his figure, leaving exposed his highly tattooed
face, and head profusely covered with long black curling
hair, adorned with a quantity of white feathers. He
was altogether a fine study.

AUGUSTUS EARLE (1798-?)
A Narrative of a Nine Months' Residence in New Zealand in 1827

THE DEMON RUM

We regaled the other New Zealanders on the quarter-
deck with biscuits, meat, gruel and rum. They all ate
very heartily, but one glass of rum was sufficient for
all of them. Such sobriety serves to prove that they can
only have been visited rarely by the enlightened Europeans who, wherever they settle, always teach the
natives to drink alcoholic liquors, and to smoke and
chew tobacco; then, when these ignorant people begin
to show the bad effects of strong drink, they start to
explain to them how disgraceful it is to give way to
drunkenness and other evil habits.

THADDEUS BELLINGSHAUSEN (1779-1852)
Voyage to the Antarctic Seas 1819-21
Translated by Frank Debenham

AN AUCTION FOR THE MAORIS

As soon as they saw our boats anchored, the natives
rushed to meet us, thinking, simple savages though
they were, that there might be a chance of getting
something. So on stepping ashore we found ourselves
surrounded by a great crowd. All of these good folk
came running to meet us pushing a lot of swine in front
of them, and there soon began one of the funniest
markets I have ever seen. A few paces from the river
there happened to be a wretched straw hut, without
any roof, and the steward, who was afraid of thefts,
rushed to it to set up shop there. As it was quite narrow,
the big box of materials took up all the space at the back.
In front we set up some sort of a platform on which
one of our sailors, an amazing chap called Tauzier, a
true Gascon, took his stand. He began to offer goods
for sale with a performance that would have done
credit to the most enterprising cheapjack at our own
fairs. . . . "Now just look", said Tauzier to all these
painted or tattooed savages, "just look at this coverlet.
I'm not selling it. I'm giving it away . . . for two pigs."
It was the best foolery imaginable. The coverlets were
an enormous success. They were seized at once and a
goodly number of pigs were already grunting in the
bottom of the boat. Unfortunately we hadn't a very
good supply and he had to start on lengths of material,
which the natives did not want. But Friend Tauzier,
still mounted on the boards, gave them such a spate of
oratory, accompanied by facial contortions and per-
suasive gestures, that very soon they were tumbling
over one another to get the stuff. For 10 yards of material we secured a big pig. Before paying up, the savage
examined his material with as much care as a good
housewife buying an ell of calico, and, to complete the

A PASTORAL SCENE

Sheep on the Rees Valley Station below the Humboldt Mountains at the head of Lake Wakatipu, the longest lake (fifty-two miles) in New Zealand. Queenstown, a popular holiday resort, is situated on the eastern shore of the lake.

SCHOOL FOR SHEARERS

Annual refresher courses are held by the New Zealand Wool Board for shearing instructors at one of the two agricultural colleges. Godfrey Bowen who established a world record by catching and shearing 559 sheep in nine hours, is seen here pointing out shearing faults.

HARVESTING IN SUNSHINE
A hay-rake (near camera) and a hay-baler at work in a field on the Makaroa Station at the head of Lake Wanaka, in Otago.

CITRUS-PICKERS
Maori fruit-pickers at work in a citrus orchard near Tauranga. Tauranga's mild climate and light soil make it ideal for the production of sub-tropical fruits; there are about 200 commercial orchards in this district.

picture, two or three Englishmen wandered round scowling and grumbling that we were sending prices up and it was a scandal. But there was a great crowd and everyone was pushing to get near the shed. The confusion was incredible. The women refused to be left out, and in addition to their pigs and their flax cloaks, they offered to anyone who fancied them their personal charms. All the men wore the national costume, if costume it may be called. They were wrapped in their flax cloaks and among the number there were some remarkably fine specimens. The costume consisted of two lengths of woven flax; one covered the body from the waist to the feet, the other was thrown over the shoulders; a few had cloaks of dog-skin. They were very nearly the New Zealanders described by Cook. They were magnificently tattooed and wore their hair gathered into a knot, attached to the top of the head. Round their necks and from their noses hung small pieces of green jade curiously carved. One of them, the chief of the tribe, carried in his hand a stick about four feet long, made of fine red wood and surmounted by one of those extraordinary little figures representing a little man with his tongue out and his legs apart. It was like a gingerbread man at home. . . .

At noon, I had as many pigs as the boat could reasonably hold, and I made for the corvette, to the great sorrow of the New Zealanders, who were still bringing us more and more pigs.

ENSIGN DUROCH

The Voyage of the Astrolabe 1840. (*The journals of Dumont D'Urville and his officers of their visit to New Zealand in 1840*) translated by OLIVE WRIGHT

A NATIVE CONGREGATION

Sunday, 27th November, 1842. A noble congregation, amounting to at least one thousand, assembled amidst the ruins of the chapel of Turanga. They came up in the most orderly way, in parties headed by the native chiefs and teachers, and took their places on the gound with all the regularity of so many companies of soldiers. We were placed under an awning made of tents, but the congregation sat in the sun. The gathering of this body of people was a noble sight, and their attentive manner, and the deep sonorous uniformity of their responses was most striking. I preached to them from Acts xv. 16, 17, on Christ's repairing the breaches of David's fallen tabernacle, that the Gentiles may seek the Lord. I am afraid that the subject was more appropriate to the occasion than my language to the subject. During the service Mr. Williams was duly installed as Archdeacon of Waiapu, or East Cape. . . . After the morning service, the natives formed into their classes for reading and saying the Catechism. The native character appears in this in a most favourable light— old tattooed warriors standing side by side with young men and boys and, submitting to lose their place for every mistake with the most perfect good humour.

GEORGE AUGUSTUS SELWYN[1] (1809-1875)

NOT SAVAGES

The inhabitants of New Zealand are great talkers, they spend the night relating what they have seen, they forget nothing, not even the blockheads; they will tell you how many potatoes they had at one meal; they

[1]Selwyn was the first Anglican Bishop of New Zealand.

relate the stories they have heard, and all the time, imitating the voice, gestures, mannerisms, and faults of the people whose words they repeat; none can surpass them in the art of imitating others.

They are very industrious. Thus, they have found ways of making mats for themselves with New Zealand flax, a very hardy kind of plant. These mats resemble those made in France from cotton. It is mainly the Chiefs and the women who wear them. They tattoo their faces and bodies, in very symmetrical designs.

To sum them up in one word, they are much superior to our peasants, in every respect. Here I see children as well developed as city children. They have a fine appearance, speak well, and understand a mere sign. They are not, as may be thought in France, savages living in the woods like animals. There are exceptions, but generally all are together in tribes; they have Chiefs, cultivate a small plot of land, and keep pigs. The houses, made of straw, are together in one place.

The Europeans are harmful rather than helpful to them; they teach them to scorn what is most sacred, to give way to drink, and furnish them with brandy, rum and tobacco. Happy are the Islands that are not confronted with these things. However, these good savages know well that these people are disposed to evil.

Fr. ANTOINE GARIN, in a letter of 1841
Fishers of Men,
ed. P. B. McKEEFRY

THE DEFENCE OF ORAKAU
1864

For three days and two nights the Maoris held the fort, a noble three hundred and ten against six times their number of well-armed, well-fed soldier foes. " We lived in a circle of fire and smoke," said Paitini, a man of the Urewera, who was severely wounded there. There was a supply of food, but the water was exhausted by the end of the first night. To the rifle-fire of hundreds of soldiers, a bombardment with two six-pounder Armstrong guns was added, and on the third day hand-grenades were thrown into the *pa* from the head of a flying-sap dug up to the northern outwork. Ringed with a line of steel, earthworks battered by shell fire, men, women and little children tortured with thirst, the valorous little band held out. There was no thought of surrender. The defenders ran short of ammunition for their double and single-barrel guns, so short that in the night firing they used small pieces of apple and *manuka* wood as bullets, saving their lead for the day time; and they even broke off the legs of their cooking-pots to serve as projectiles. . . .

The story of the afternoon of April the second, 1864, imperishably remains as an inspiration to deeds of courage and fortitude. Nowhere in history did the spirit of pure patriotism blaze up more brightly than in that little earthwork redoubt, torn by shell fire and strewn with dead and dying. The grim band of heroes proudly refused the surrender demanded by General Cameron.

To the General's request, delivered by the interpreter from the head of the sap, the reply was made by a chief who was Rewi's mouthpiece: "Peace will never be made, never, never, never!" A further reply, in words that will forever live, was delivered: "Friend, I shall fight against you for ever and ever!" (in the Maori: "E hoa, ke whawhai tonu ahau a koe, ake, ake!")

The interpreter, Mr. Mair (afterwards Major) said: "That is well for you men, but it is not right that the women and children should die. Let them come out."

A voice asked: "How did you know that there are women and children here?"

Mair replied: "I heard the lamentations for the dead in the night."

The chieftainess Ahumai, daughter of the old chief Te Paerata, called out to the interpreter: "If the men are to die, the women and children will die also!"

So went on the hopeless fight, but not for much longer. Rewi gave the word; his warriors loaded their guns, with their last cartridges, and with the women and children in their midst, they charged out in a body, going at a steady trot at first, until the amazed soldiers opened a fearful fire upon them. That retreat through the fern and swamp to the Puniu River and beyond was, like the defence of the *pa*, full of deeds of gallantry and self-sacrifice. . . .

When the sun went down on Orakau a hundred and sixty Maoris lay dead on the battlefield, and on the line of retreat to the south side of the Puniu River. . . . Of the British soldiers seventeen were killed and thirty-five wounded. The dead and wounded soldiers were carried in rough transport carts back along the road to Te Awamutu camp. An Irish soldier walked by a cart, keening in his native tongue. His brother lay in the cart with a bullet through his head. Maori wounded were carried to the camp, some with limbs shattered by shell and grenade.

The Maori dead were buried where they fell, scattered over more than a mile of country. Nearly forty men and women were buried in the field on the north side of the road as you drive over Orakau. Their parapets were just tumbled in on them. When the trench graves were filled in, the clenched hand of a Maori protruded above the ground, and a soldier tramped on it to tread it under. The last gesture! Defeated, but unconquerable.

JAMES COWAN (1870-1943)
Hero Stories of New Zealand

TO-HI

One of our Rotorua acquaintances was a very remarkable
man named To-hi. He had some years before (since
coming into the country) been concerned in an act of
cannibalism. It was hard at first not to shrink from
welcoming him. He was a thickset short man, with a
keen, strong-willed expression, the eyes bloodshot and
fierce, but the whole expression was rather thoughtful
and intelligent than savage.

The cause of his cruel raid on a neighbouring tribe
was that a fine boy of his had started on a journey to
them and was never heard of again. He was probably
drowned crossing some river, or lost in the forest. In
the wild, passionate grief of a father, he took up the
notion that they had killed and eaten him. They had
been hostile in old days. Soon this notion, confirmed
by wild rumours, grew into belief, and he and his men
surprised and killed a number of his old enemies, and
had a cannibal feast afterwards. When the Judge spoke
reprovingly to To-hi of this deed, he grew wildly
excited—his eyes glowed like embers. He took up a
ruler that lay near, and striking rapid blows on the
table, he burst out: "Why should I not? They took
my child and slew him, and roasted his liver in the fire.
Why do you condemn the practice? Beasts of prey eat
beasts, birds eat birds, fishes eat fishes—why should
not men eat men?" Then, suddenly softening, he said
quietly: "But I know it is contrary to English ways of
thinking and it shall be done no more." After a while he
looked round at the various ornaments in the room, and
said: "Friend, I am a son of Mate-te-Kapua (the mythic
ancestor of his tribe, and a mighty lifter of property)
"My fathers, when they desired a thing, stretched

forth their hands and took it. I do not do this, but the hands of my heart go forth towards them. Take my child" (a boy of ten, his only remaining one) " and teach him your ways, that neither the hands of his body nor of his heart may covet."

This wild man had good stuff in him. He put himself under Christian teaching, though he was never baptised. He became a very efficient magistrate under the Government, took the names of the Police Magistrate and the Acting Governor, and always signed his name, Beckham Wynyard Tohi. He died, fighting on our side, in the war of 1863. His wife was beside him when he fell, and directly shot the man who had killed him.

LADY MARY ANN MARTIN[1] (?-1884)
Our Maoris

COLOUR BAR

To view men whose skin differs in colour from our own as " damned niggers" is a weakness of our Anglo-Saxon character, which proves our civilisation and Christianity far from perfect. It destroys all chance of our gaining the affections of our native subjects in any part of the world; for uncivilised men will forgive any amount or kind of wrong sooner than a single personal insult. The Maories are exceedingly sensitive to any appearance of personal slight. I once heard a company of them discussing the character of a most estimable missionary, the only drawback to whose usefulness is, that he has a stomach so delicate that he cannot eat food prepared by natives. This was the very point in his conduct with which those whom I overheard seemed most impressed. Nothing can exceed the kindness and respect

[1]Lady Martin was the wife of William Martin, New Zealand's first Chief Justice.

with which men like Sir George Grey and the Bishop
of New Zealand behave to natives; they treat them as
"gentlemen". The same remark applies to the superior
officers of the Government, the clergy, the more highly-
educated colonists, and the older settlers. But the
ignorant mass of townspeople judge of the natives from
their not very prepossessing exteriors, and never having
had experience of the good qualities which, as all who
have lived amongst them acknowledge, lie concealed
beneath, give free vent to their arrogance and contempt,
and speak of the Maories, both publicly and privately,
with disgust and dislike. Men habitually told that
they emit a disagreeable smell, are not likely to feel a
very strong affection towards the race that smells them.
I know that the petty rudeness of Europeans is so
disagreeable to many chiefs in Waikato, that they
dislike going into Auckland, or any of the English
villages, and are very shy of visiting at English houses.
Their own behaviour to strangers affords a striking
contrast, not very creditable to ourselves; a chief of
the highest rank will unsaddle the horse of his guest
with his own hands, and either pitch his tent or give
him the best house in the village to sleep in, covering
the floor with freshly gathered fern and new flax mats.
The women set to work to cook, or, if their own meal
is nearly ready, a portion is set aside for the stranger
before the others partake. Anyone who in return
invited one of the principal men in Waikato to accompany him to Auckland, could not fail to be shamed
on the road. A shakedown of straw in an inn stable,
bread and meat bought at a shop, or a meal in the inn
kitchen, given as a great favour at the Englishman's
solicitation, would be all the hospitality he could
procure. I have heard the Bishop of Auckland say he
is quite ashamed to travel with his native deacons,
men who dine at his own table and behave there like
gentlemen, because he could not take them into public

A FIRE LOOK-OUT ON THE KAINGAROA FOREST

The growth-rate of radiata pine in New Zealand greatly exceeds that of other countries. Huge state forest plantations yield over fifty million cubic feet a year in growth. Firewatchers regularly scan the plantations for signs of what could be immensely costly outbreaks.

A SHEEP SALE

Sale days are regular features of New Zealand agricultural life. Here farmers inspect ewes which have been bought for shipment to Kenya.

MOVING CATTLE

A familiar scene in New Zealand country districts. Cattle are being driven down the main road between Ohingaiti and Mangaweka, close to Taihape, in the North Island.

WATTLE IN BLOOM

Many varieties of exotic flora flourish in the warm climate of the North Island. The Australian wattle, for instance, is well established. Here are black wattles in bloom beside the Tram Valley Road, in Swanson.

rooms where a tipsy carter would be considered good society.

J. E. GORST (1835-1916)
The Maori King

THE MAORI CHARACTER

As for the Maori people in general, they are neither so good or so bad as their friends and enemies have painted them, and I suspect are pretty much like what almost any other people would have become if subjected for ages to the same external circumstances. For ages they have struggled against necessity in all its shapes. This has given to them a remarkable greediness for gain in every visible and immediately tangible form. It has even left its mark on their language. Without the aid of iron, the most trifling tool or utensil could only be purchased by an enormously disproportionate outlay of labour in its construction, and, in consequence, became precious to a degree scarcely conceivable by people of civilised and wealthy countries. This great value attached to personal property of all kinds increased proportionately the temptation to plunder; and where no law existed, or could exist, of sufficient force to repress the inclination, every man, as a natural consequence, became a soldier, if it were only for the defence of his own property and that of those who were banded with him—his tribe, or family. From this state of things, warfare arose, as a matter of course; the military art was studied as a science, and brought to great perfection as applied to the arms used; and a marked military character was given to the people. The necessity of warfare, and a temperate climate, gave them strength of body, accompanied by a perseverance and energy of mind perfectly astonishing. With rude and blunt stones they felled giant kauri—toughest of pines; and from it, in process of time, at an expense of labour, perseverance and ingenuity perfectly astonishing to those who know what it really is, produced—carved, painted, and inlaid, a masterpiece of art, and an object of beauty—the war canoe, capable of carrying a hundred men on a distant expedition through the boisterous seas surrounding their island. As a consequence of their warlike habits and character, they are self-possessed and confident in themselves and their own powers, and have much diplomatic finesse and casuistry at command. Their intelligence causes them theoretically to acknowledge the benefits of law, which they see established amongst us, but their hatred of restraint causes them practically to abhor and resist its full enforcement amongst themselves. Doubting our professions of friendship, fearing our ultimate designs, led astray by false friends, possessed of that "little learning" which is, in their case, most emphatically, "a dangerous thing," divided amongst themselves—such are the people with whom we are now in contact—such are the people to whom, for our own safety and their preservation, we must give new laws and institutions, new habits of life, new ideas, new sentiments, and information— whom we must either civilise or by our mere contact exterminate. How is this to be done? Let me see. I think I shall answer this question when I am Prime Minister.

F. E. MANING (1811-1883)
Old New Zealand

THE TIMBER-DRAGGERS

It was a wild and exciting scene. The huge log the natives were dragging out was of unusually large dimensions, some three feet in diameter and some eighty in length, the largest spar of the *Delhi's* cargo, and the last required to make her a full ship. Every available man of the tribe had been mustered to drag the spar out and then feast afterwards. The head of the spar was decorated with branches of flowering trees, and waving tufts of feathers had also been fastened on, adding to the effect of the "headgear." At this decorated end of the spar, and on it, stood the oldest chief of the tribe. Round his waist he wore a short mat of unscraped flax leaves dyed black. It looked like a bundle of thatching more than anything else as it hung down to his knees. This constituted his whole attire. In his right hand he brandished a *taiaha*, a six-foot Maori broadsword of hardwood, with a pendulous plume of feathers hanging from the hilt. High overhead he brandished his weapon, imparting to it the peculiar Maori quivering action, with outstretched arm raised aloft like unto a soldier leading his men on to battle. He kept repeating a long string of words in quick succession, lifting up one foot and stamping it down again, the body thrown back on the other leg. Every moment his voice became louder until almost reaching a scream; then he grasped the weapon in both hands, sprang into the air, and came down as if smiting an enemy to the earth. At this instant some eighty or more men, minus a flax mat like the chief, or even fig-leaf, yelled forth one word as ending chorus. As one man they simultaneously stamped on the ground, and then gave one fearful pull on the rope doubled round the end of the spar—a pull that you thought would snap the rope in two; but it stood the tremendous strain, and the huge mass forged ahead several feet. The chief sprang into the air again, flung his arms on high, yelled out one word, the gang repeated it with a louder yell, the earth almost vibrated, as springing into the air, they landed as one man; then another strain, and away slid the spar a few feet more. Again and again this was done, the old chief becoming more and more excited and even more agile instead of less so, his voice attaining to a higher and higher key until he positively screeched, and after each tug the spar advanced several feet. At last, after one tremendous pull, the gang ended their shout by prolonging it until it died away in a comparatively softened tone, and the chief accepted this as an intimation that they must have breathing-time before beginning again. So they rested; meanwhile a tribe of young children brought kits full of wet mud to besmear the sleepers in front of the spar to make it slide along more easily. It had only to be dragged a few hundred feet farther when it would be launched down a declivity to the sea-beach. So we took a stroll farther into the forest to see the other trees in the course of being felled. . . .

On getting back we were just in time to hear the old chief begin his long recitation to work the men up to proper pitch. This he did, and after some vigorous strains on the rope we saw the branches, flowers and tufts of feathers suspended, as it were, in mid-air; then the other end of the spar tilted up, and away rushed the stupendous mass, sweeping everything before it, snapping young trees like carrots, and then passing clear of the forest, it flung a cloud of dust into the air as it swept across the narrow belt of open ground, pursuing, like an avalanche, its wild career, and by the time the prolonged shout with which it had been sent on its last swift journey had died away the spar had reached the beach, and its garlanded head, now sadly despoiled, sent a shower of spray into the air, showing it had reached the water's edge, and then another loud, long, and joyous shout rang through the forest.

Nota bene—The old warrior chief was *not* standing on the end of the spar when the last long and strong tug at the rope was given.

SIR JOHN LOGAN CAMPBELL (1817-1912)
Poenamo

SUBDUED, NOT EXTERMINATED

The Maoris were very polite. I was assured by a member of the House of Representatives that the native race is not decreasing but actually increasing slightly. It is another evidence that they are a superior brand of savages. I do not call to mind any savage race that built such good houses, or such strong and ingenious and scientific fortresses, or gave so much attention to agriculture, or had military arts and devices which so nearly approached the white man's. These, taken together with their high abilities in boat building, their tastes and capacities in the ornamental arts, modify their savagery to a semi-civilisation—or at least to a quarter civilisation.

It is a compliment to them that the British did not exterminate them, as they did the Australians and the Tasmanians, but were content with subduing them and showed no desire to go further. And it is another compliment to them that the British did not take the whole of their choicest lands but left them a considerable part and protected them from the rapacities of land-sharks, a protection which the New Zealand Government still extends to them. And it is still another compliment to the Maoris that the Government allows native representation in both the legislature and the cabinet and gives both sexes the vote. And in doing these things the Government also compliments itself. It is not in the custom of the world for conquerors to act in this large spirit towards the conquered.

MARK TWAIN (S. L. CLEMENS) (1835-1910)
Following the Equator: A Journey Around the World

MAORI WOMANHOOD

This settlement (Ohinemutu) has always been famed throughout Maori land for the beauty of the women, from the days of Hinemoa down to the present time; and during our stay we saw a few young girls with complexions like southern gipsies, just fair enough to let the warm colour show through the clear olive skin, and large dark lustrous eyes, with great and ever-changing expression, rosy lips, as yet undefiled by the blue tattoo, and beautiful, snow-white, regular teeth. But even the best-looking Maori girls rarely keep their beauty long—they have hardly reached womanhood or maternity, ere the once firm bust has lost its shapeliness, and the clear white of the eye becomes dimmed and tarnished. Many are leaving off now the old barbarous unkempt shock head of hair, and comb their abundant locks in the more cleanly and becoming mode of the pakehas. They have generally small and well-shaped hands and feet.

The custom of tattooing is now falling out of fashion amongst the rising generation of both sexes, and it is to be hoped that before many years have passed, the nickname of "Blue-lips" will no longer be applicable to the native girls of New Zealand. Where the tattooing is confined to the slender lyre-shaped line on the fair one's chin, the effect is really not unpleasing; but the tattooed lip is an abomination.

HERBERT MEADE (1842-1868)
A Ride Through the Disturbed Districts of New Zealand 1864-65

A MAORI MATRIARCH DIES

SEDGWICK:	No one can tell the hour of death.
AROHA:	I have willed it.
SEDGWICK:	But why? Why?
AROHA:	Who lives by the sword, shall die by the sword.
SEDGWICK:	What do you mean?
AROHA:	Your cross, a sword. To cut my people down. The Light of the World, no light. Only dark, dark, dark. What has your Christ brought me? Affliction. Disgrace. Shame.
SEDGWICK:	Then offer Him your shame. Think of Him on the Cross, naked and mocked. Think of that shame, then of yours.
AROHA:	I gave Him my whole life. I made His pain my own. The thorns. The nails. The wounded side. I ate His flesh. I drank His blood. What more does He want?
SEDGWICK:	You, Aroha.
AROHA:	He cheated me.
SEDGWICK:	*gently:* No, Aroha. You cheated Him. *A pause. Something stirs in Aroha.*
AROHA:	How?
SEDGWICK:	By pride. Your Christ had the face of a Maori chief. Was it love he counselled? No. Thundering in your soul was pride, pride. This land of yours, a green pocket in a conquered land, a wilderness, unused, untilled: a sanctuary to pride. From pride you built a world for your children out of the air; no wonder they found it would not hold them. And the Christ you found

in the Church you fashioned in your own image; no prince of peace, no healer of wounds; an avenging chief who must never be slighted, never humiliated, never crossed.

AROHA: Must your Christ have everything, then?

SEDGWICK: Everything. Strip yourself of pride, honour, dignity and respect. Find them again in Him. Live, Aroha.

AROHA: Live! Live! How shall I live? You want me to go to Tamatea; grow fat and swing pois; you want me to see my race a lot of laughing clowns, swilling beer and going to seed and I an old clown with them. I will not. I will not.

SEDGWICK: Laughing clown; that you could never be. Mother, leader of your people; there's your path. Everything pulls you to Tamatea. Johnny: Queenie: not even this land will remain in your hands. Accept the pakeha's conquest by force; make in yourself a new conquest that will redeem in the grace of laughter. Forget greatness; forget history. Find harmony and a lasting peace.

AROHA: *after a pause:* Is that my choice then?

SEDGWICK: Yes.

AROHA: On your honour and your faith?

SEDGWICK: On my honour and my faith.

AROHA: *rising slowly form her chair, supported by the taiaha:* Then, on my honour, I choose. I choose, if it must be, the way of pride. I will go proud down to my death, for that is all I have left. I will not be humbled; I will die true to my past. No, not even for Him will I weaken; I will not carve up my life, slice by slice from the whale. I go

to Whetumarama and the gods of my
people. I have been too long away. That is
my choice. That is my victory.

She sinks feebly, exhausted.

SEDGWICK: There will be no victory in that death.

AROHA: Not your victory; mine. The only one
still left open to me. Don't try to frighten
me by talk of hell: where I am going, there
is no hell. I am calm and clear, and the
path ahead I have struck out for myself.
And you, young man, who serve Him and
spread the Light; there is great goodness
in you. Keep to the Light, I go to dark, my
only home.

SEDGWICK: Then I can do nothing more for you.

AROHA: No.

BRUCE MASON (b. 1921)
The Pohutukawa Tree

MODERN

Hori Tenawiri
Sits against the post
Of the veranda
Of a house built by
A pakeha.
The piles stand starkly
So that the house is on
Stumpy stilts.
Rank grass grows there
On the muddy track.
One wild jonquil
Beneath his foot.
(Ancient canoes passed
By this spot
Seventy years ago.

Swift massacre—revenge—
Sacrifice—blood at full heat)
Hori Tenawiri
Is going to the pictures
To-night
To see "Texas Moon";
He has three and ninepence,
But that will suffice
For a ticket for two,
And sweets.
(There is a grave nearby
Where a splendid warrior rests;
His flashing eyes, his grim face
Carved as of brown stone
Now dust). . . . His flesh and blood
Passed on to Hori Tenawiri,
Who is leaning on the post
Of the veranda,
Crushing the wild jonquil
And waiting for nothing
In particular.

F. ALEXA STEVENS

MAORI TIME

The modern Maori adapts himself to two concepts of
time. One is the pakeha concept: time is something
solid, fixed, definite, to which other activities must be
geared. You adapt to pakeha time when you want to
catch a train or a bus badly enough, or go to the pictures,
or knock off work at the end of the day. "Maori" time,
on the other hand, is a plastic medium that flows round
and adapts itself to the activities of the day. The "Maori"
time for anything is when you are ready to do it. An
appointment to be at a place or meet a person (a friend,
for instance, for a social evening) at, say, seven o'clock

in the evening, may be kept at eight or nine o'clock—just whenever you get round to being at the place in question. Conversely, pakehas invited to a Maori house for the midday meal need never worry about being punctual. A pakeha hostess may become worried if her guests do not arrive on time. Not so the Maori hostess. The food will be ready to eat whenever anyone is ready to eat it. The first course may be served and then someone sent down to the shops to buy cake and beer for dessert. Why worry about food hot or cold? Food is food, and time is what you make it. It is not that the Maori does not have clocks about the house with which to order his life. Most houses have rather an elaborate mantel-piece clock: large frame, gables, gilt decorations all complete. These clocks are occasionally checked by wireless time and thus are generally accurate enough for trains and the pictures, as long as you remember that the clock is probably so much fast or slow. It is this "Maori" time then that rules the casual life of the Maori. Pakeha time is a sort of necessary nuisance to which you adapt yourself so as to be able to do other desirable things.

ERNEST (b. 1901) and PEARL BEAGLEHOLE
Some Modern Maoris

THE TANGI

Poor old Tawa. He was said to be near a hundred years of age when he died. They had laid him in state there in front of the fine new meeting-house that he had named Fount of Life and Wisdom in memory of the sacred house of his ancestors in the old homeland of far Hawaiki. He had raised most of the money for it, and it had been his ambition to see the place completed with all its traditional carvings and its bright reed decorations, and its modern tile roof and electric light.

And now, since he had performed the opening ceremonies only a few months ago, this tangi of the old men was the first public gathering to assemble around the big new meeting-house of the tribe.

Lying there in state, he looked strangely different from the feeble old man in the rather shabby pakeha clothes who had tottered through the last few years of his life. Now they had covered his shrunken body with fine kiwi-feather cloaks, and beneath the plumed head-band his sharp features had regained in death the calm dignity of a true son of a noble line. Near his head were photographs of his relatives. His greenstone mere and his taiaha lay beside him, also an old-fashioned double-barrel gun which was a souvenir of the days when he had chased rebel bands along the neighbouring beach.

Now the last party of visitors was arriving, welcomed to the rain-sodden village courtyard by the mourn-ing women. The wreaths of bitter kawakawa round their heads were not more bitter than their tears of grief.

"Haere mai!" the keening voices called to the visitors. "Come hither into the presence of death, into the home of the mourners. Come and behold the face of our departed one!"

The big gathering of friends and relatives waited in silence. Whereupon the leading woman of the visiting party went to the side of the dead man and intoned the old farewell beginning: "Depart, O father, to the Beings, to the far Hawaiki, to the Lord of the Dead." And she repeated all the old mysterious sayings that the young people know by heart but can scarcely explain. However, the finish of it is plain and final enough for anyone: "Therefore go, O father, go to the home that awaits us all."

And then the whole party drew round the dead man and raised their voices in an old mournful family dirge.

And some, overcome with grief, threw their shawls over their heads and wept. The chieftain's old widow sat on the ground beside her dead lord. She covered her head and rocked to and fro, but uttered no sound. And the whole company round about shared in this grief and swelled its tide.

Manunui summed it up well as he stood before the big crowd at the tangi for his old friend with a heart as heavy as the rain clouds that the mid-day sun was now banishing from the dark hills. " Alas, alas!" he cried, " the giant totara is fallen; the strong tree that Tane loved is laid low, its place in the forest cannot be filled, neither can we shelter under its branches any more. The crash of its fall echoed throughout the land; the shock of its fall has shaken the earth and loosened the roots of the lesser trees. Aue! aue! aue!"

" Aue! aue! aue!" echoed the mourners in their anguished keen.

But quick as the storm of grief had arisen it soon vanished. And presently laughter was heard among the young people, and only tired and hungry babies wailed monotonously as the crowd started to drift away.

RODERICK FINLAYSON (b. 1904)
Brown Man's Burden

MAORI AND PAKEHA

There is some scope for reflection upon the proposition as to whether the Maori people have accepted us, rather than as to whether we have accepted the Maori people. History shows that the Pakeha has not always stood too well in his dealings with the Maori race, while the Maori looked with a patient, contemplative and still trusting eye upon the strangers' actions, speculating, there is no doubt, at the motives of the incoming Pakeha. It would also not be out of place to repeat that, when past difficulties were contributed to so largely by the impatient intolerance of early settlers rather than by omissions or commissions of Government, we should never neglect to ensure that past failures are fully understood and security against their repetition provided for. The Maori has a high intelligence, a keen perception, and the facility for determining, probably better than any other race, the motives of the human mind. He can detect straight-forwardness and honesty of purpose as easily as he can dishonesty and insincerity, and form his own conclusions upon the contrast. He judges us by our deeds and not by our words. He forms the best estimate of our purpose, from the attitude of the newspapers, from the attitude of the public around him, from the actions of those who have it in their power to regulate his life, or to control his business.

The Maori has a keen desire for the elevation of his people, and to rise to and maintain a social equality with his Pakeha brother. He is not a child to be humoured and spoiled as some would make him out to be, but a grown man who has come to recognise that he has not yet completed his journey, but still has a way to go before he reaches his destination. Those members of the race who have reflected upon the subject, realise that the march of progress has been accelerated, but have the perception to see that the pace should not be made too hot, or the remainder of the way rendered more difficult by undue haste or undignified impatience; and I believe that whatever mental reservation might exist in the mind of the Maori, it consists of no more than a deep and abiding feeling, not of hostility, but of wonder tinged with some misgivings as to when the Pakeha will reach that happy state when his knowledge and understanding of the Maori people their past wrongs and grievances, their future hopes and aims, is full and complete.

NORMAN SMITH (b. 1902)
The Maori People and Us

THIRD STEP

When Timi knew that the sun would be shining full on the whare's only door, he emerged to bask on the bottom step.

The daily ritual of shedding first the red blanket and then the soldier overcoat was usually completed by the time the sixth match had got the dampish tobacco in his pipe going properly. Then a man could relax with never a wish for change.

There was only one thing—soon Mrs. Timi would waddle up from the creek with the basket of peeled potatoes and say, "When the hell you going to put in the middle step, eh?" Then she would grunt heavily, climbing across the gap to make him move one elbow. And he would think, "Yes, I will do it soon because the middle step is good for leaning on and the space is too wide for comfort."

From a mile away the muffled noise of the bulldozer making the forestry road comes and goes. As Timi sprawls lower and closes his eyes, its snort coming closer each day brings uncomfortable mind pictures. They are like small bad dreams, just like the ones that came long ago from the words of old Mahu the grandfather.

That was back in the years when Timi was a young man and there were three good steps for the whare; back at the Land Court of the inland town with the forestry people wanting the flats and the foothills. Timi's visits with the relations to the Land Court were special events that made one year different from another. There you met strange cousins and uncles, and some who were not in the hapu at all but saying they were.

Good visits those, with much laughing, but not all of it happy because of talk about the land going to the pakeha some day; and the old grandfather Mahu giving his oration outside the Court House veranda, a tanekaha stick helping the words—ten steps this way with the warnings, then the pause and ten steps back again.

That was the scene the mind always remembered— the young ones only half listening and a little shy, thinking of the shops of the town, and yet not going because of the fear that kept them there to listen.

Though the questions and answers all happened inside the court-house where you tried to please the pakeha, it was outside on the veranda where the decisions were made. In old Mahu's oration saying that defeat lay in any land surrender, there was also the sound of despair, as if he knew the battle was already lost. You sensed that he knew it was his last fight. When at last he put the question and all waited for someone to answer, some fool laughed, muttering, "Aw, what the hell?" There was the shocked quietness with old Mahu waiting. Then another laughed, and all laughed, forgetting the grandfather and thinking instead of taxis and good times about the towns.

Old Mahu wiped the sweat from his forehead with the back of his hand, put on his hat and walked quietly down the courthouse steps, back over the hills and the estuary to the whare to die.

Sometimes Timi's youngest son would come home from the forestry plantation with a good suit and tie. A good boy, young Mahu, working hard at driving the bulldozer to cut the forestry road, bringing the crayfish home on Friday night but restless to be gone on Saturday.

THE BIRTHDAY PARTY

An oil painting by Bryan Dew (b. 1940), "The Birthday Party" combines keen observation with a sardonic comment on New Zealand family gatherings.

SIR EDMUND HILLARY

A portrait-bust in concrete of Sir Edmund Hillary, the famed mountaineer, explorer and conqueror of Everest. This is the work of Alison Duff, an Auckland sculptor, and is part of the sculpture collection in the Auckland City Art Gallery.

Young Mahu walking about with the creased pants would look for a while at the estuary, kicking the sand and never still. He would talk a lot about the young trees all in lines, happy in telling Timi of the forest coming closer and the road gashing straight through the ancient kumara land. Then, looking at the grave of the grandfather he would be silent and say, more quietly, "But not there," after which he would depart to catch the bus for the town; being cheerful because of Mrs. Timi's easy weeping, meaning nothing much.

Young Mahu too, with the same name as the grandfather, felt uneasy dreams with his words, but not all unhappy and not of despair. But always Timi wondered what the grandfather would be thinking of him not doing anything, spoiling the sleep perhaps, what with the machines roaring in the places that had always been quiet. But the young man's words telling of the forest growing again might be a better thing and the grandfather not worrying any more.

As the morning goes, the long shadows of the young trees grow smaller and the sun shines on the brown scar of the fire-break going away.

Soon the noon whistle will echo and Mrs. Timi will come out saying, "You getting that board yet for the step, saving me the fall one day, tomorrow?"

E. H. AUDLEY (b. 1895)

Humour and Sentiment

INCIDENT IN THE HOUSE

I must not forget a veritable incident of the first session of the Provincial Council of Otago, which old identities have often laughed over. I will try to relate it as it occurred, not as it has sometimes been told. The story respects an honourable member yet living, and not an iota the less respected for it. A worthy man he was—a worthy man he is—and so innocent of sham, that I am sure, while he laughs over it with others, he is in no ways ashamed of its occurrence. The honourable gentleman in question had left the shop in the charge of his daughter to attend to his Parliamentary duties. The House was in debate, and he had possession of the chair. An orator of weight and no little sledge hammer energy, he was in the very height of his argument, demonstrating certain consequences sure to succeed to a certain course of procedure, and sending home his conclusions with real and genuine earnestness, in a full, rich broad Doric, the tone and gesture that of the Titan plebs of the North—when, behold! the audience in the gallery, entranced by his eloquence, were disturbed by a sweet-faced *hafflins lassie* squeezing and *wrastlin'* her way through among them and towards the forum. She won her point, not without difficulty, and a little out of breath—little recking she of any importance attaching to any business save her own. Impassioned, he, and lost to all meaner things, at his full height, and holding in close attention the Honourable the Provincial Councillors seated around the green baize covered table, he was interrupted now by a smart tug at his coat tails—a tug intended, with most contemptuous indifference to the effects which might ensue, to interrupt all the glowing flow of eloquence; and an exclamation, loud enough for everyone to hear. Faither! Faither! No attention, however, followed. A vexed disappointed look on the part of the emissary, and another tug came, smarter than the first, with another similar exclamation, Faither! Faither! This elicited an impatient gesture—as if to intimate that on no account could he be disturbed. But the beseiging party was not to be turned off discomfited in that way. And so, with an air of still greater determination, and a dash of the imperative thrown into it, the exclamation was again repeated of Faither! Faither! This could not be withstood. It brought out the angry retort and enquiry in one breath, "Be off wi' ye, lassie; what dae ye want?" "Want?"—and forth came the urgent necessity of the case—"I want ye alang wi' me this very meenite. *The man's come for his breeks!*"

JAMES BARR (1820-85)
The Old Identities

GRIT IN HEXAMETERS

Earth too haply will meet him in converse ratio shortly,
For as he drives up the long straight track that leads
    from the mountain,
Minute millions of grit, and sand, and cart-pounded
    shingle,
Driven by shrieking nor'-wester, will find a retreat in
    his eyelids,
And while he tries to remove them with hopeless corner
    of handkerchief,
Rolling boulders of stone will jolt and confuse his
    perceptions,
Plainly proving the fact, as the rattling conveyance
    advances,

That earth, in the shape of shingle, exists in spite of
    Road-Boards;
And let him venture to live by a river-bed edge, or a
    back street,
He will discover an earthy sand omnipresent and gritty,
Whirled by the summer wind through invisible crevice
    and cranny,
Coating his table, his chair, his chimney-piece, side-
    board and book-case,
So that upon them his children draw horses and men
    with their fingers;
Appearing, too, like pepper on all his papers and letters,
Dusting his melting butter and hid in the crust of his
    quatern,
Floating on top of his milk, and lying await in his
    tea-cup,
Strewing his beard and hair, and spreading his counten-
    ance over,
Imparting a pallid, dried-up look to his wind-beaten
    visage,
And grinding between his teeth as homeward he comes
    of an evening. . . .

LAURENCE J. KENNAWAY
Crusts: A Settler's Fare Down South

SAVED BY A PLAID

Soothed yet subdued by the grave harmonies of Nature,
Mary wandered on from the rock to the edge of the
Terrace, where she stood, looking down on the shrunken
stream, chafing and fretting amidst the rocks that
obstructed its course a hundred feet below. . . . So
absorbed was she in her thoughts, that she failed to
hear stealthy footsteps approaching, and was unaware
of another's presence till a hand fell heavily on her
shoulder. Whether startled by the shock she missed

her footing, or whether she was pushed over, Mary never could tell, but the next instant she fell over the precipitous bank. In her descent she clutched a small shrub, and clung to it with the tenacious grasp of desperation. Then she looked upward to see whom her assailant might be; and her heart sank within her as she recognised the features of Bess Humphreys.

"For mercy's sake help me to get up, Bess," she cried. "What on earth made you frighten me like that?"

"Because I hate thee," came the reply, in deep stern tones, hissed, rather than spoken, through the close-set teeth. "Because thou robbed me of the man I cared for, and who cared for me till thou came between us with thy white face and mincing ways. He would have made me his lawful wife belike, only for thee, as he had a right to do, for I carry his child, who will never know his father. Now thou canst go to him, if thee likes, for thou shall drown in the river, and I'll stop to see thee." ...

"Oh! no, no, Bess: don't let me drown. I've never done you any harm, I swear it," the girl appealed once more.

But appealed in vain. Bess stamped the ground with her foot as if impatient of the delay—"Oh! I wish I could reach thee," she cried. "If I could, I'd push thee down, thou smirking devil. But I can't; so I'll just hide and watch thee till thou tumbles into the river. Lord! what a pretty corpse thou'lt make for a crowner's quest."

And she shrieked exultantly with diabolical mirth, as she stood, with clenched hand upraised, looking down upon her victim.

Poor Mary held on with all her strength to the frail branch, with her pale face upturned to the pitiless moon, and the yet more pitiless woman above her; and a great horror seized her as she listened to the angry roar of the boiling flood below, tossing its white foam aloft as if reaching for its prey. She felt her grip relaxing and cried aloud for help; but human help there seemed none. . . .

Hark!—What was it she heard?—Tramp—tramp—tramp came the sound of many feet, hurrying over the frozen ground; and a welcome voice cried aloud—"Hell-cat!—what are you about?" Another moment, and the figure of Bess Humphreys disappeared, and Mary's brother bent over the cliff.

"Good God!" he exclaimed, as he marked her position about ten feet below the brink. "I can't reach her. Hold on, Mary dear, till I fetch something to pull you up with."

"I can't," she sobbed faintly. "I can't, Ned. I must let go if you don't help me quick."

A burly miner came to the rescue. Unwinding the long plaid in which he had carefully enwrapt himself, he lowered it to the girl; saying in grave, quaint tones:—"Tak' a guid grip of that, lassie, and hauld on tae the bit bush, till ye hae it weel in han'."

And thus was Mary rescued.

VINCENT PYKE (1827-94)
White Hood: A Tale of the Terraces

TAUMARUNUI

A New Zealand Joker's Lament for his Sheila

I'm an ordinary joker getting old before my time
For my heart's in Taumarunui on the Main Trunk Line.

You can get to Taumarunui going north or going south
And you end up there at midnight and you've cinders
  in your mouth;

You got cinders in your whiskers and a cinder in your
  eye,

So you hop off at Refreshments for a cupper tea and pie
In Taumarunui, Taumarunui, Taumarunui on the Main
    Trunk Line.

There's a sheila in Refreshments and she's pouring cupsa
    tea
And my heart jumps like a rabbit when she pours
    a cup for me;
She's got hair a flaming yellow and a mouth a flaming
    red
And I'll love that flaming sheila till I'm up and gone
    and dead
In Taumarunui, Taumarunui, Taumarunui on the Main
    Trunk Line.

You can get a job in Wellington or get a job up north
But you can't in Taumarunui though you try for all
    you're worth;
If I want to see this sheila, then I got to take a train;
Got ten minutes for refreshments then they cart me off
    again
From Taumarunui, Taumarunui, Taumarunui on the
    Main Trunk Line.

Well, they took me on as fireman on the Limited Express,
And I thought that she'd be jake but now it's just a
    flaming mess;
The sheila didn't take to me; I thought she'd be a gift;
She's gone and changed her duty hours and works the
    daylight shift
In Taumarunui, Taumarunui, Taumarunui on the Main
    Trunk Line.

I'm an ordinary joker growing old before my time
For my heart's in Taumarunui on the Main Trunk Line.
                        PETER CAPE (b. 1926)

MATAI BEER

In the rip-roaring times of the King Country, Matai beer was a favourite with those who were strong enough and tough enough to drink it. It went out of favour when "cruisers" for the various timber mills complained that much good yellow pine was being ruined through the number of deep axe cuts and even auger holes in the standing trees, made to let the potent juice run into waiting pannikins or buckets. The favourite recipe for this form of wood alcohol represented the addition of three or four cupsful of the sap to each gallon of "ordinary" liquid refreshment. That the resultant mixture had a pretty hefty kick to it may be judged from this description handed in to the Taihape newspaper (1912): "Matai beer is the term used to describe a certain brand or grade of alcoholic brew. It may be identified easily. It smells like an ancient bar room the morning after. It tastes like used machine oil, only a very low grade of machine oil. When a deep swig is absorbed, one has all the sensations of having swallowed a lighted kerosene stove. A sudden violent jolt of it has been known to stop the victim's watch, snap his braces, and crack his glass eye right across—all in the same motion. If it must be drunk, drink it while sitting flat on the floor. Then you don't have so far to fall."

Those boastful Southerners will have gathered that their far-famed Hokonui is as ice cream soda to that virile product of the King Country palmy days.

There was, some old-timers may remember, the classic yarn about the pioneer city angler engaged in prospecting one of the back country Ohakune streams. He was waylaid by an aggressive-looking bushman who

THE KIWI

Adopted by New Zealanders as their national bird and giving its name as a synonym for the average man, the tail-less, wing-less Kiwi is a nocturnal bird, blind in the daytime. Its sensitive nostrils at the tip of its bill allow it to seek the worms which it consumes in large quantities.

DEER-HUNTERS

Some 100,000 deer are shot every year in New Zealand, about half by amateurs, the rest by professional deer-cullers employed by the government. Here four cullers display wapiti and red deer antlers destined for the Dominion Museum, Wellington.

ON HORSEBACK

Many New Zealand beaches are suitable for horse-riding and racing. In this scene, a group of Maori youngsters ride along the beach at Wainui Bay, Northland.

A YACHT RACE ON THE WAITEMATA

Auckland's Waitemata Harbour is a yachtsman's paradise: the Anniversary Day Regatta (29th January) claims to be the largest one-day regatta in the world. The picture shows the Royal New Zealand Yacht Squadron's twenty-seven-mile "Round the Island" race. The Squadron was granted its Royal Charter in 1902.

carried a bottle in one hand and a shotgun in the other. "Here, sport," said the bushman, "have a drink on me!"

The angler protested that he didn't drink. Levelling his gun at him, the owner of the bottle ordered, "Drink!"

The man from the city drank, then shuddered, shook, shivered and coughed mightily. "Well!" he spluttered, "that's horrible stuff!"

"Ain't it?" agreed the bushman. "Now you hold the gun on me while I take a——gulp!"

IAN MACKAY (b. 1909)
Puborama

SONG OF THE BOOB

I'm the sort of silly boob that chases
        Races.
I get tips from all the surest sources—
        Horses
So sure that no four legs can whack them—
        Back them:
Then something happens and it's no
        Go.
I've lost my money at the trots,
        Lots;
I've lost more money at the sprints,
        Mints;
And, oh, the simple thought of hurdles
        Curdles
My blood and makes my very liver
        Quiver.
It's all the same, no matter what. . . .
        Hot
Favourites know I'm on them, and
        Stand

Still at the post—they'd rather burst,
          First
Than let me see them coming in a
          Winner!
My dark horse never comes to light—
          Spite!
I double up, I stick to owners—
          Jonahs!
I follow a jockey—vain! A trainer—
          Vainer!
I'm easily the biggest of the tote's
          Goats. . . .
I'm the sort of silly boob that chases
          Races.

                    J. H. E. SCHRODER (b. 1895)

CHARITY

"Dear Brethren." So the stately prelate starts his
     sermon:
Then, looking round the rather mongrel congregation
With slight distaste,
Adds, with the faintest alteration of inflection,
"In Jesus Christ."

                    HELEN BLACKSHAW

AFTER THE CHRISTENING

After the christening, the vicar handed the baby to Mrs.
Drake, which was rather unfortunate, because she had
not yet recovered from the shock of its premature
arrival. Once outside the church she thrust the bundle
at her husband.

"Here—you've got to carry it."

Mr. Drake looked at his wife in dismay. Carry the

baby! Not he! He examined his elegantly suited self—beautifully polished boots, pin-striped trousers, frock coat, immaculate shirt with its starched collar and cuffs, silk hat, gloves, stick. Carry a baby in the street? What did Jo think he was? The next thing she would expect him to push the perambulator like some of the chaps at the office. Not if he knew it. He was about to expostulate when he caught sight of his wife's face. Poor Jo! This had been a terrible blow to her. Not that they could help it—or the poor mite either, for that matter. It was nobody's fault, but it was a jolly shame, all the same. People naturally expected fine healthy babies and, when you were as adorable as Jo and a decent chap like himself—well, you had a right to expect the best. By Jove you did! He took the child, and as he did so, dismay struck him again. To be seen carrying this through the streets—these yards and yards of white embroidery with nothing inside—or next to nothing. No, sir! Not James Charles Henry Drake! Quickly he gathered the length of the gown, rolled it cocoonwise round the tiny bundle at the top end, and thrust the small querulous roll under his arm. They set off, his wife in earnest conversation with Mrs. Morgan.

Quite suddenly she noticed that the crying had ceased. She turned to her husband and failed to notice the baby tucked firmly out of sight under his arm. Unreasoning panic seized her.

"Jim, where is the baby? What have you done with my child?" With cheerful pride he turned to show her the baby, apparently comfortable for once. Josephine Drake was furious.

"Oh you brute! How dare you do such a thing? Look at her gown!" She almost snatched the baby from under his arm, and set about unwinding the once beautifully laundered garment.

"Look at her gown! Just look at it! It's the last time

I'll ever ask you to carry a child of mine, you great brute."

"Now, now, Jo," soothed Mrs. Morgan. "You shouldn't have asked him. Men hate to be seen carrying babies in the street. I'm really surprised at you. Why, I wouldn't have dared to ask Dad to carry our boys when they were babies. Give her to me. I'll carry her, poor mite."

To Dad Morgan the young husband was complaining, "I don't know what has come over Jo these days. I never seem able to do the right thing, no matter how I try. One would think that it was all my fault."

"Women are like that," replied Dad Morgan feelingly. "Why, even Ma has her funny little moments when I can't do right. But you know, Jim, this baby has been a great shock to Jo, and it will take her a while to get over it. You be patient with her, boy, and she will be all right."

"I suppose you *are* right," said young Mr. Drake more cheerfully. "You know, Dad, if she does live, I shouldn't be surprised if she becomes quite a jolly little kiddie. There is something about that baby, even now. I think she's got sense. Did you notice"—with great satisfaction—"how she stopped crying when I had her under my arm. I rather think she liked it."

IRIS HUGHES-SPARROW (b. 1906)
The Signature was Joy

GEORGE IN CHARGE

The farmer swung to the saddle
'Mid the dogs' unholy row.
"Now, Son, you'll attend to the buyer,
When he comes to see that cow.

Remember the price I've told you—
Do you hear? Or I'll skin you alive!
It's seven pound ten you'll ask for,
But we'll come as low as five!"

Now George was a simple fellow,
But for once his course was clear,
And his permanent grin got wider
As the scheduled hour drew near.
His memory George was stirring,
Just to see that it kept alive:
"It's seven pound ten we're asking,
But we'll come as low as five."

The buyer looked her over,
While his mind revolved a sum;
Then at last he popped the question,
And the fateful time was come.
Quoth George in a glow of triumph,
At the bargain he meant to drive,
"It's seven pound ten we're asking,
But we'll come as low as five!"

D. J. DONALD (d. 1938)

RINGING THE BULL

When Ned Wilson arrived, he took the situation in
hand. As the bull was nervous, not wild, just nervous
(Ned showed me how to tell a nervous bull from a
wild one), we decided to throw him down and tie his
legs. The only thing every man had to be careful about
in ringing a bull, was to be sure not to lose the small
screw that fastened the ring together after it was through
the nose. Gus trusted me with it; he said he would
fix the ring in place, and when he held his hand out I

was to put the screw into his fingers. Then there would be no mistakes.

The reason Ned reckoned the bull was nervous was because he ran round and round the stockyard, trying all the spaces between the rails. If he were out and out wild, it would be a different tale; we wouldn't be in the yard with him. Ned could tell us that. As it happened, we weren't in the yard very much longer, because when Gus coiled up the rope and made a move to lasso him, things began to happen. Now Ned Wilson has a fad for clay pipes, and in his hurry to get through the rails he bit the stem of his pipe in two; the way he went off about it was a scorcher. Gus said he would buy him a gross of the things if he would only shut up about it, but that was no good. That clay pipe was the only one Ned had managed even to colour properly in thirty years' experience with clay pipes. He wouldn't have taken ten pounds for it, and there it was all smashed up because Gus didn't have the brains to know a wild bull when he saw one.

When Gus left the yard he forgot to take the rope with him, and we had a bit of an argument as to who would get down off the rails and get it. I would have done it myself only, as I pointed out to Gus, he was careless enough to leave it there, so it was up to him to go back for it. Ned said he'd let us get killed our own way; he didn't care. We finally compromised by raking it through the rails with the aid of a garden rake lashed to a long pole. One of the little things I've been intending to do for the last year is to build a strong race in my yard, so that I can run wild cattle into it and shut them in. We put in over an hour trying to snare the bull from the rails, and finally Ned got impatient and took the rope away from us. He coiled it up in two neat coils, and held it in one hand with two fingers separating the coils. That was the proper way to hold a lariat!

As soon as the bull turned his head towards Ned he shouted: "Now watch closely, boys," and threw the whole thing at the bull.

It landed on his horns, and if Ned had only hung on to the end instead of letting the whole thing go, he'd have saved us a lot of trouble and worry. After the bull had shaken it off and made a careful examination of it, it was Ned's turn to get the rope, but he jibbed on it. He said he wouldn't have minded going down into the yard with that bull if Gus and I had only done what he wanted us to do at first. Now the bull was excited after the way we had been messing round with him. Ned said our stupid folly was the cause of it and we could finish the job ourselves. We raked the rope out again and before we tried any more lasso work we tied one end of the rope to the top of the rail of the yard, and then I had a go. I used to be pretty good at that sort of thing. I remember lassoing our big rooster at home once when I was a boy. He was just in the deep notes of a very impressive crow when I got him round the neck and everyone that spotted him for the next week or so thought some dog had been worrying him. I must have lost the art since then, because I didn't make much of a show at snaring the bull. Gus did the trick in the end, and you should have heard him telling Ned and me why it was we had been so long over it. If we had only let him do it instead of having a go ourselves, the bull would have been rung hours ago. If we wanted to practise that sort of thing, why didn't we practise on a post somewhere, in the evenings, instead of wasting valuable time when he wanted to get his pedigree bull rung.

The next job was to throw the bull and get him tied up securely. That didn't take very long because we hauled him to a post and then got down into the yard and surrounded him. Ned got kicked in the pocket-watch while he was stooping down explaining to Gus how to make a slip knot.

I thought the poor chap was done for. I remember wondering who would be responsible for the funeral expenses, while I was nipping to the house for a billy of water. Fortunately, Ned was only winded, and after I had heaved the water over him, he soon let us know he wasn't dead. We helped him through the rails, and he lay on his back and cursed Gus and me while we threw the bull and ringed him. I remembered the little screw and put it in my mouth for safety. I was leaning over Gus to see that he did things right, when the bull made a desperate struggle for liberty, and Gus's head came up and caught me in the face. I spat blood, and cried and blew my nose for about half a minute, and then Gus got wild because I couldn't find the screw. It was getting near milking time and we fixed things in the end by weaving a fine piece of wire through the bull ring and twisting the ends. Gus said that of all the born fools I was one of them. Next time he had a little job to do I was to keep away. I only got in his road, and worried him.

FRANK S. ANTHONY (1891-1925)
Me and Gus

THE FULL CUP

My strength can never fail me,
Nor foul disease assail me,
Nor loathly germ attack me,
Nor pain nor sorrow rack me;
My ways are safely guided,
My needs are all provided,
A kindly State supports me,
No person ever thwarts me,

No dunning duty calls me,
No threat of hell appals me,
No daily toils fatigue me,
No nasty noises plague me,
No spectre of poverty haunts me,
No looming danger daunts me,
No force unseen frustrates me,
No man or woman hates me,
No god or devil frights me,
No fierce ambition bites me,
My lovely wife adores me,
And, Lord, how living bores me!

ARNOLD WALL (1869-1966)

THE BUSH-FIRE

The Swede made a final rush, found a door, opened it, and stumbled, half suffocated, into clearer air. Through the window the light of the blazing forest poured as bright as day, but every pane of glass was cracked and splintered by the terrific heat. On a broad bed in one corner sat his eldest boy, sobbing aloud and monotonously shaking his three sleeping brothers. "They won't wake, father," he said piteously; "and this is the end of the world."

Andersen caught them up in his arms, bed-clothes and all, but the weight was beyond even his strength, and he set the eldest boy down. "I kom back, Sven," he said, looking into the child's eyes.

"Let me come with you, father; I can walk."

"Ach, you can't walk on the burning floor; you got no boots, my poor one. You be goot boy. I swear to mine Gott, I kom back."

"Oh father, take me with you now. You will never come back; you never did come back."

The Swede looked through the window into the heat

of the hell without. "Hear me, Christ Jesus," he said hoarsely; "dis I leave here is mine eldest sohn. With you I leave him."

Again he caught the three boys in his arms and dashed down the passage on to the veranda. The left side of the house was already in flames, and forks of light darted at him as he ran. Beckwith took the children from him and hurried with them back to the road, and once more Andersen turned to the burning building.

Whatever it had been before, it was an act of sublime heroism now. Over the roof the flames were pouring in a living sheet that in a few minutes must envelop the whole house. From the passage, as from the mouth of a tunnel, the red smoke rolled acrid and insufferable. The Swede gathered himself, and with his arms before his face dashed through flame and smoke to the room. He seized the boy, rolled him in the counterpane, and again turned to the exit. Nor was he an instant too soon, for even as he fled the flames broke through the partition walls and wrapped the right side of the house as the left in a cyclone of fire.

Choking, scorched, half blinded, he reached the veranda and leapt down. He saw a group of persons across the road, and Beckwith hurrying forward to meet him. All around the scene was brilliantly illuminated, he could make out the approaching man's face as clearly as if it were mid-day. And even as he caught sight of him he saw him pause and his face stiffen in sudden horror. Then he became aware of a stupendous roaring, of a dazzling light above, behind—where exactly he knew not—and of voices calling to him warningly, supplicatingly, despairingly, from the group on the road. Of what was happening he had no knowledge, but in that instant there came to him an inspiration, and he acted on it. Drawing back his arms as he ran he hurled the boy forward full into Beckwith's breast. It was a feat of tremendous strength, such as none but a frenzied man would have attempted or succeeded in performing. And as the child left his arms there sprang up all around him a great and dazzling glory as of the kingdom of heaven opened. For an instant he gazed into it, knew it was his heritage, and in that knowledge passed into eternal sleep.

But the agonised group on the road saw only the horror and splendour of the falling tree.

WILLIAM SATCHELL (1860-1942)
The Toll of the Bush

WINTER NIGHT

The candles gutter and burn out,
   and warm and snug we take our ease,
and faintly comes the wind's great shout
   as he assails the frozen trees.

The vague walls of this little room
   contract and close upon the soul;
deep silence hangs amid the gloom;
   no sound but the small voice of the coal.

Here in this sheltered firelit place
   we know not wind nor shivering tree;
we two alone inhabit space,
   locked in our small infinity.

This is our world, where love enfolds
   all images of joy, all strife
resolves in peace: this moment holds
   within its span the sum of life.

For Time's a ghost: these reddening coals
    were forest once ere he'd begun,
and now from dark and timeless boles
    we take the harvest of the sun;

and still the flower-lit solitudes
    are radiant with the springs he stole
where violets in those buried woods
    wake little blue flames in the coal.

Great stars may shine above this thatch;
    beyond these walls perchance are men
with laws and dreams: but our thin latch
    holds all such things beyond our ken.

The fire that lights our cloudy walls
    now fails beneath the singing pot,
and as the last flame leaps and falls
    the far wall is and then is not.

Now lovelier than firelight is the gleam
    of dying embers, and your face
shines through the pathways of my dreams
    like young leaves in a forest place.

A. R. D. FAIRBURN (1904-1957)

SCULPTRESS

One year ago he died, yet just to-day
She took the cloths from the unfinished clay;
And for one pitiless instant, lost, undone,
Her forehead rested on the graven one.

RUTH GILBERT (b. 1917)

MR. GLOVER'S WELLINGTON

I think I can best express my opinion of Wellington in terms of a short fable. Now suppose I go into a fish shop and without noticing it buy a crayfish with one claw, and suppose I wish to make representations to the proper authorities that I have been taken down. I ring up a friend of mine in the Procrastination Department of the Ministry of Frustration and he puts me on to somebody whom he knows in the Constultification Division of the Ministry of Ineptitude. He happens to know somebody, just the man I must see, the Crustacean Comptroller in the Submarine Division of the Ultramarine Department (Fisheries), who will certainly advise me what steps to take about having inadvertently bought a one-clawed crayfish. Well, he's helpful and says that I ought to see Herb in the Hygiene Branch of the Department of Health, because if one-clawed crayfish are to be found round the coast they are not the scavengers they are expected to be, and furthermore, the question arises in conjunction with someone from the Ministry of Housing because the fish shop from which I bought it is owned by a Greek. (I am not referring to Archbishop Makarios). The Ministry of Housing, if you ask, because the fish shop happens to be next to a State house whose tenants complained of the smell and it may just be that the missing claw has found its way under their floor boards thus contravening the Fresh Fry and Stale Fat Amendment Act to the Fish (Fried or Fresh) Mongers and Poultry Purveyors Licensing Amendment Enactment of 1923. I am also referred to the Labour Department, which insists that the provisions of the Crayfish-Takers Industrial Union of Workers' Award, Clause 10, Subclause (d) clearly state that one-clawed crayfish may only be lawfully taken by a one-armed crayfish-taker if not under 10 inches measured from top to tip.

I don't know what Security has to do with this, until a type looking like a failed major calls on me discreetly to inquire whether the crayfish was red before or after it was cooked. And the Scales (Fish) Inspector of the Weights and Measures Department is called in to investigate the weight of the crayfish because 3s. 6d. a pound minus one claw might contravene the P.T. ruling on the retail price. All this is good clean Wellington fun, but what a nice lot of chaps you meet—and look how many men you have kept in gainful employment.

DENIS GLOVER (b. 1912)
Hot Water Sailor

BIRTH IN THE BUSH

"What do you think of this, Mrs. Holt?" asked Geraldine, waving her hand in the direction of the gumfield. She knew Marion had never seen anything in the view.

"Much better than being down in a gully as I was for so many years. It's lonely in a gully, and things come at you out of the bush. My nearest neighbour was ten miles away at first, and only men at that, and when it came to my time with the first there wasn't anybody to get regular, and it came unexpected, too. Bill rode off for help, but it came with me on my back alone. . . ." Marion fidgeted, fearing her guests would be bored, and it was hardly the thing to be telling with a man there. "And then it died before anybody could come. It was rather hard on me, a young girl and my first, and Bill had to make a little coffin and bury it. It was two months before any parson could come to say a few words. It took me a long time to get over it. I kept seeing Bill putting the little coffin into the grave, no name or anything. I suppose I was a bit of a baby, for I used to go and cry there when Bill was away. It did seem as if I might have had the child in that lonely place. However, the second came all right, and then we got neighbours. Things don't stay bad for ever. I tell my daughter she needn't talk about it being quiet here."

JANE MANDER (1877-1949)
Allen Adair

HOME AND SCHOOL

"Tell me," I ask, "did you get the strap to-day?"

"No," says Susan wistfully, "nothing exciting happened to-day . . . Oh, yes, I remember, Andrew Metcalf said a rude word."

"Did he?" I ask, all ears.

"Yes, he said Backside." Her eyes are awed.

"Did he get the strap?" I ask.

"Do you know what? We were having gramophone records and he asked Mrs. Griffin to put the backside on. Wasn't he *awful*?"

"Did teacher think he was awful?"

"No, she didn't," says Susan disgustedly. "Do you think he was awful?"

"Of course not."

"I'll tell Mrs. Griffin you don't think Backside's awful."

"Don't bother," I say hastily.

"No bother at all," says Susan. "Mrs. Griffin will be interested. She says she likes to know what our parents think about things."

Does she indeed, I think grimly, but dare not say it aloud for fear it may be regarded as relevant to the Parent-Teacher relationship.

I tackle my eight-year-old. "Tell me," I ask him, "does Mr. Donald give people the strap much?"

"Don't be silly, mum. Only the Headmaster's allowed to give people the strap."

"Well, what does Mr. Donald do if you behave badly?"

"He sends us to the Headmaster, or"—his voice is husky with emotion—"he doesn't let us play footie in the lunch-hour."

There is comparative silence while he ruminates.

"Tell me," he barks, aiming a barristerial finger, "do you think the earth came off the sun?"

"Of course," I say stoutly.

"Then you're wrong!" he yelps, bringing his fist down heavily and shattering a biscuit. "It didn't. It came off a twin sun."

"Indeed," I say coldly. "Who says so?"

"Mr. Donald. And a man called Hoyle."

"Actually," I defend myself, "I did listen to some talks over the air, but I didn't think that was quite——."

"You couldn't have been paying attention," says George firmly. "Mr. Donald says it's very important to pay attention, otherwise you'll join the ranks of the intellectually unfit. Are you intellectually unfit?"

"Tell me, how many marks did you get for writing to-day?" I ask, counter-attacking. (Writing's his weak subject.)

"Missed writing to-day. Had to go to the Murder House instead."

"The Murder House?" My hand falters to my throat. "You mean the Headmaster's Study?"

"No, the Dental Clinic. See?"

He bares his gum, and through the crumbs I see two bleeding holes which lately housed two obstinate baby teeth.

"See?" He produces from his pocket something

shrouded in off-white gauze. "I'd better put them under the mat straight away." He dashes out.

My eyes follow him fondly. Only the young, I reflect, are capable of believing in an expanding universe, and fairies at the same time.

He pokes his head round the door. "And the fairies just better not forget!" he threatens darkly, and withdraws.

MARIE BULLOCK (b. 1918)
It's Been Nice Not Knowing You

REVERIE ON THE RAT

I want to talk about the Rat.

You've heard me talk of this and that.
Just for a change I'd like to speak
Some words about the Rat this week.

The Rat is different from the Cat,
He dare not sit upon the mat;
He sees with anxious eyes the feline,
And for his hole he makes a bee-line.

And yet he differs from the Bee,
He does not give us honey, see?

And then, again, he's fond of cheese,
A food that is not liked by bees.

The Rat's a rodent beast—his habits
In this respect are like the Rabbit's.

However, in a stew, I feel,
The Rabbit makes a nicer meal.

The Rat is different from the Rhino.
You ask me why? I'm damned if I know.

He differs from the Hippo, too.
I find that very odd, don't you?

The Rat is different from the Cat . . .
I think I may have mentioned that.

I do not like this quadruped,
I feel that he is better dead.

It would not be a serious loss for us
If all his family dined on phosphorus.

A. R. D. FAIRBURN (1904-57)

RON SOMETHING-OR-OTHER

Jim's speech was getting pretty colourful by this time,
but minus one or two of his favourite words, this is
what he told us:

"I was shooting with a bloke called Ron something-
or-other in South Westland just after the war. Biggest
lying coot I ever come across. If he told you the billy
was boiling you could bet fifty rounds it wasn't. If
he said the river was flooded you'd know it was low
enough to cross without getting a boot full. Only
good thing about him was he lied all the time; you
could count on it.

"The one time he went up to the tops he got himself
lost and didn't get back till next day. Said he'd been
floundering around in a blizzard and almost collided
with an enormous stag. He'd shot it, skinned it, and
warmed his hands on the body. When it got dark,
he'd gutted the deer, wrapped himself in the skin, and
crawled inside the carcass out of the weather. In the

morning he'd found himself buried in three feet of
snow, and the carcase frozen solid. His knife was
outside and his hands were too numb anyway to bend
the flaps back. He was trapped.

"By the time he'd chewed himself free, climbed down
to the river and got swept under a log-jam, it was late
in the afternoon. He'd swum up through the logs,
shifting them aside as he came to the surface for air,
dived again for his rifle and pack, and then gone off
for the evening shoot. He'd cleaned up a mob of twenty-
five deer, but lost all the tails at his last river-crossing
on the way back to camp. I found the place later on
where he'd spent the night, and most of the next day
in his sleeping-bag, about twenty minutes up-river
from the hut.

"Later on he took our pack-horse up the river-flats
to get a bundle of skins we'd left behind. Tied the nag
up and went out for a shot, got nothing, came back,
saw the horse through the trees, and dropped it for a
deer.

"Story he told me was the beast went mad and
attacked him, so he had to shoot it in self-defence. I
said the horse's body was still tied to the tree, and it
looked to me as if it had been shot from the side. He
had the cheek to say he'd tied it up after it was dead
to stop the pigs dragging it away with our pack-saddle.
The hole in the horse's shoulder was where the bullet
had come out. It had gone in its mouth! I booted him
off the block for pointing his rifle at me in the finish,
and I wasn't too sorry for the chance when I got it
either.

"That wasn't the finish though. A few days later a
crowd of police came in to get me, armed to the teeth.
My mate had been spouting in a pub about how I'd
been blazing away at him for two days, riddling the
hut with bullets, and just missing doing him a serious
injury. He'd crept out in the night and run for safety,

followed by a screaming hail of .303s. Someone had heard this yarn, told the police, and they'd come to get me. It took a while explaining about our Ron, and by the time they got back to town it was too late. He'd done a moonlight on the publican, owing a week's board, and wearing the barman's shoes and coat. Don't know where he got to, but he was a beaut."

BARRY CRUMP (b. 1935)
A Good Keen Man

Amusements and Sports

EARLY THEATRE

In the palmy days of the Theatre the world knew no
Hitler; life in general was not very exciting; there
was no movie industry and no broadcasting; and the
Stage was one of the chief joys of life. There was always
either something good in town, or something coming,
or the memories of a show that had passed on, to talk
about. This applied to all classes; in those days you
could see a lot of fun at small expense. In the main
centres vaudeville was always to be seen, and the pro-
grammes were changed weekly; there was a continuous
flow of new acts and stars from Australia and further
afield. Good visiting companies playing dramas and
comic operas were seen frequently; the stars of the
concert platform, accompanied by echoes of London
applause; and in between, lecturers and elocutionists,
concert parties and circuses, grand opera companies
and the performances of local dramatic and operatic
companies which often compared favourably with those
of the people from overseas. The provincial towns saw
a good proportion of this entertainment; they had no
permanent vaudeville, but touring variety shows were
seen instead. The world went very well then.

Old-timers among theatre-goers recall that the
theatre in the pioneering days, and even down to the
1890's and later, offered much that was crude and
second-rate—that the theatres were often make-shift
halls with hard seats, poor lighting, and leaking roofs—
that scenery and effects were ludicrously scanty and
even lacking altogether.

An English author, David Christie Murray, who was
in New Zealand in the early 1880's, toured with a

theatrical company and has recorded some of his experiences. "I remember," he wrote, "that we played once in a schoolroom built of corrugated iron and without a vestige of scenery. We put on *Chums*, and the settler's parlour, the forest scene, and the outer view of the Otago homestead were each and all represented with the help of a green baize cloth, which hung at the rear and on either side of the stage, three upturned petroleum tins, three chairs, a tub, and a little oblong deal table with red legs. We had a stage space of about four yards by three." Of another performance he relates: "I have seen the house drowned in tears over that lugubrious and hollow *East Lynne* when the stage has been enclosed in green baize and there has not been a stick of respectable furniture on the boards."

MAURICE HURST
Music and the Stage in New Zealand

A PIG-HUNT

Selecting an opening between two bushes, Gilbert was able to gain an entrance into the thicket, but it was so dense that he had to proceed in a crawling position for some distance, when he got into a kind of run or track made by the pigs, and, looking along this, he saw at no great distance a fierce-looking boar whetting his huge tusks and disdainfully regarding the dogs which were yelping at him. The advent of a new enemy on the scene attracted the boar's attention, and immediately two dogs fastened on his ears, but he succeeded in shaking them off, and at the same time advanced somewhat nearer Gilbert, who felt his position an exceedingly uncomfortable one, hemmed in as he was by surrounding scrub. He was afraid to fire in case he should hit the dogs, and he felt that if either of them was rendered *hors de combat* in any way, his own chances of getting

out of the gully alive were small. Yet though tempted
to retreat at once, he did not like to do so; he thought
he would risk a shot, and did it. From the position of
the boar, Gilbert was unable to take aim at any place
but its head; he waited for some minutes in the hope
that he would get a chance of shooting it behind the
shoulder, but it was no use, so he resolved to aim at
its eye. He lay down and took as steady an aim as he
could, seeing that he was haunted by the dread of
being ripped by the savage-looking tusks of the creature
if he missed. Gilbert fired; he heard a shriek from the
pig, accompanied by the sound of a rush and crashing
of branches, and through the smoke he saw the huge
boar hurling itself towards him. He thought his hour
had come, yet he could do nothing. He drew his revolver
and lay close to the ground, in the hope that the brute
would pass over him. Before he had time almost to
do this the boar was upon him, but just as it reached
him it fell dead, with its fierce snout touching him,
while the blood spurted from the wound in its head
over him. It gave one convulsive struggle, and then
lay perfectly still.

ALEXANDER BATHGATE (1845-1930)
Waitaruna, A Story of New Zealand Life

DANCING IN THE 1880's

As we grew older it was not the picnic that appealed to
us so much, but the dance that followed at night. How
fine and grown up we were the first time we were
permitted to dance. And actually to go home and
dress for the dance. It had a marvellous sound. What
matter that the milking and the feeding of the pigs
and fowls had to be done first! We persuaded ourselves
that we really went home to dress! True, our dresses
for some years were only our ordinary "Sunday dresses"

freshly starched and ironed, but there was always a new bit of ribbon for our hair or a new lace collar or some little ornament to transform it from a day-frock into a glamorous evening gown.

Our mothers sat sedately round the room on stiff, hard forms admiring their daughters, and keeping an eye on their behaviour! "Don't you dare go outside between dances, Trixie!" "Maggie! don't let the boys swing you off your feet like that. It isn't decent, acting like great tom-boys!" And we would say, plaintively, "But it's so hot, Mother. Can't we go out and get just a teeny breath of fresh air?" And "I can't help it, Mum. They *will* do it, we just can't keep on our feet."

Those old dances! Do people really enjoy the modern dancing—the shuffling gyrations, the convulsive stepping, and, worst of all, the standing practically in one spot, faces together, bodies in a close clinch, shoulders and rumps heaving, feet lifting occasionally like a horse stamping away flies! In the old dances there was grace and dignity, splendid steps and intricate patterns of movement, and withal plenty of fun and merriment. Match to-day if you can the grace of the mazurka, the dignity of the maxina, the liveliness of the polka, and the swinging rhythm of the schottische. And the grand old square dances: the vigorous lancers and the quadrilles; the graceful langorous d'Alberts. Listen to the music; watch the instant response to the orders of the M.C.: "Top and bottom couples visit to the right", "Swing corners", "Ladies to the right, gentlemen to the left and swing partners," "Waltz to corners, and waltz the room," all to the sobbing of the old accordion and later to the challenging rally of the fiddle. There was a little roughness sometimes, a bit of horseplay, perhaps. "Swing 'em off their feet, boys"—soon suppressed by the M.C. if it threatened to get out of hand, but no vulgarity. Compared with the black bottom and the big apple, with their obscene suggestiveness, our wildest romping was decorum itself.

JEAN BOSWELL (1876-1963)
Dim Horizons

CLIMBING IN THE SOUTHERN ALPS

The whole chain of great snowy peaks stood forth clearly against the crimson west, and was again mirrored in the placid lake at our feet. So peaceful was the evening scene, that, as I gazed, I could scarcely realise that these white, glittering peaks had been the theatre of so much hardship, so much privation, and so much peril during the last few months. I felt amply rewarded, however, for the long marches and hazardous climbs, for the cold, the wet, and the general discomfort of my sojourn, by the closer knowledge I had obtained of these majestic heights; these seemingly impregnable fastnesses of ice and rock; by the sights which had been unfurled before my eyes of the wonderfully contrasting zones of glacier and vegetation on the west coast, unparalleled by all that I have yet seen or heard described in the extraordinary proximity in which one climatic region is brought to another. I remember, too, how, when some new summit scaled, seated on a lofty point

"High between the clouds and sun"

I would forget briefly the toils of the ascent, and the precariousness of the descent before me, lost in the momentary triumph of the accomplished aim. There is this, at least, to be said in favour of the pursuit of Alpine climbing—that the end obtained is in many cases definite, and, in a certain sense, attainable. Once a peak scaled, the whole enterprise passes in one's mind into the condition of definite achievement, and the climber turns his attention to fresh things yet to do. In this respect Alpine climbing contrasts strangely with most human pursuits in which the question of success is rather one of degree than absolute in its nature, and the long, patient, and laborious pursuit of truth by which the end is never gained, but continually approached, sometimes by almost imperceptible steps, is foreign to the nature of this part of our undertaking.

E. A. FITZGERALD
Climbs in the New Zealand Alps

FARMER'S DAY OUT

When the farmer is asked how long he works, his reply is invariably "From daylight till dark." This is the usual formula—a rationalisation that is not strictly true; but the early dark of the winter months certainly brings greater opportunities for leisure. . . . A sheep-farmer who solemnly declared that he had no leisure at all admitted that he spent at least one day a week at the market although he bought and sold only once or twice a year. There are some who regularly attend two markets every week. Over ninety per cent of the farmers attending the fortnightly market in Littledene are sheep-farmers. The man with the mixed small farm has little time for sales and does not attend unless he has something to sell or is anxious to buy. . . .

The big sheep fairs are held in March and April. Then the fat lambs are sold for export and the farms are restocked with ewes. The other fortnightly sales during the year supply the local and city markets with mutton, but a large proportion of the sheep in these sales are merely changing homes, altering the entries in the ledger at the Littledene branch of the Bank of New Zealand and building up the commission account of the stock auctioneer. To lean over the pens contemplating these peripatetic sheep and chuckling at the perennial witticisms of the auctioneer—then to spend an hour at the Working-men's Club before going home—this is the "day out" of the sheep-farmer.

H. C. D. SOMERSET (1895-1968)
Littledene

WHALING IN COOK STRAIT

Miss Whekenui spins round. Her owner, at the wheel, opens wide the throttle. The speed-boat leaps ahead, with a sudden deep-toned roar we have not heard from her before. The slapping of the water on her bow becomes abruptly hard and vicious. Spray flies over her in a continuous blinding sheet. She lurches violently as she plunges through the waves. Feet splayed, gun pointed slightly downwards, the harpooner rides erect on the bow, while the launch careers madly across the sea. The helmsman, hat pulled down hard over his eyes to screen them from the stinging spray, peers ahead from under the dripping brim. Suddenly the chaser rushes into a patch of oily-smooth water, where the whales have been. The engine slows, the vessel loses speed. *Cachalot*, flying on white wings of foam comes racing with the wild white horses of the sea. The two boats cruise at easy pace, on slightly divergent courses, bracketing the way they believe the whales to have taken.

They are not mistaken. Two vast black heads, wet and shining, break water fifty yards ahead. The engines roar, the launches leap for the spot at full speed. But they are still twenty yards away when the great flukes of the sea-beasts' tails go skyward, showing white undersides, as they sound. Once again the white plumes of their breath are dissipated by the sea breeze.

So the chases goes on, greyhounds after a hare. The two whales double and dodge, blowing now ahead and now astern, keeping together, the two humps showing always side by side. The end of the chase is never in doubt; it is only a matter of time. Half an hour— then, as the gunner waves his arms for *Miss Whekenui* to increase speed, two immense dark shadows can be seen slipping along ahead, with the water shoaling above them. The launch dashes recklessly alongside. A huge flat head, warty and knobbed and hideous, like that of some uncouth prehistoric monster, thrusts up through the waves not six yards away on the port bow. Two gaping nostrils open on the broad back, and the creature snorts a blast of spume into the air.

The gunner swings the muzzle round. There is a dull report, half drowned by the racing engine. A puff of white smoke is quickly blown away by the wind. We catch a momentary glimpse of the coils of rope flying through the air, of the butt of the harpoon projecting from the whale's flank. At the same time, the second whale blows, between its mate and the rocking launch, right beside us, so close one could step over dry-shod on to its back, with the bight of the harpoon-line lying across it. Then both tails fly up together, the broad flukes showering the salt sea over us, as the whales dive deep down. They leave the sea boiling in their wake.

Our harpooner, making sure that the line runs freely through the chocks in the boat's bow, stands upright, leaning against the gun. The helmsman takes another turn round the steaming loggerhead, and eases the tension with the motor as the whale takes *Miss Whekenui* in tow. A fine sight in the sunshine, with the drenching spray flying left and right, and the gunner, lance in hand, poised on her bow, *Cachalot* races past to give the death-stroke. But when the whales next come up, they are far to port of her. The harpooned whale blows first, spouting bloody foam. It is the cow to which we are fast; had we taken the bull whale, the cow would have fled, whereas the greater constancy of the male keeps him by the side of his wounded mate.

When next the wounded whale rises, *Cachalot* ranges alongside. With all his strength, the harpooner hurls his dart into the beast's side. Hardly has the whale submerged than the helmsman fires the bomb, by touching the ends of the insulated wire to electric points on the boat. There is a muffled thud under water, and while *Miss Whekenui* is still pulling up on the harpoon-line, the whale rushes to the surface, blowing dark blood in its death-flurry. *Miss Whekenui* draws up to it, and the gunner thrusts the sharp point of an air-spear in its side, leaning on the shaft and pushing it deep in, to pump air through a hose from the engine into the gigantic carcase and so ensure its floating. Many a whale of old was lost through sinking, but to-day the air-spear has lessened that risk.

Foolish, ununderstanding, the bull whale has waited at the side of its dead mate. It falls an easy victim to *Cachalot's* deadly gun. The harpoon, placed in a mortal spot, kills it and after sounding once, it floats lifeless on the surface, the waves slopping over it.

STEPHEN GERARD (1909-1941)
Strait of Adventure

MESSING ABOUT IN BOATS

In many New Zealanders' belief, man has never built anything more beautiful than a boat—or more enjoyable. Some of our earliest memories will be of splashing about in the warm shallows, gathering pipi shells along glistening, gently shelving beaches, launching some floating contrivance that was no toy but a dream-boat named for adventure, eating picnic lunch with crusts for the screaming gulls, and shivering with delight in surf braved on parental shoulders. The sun and the sand, the sea and its boats are our birthright, for we are a maritime people.

Thousands of us race unsinkable amateur-built seven feet six inch sailboats before we can muster as many years as the boat's length in feet. The Auckland Anniversary Day regatta on January 29th is said to be the largest one day regatta in the world; with over 3,000 pleasure craft from plywood midgets to sixty feet keelers and ocean-going cabin cruisers; topsail and bermuda rig, spinnakers as many-hued as Joseph's coat, ballooning past the flag-dressed Naval Base, beating back before sundown, closehauled for the finish, the stowing of gear and the camaraderie of a drop o' the doings.

Boat-building was one of the earliest of New Zealand's crafts, brought to remarkable finesse in scores of designs. Amateurs build their own craft, often in backyards miles from water; carved and clinker planked, laminated pressed-wood or fabricated fibreglass. Until recent years all our boats were built of kauri, the unique pine that brought Captain Cook ashore for spars, and which timbered the hundreds of scows and schooners of pioneer days.

Wooden ships and iron men—the saying goes; and New Zealand was developed by them.

KENNETH MELVIN (1905-69)
New Zealand

AT THE RACES

The race-course, outside the oval of track, had lost to bright fashion its summer colour and only inside the track, where a grey ambulance waited and a few men moved, was the grass still to be seen, brown and burned by the sun.

Margaret focused the glasses, won from Harry by

promises which she could never keep, until the whole race-course lay, clear and close, almost under her hand. In the birdcage the horses for the first race circled and danced, perched on by jockeys as light and as perky and as gay as parakeets, and threaded out curving and sidestepping on to the unmarked track. Above the roofs of the buildings—the totalisator, the grandstand, the members' stand, the bar—the balloon rode as no balloon ever rode, rigid from its mast, and away to the left the tide rose in patterns of light and shadow through the mangroves. The horses, rich as velvet, strained on tight reins past the grandstand, out to the barrier wires. Shredded by the breeze the tatters of music blew up, harsh and gay, to where the children sat, and with one arm hooked around the post Margaret stared through the binoculars.

—Can you see anything? Harry asked.

She did not answer.

Swinging and turning, the horses came into line, broke, reformed and burst away, running in silence, charging, while the wide line narrowed and beat against the rails and she saw them go into the bend and show again, smaller now, straining in the same amazing silence across the back-straight, and run towards her, colour after colour bright in the sunlight, to come to the hurdles where, still in silence, they stretched out and hung a moment as though carved from something solid and eternally still, and ran on. They raced in silence, or to a series of sounds—the banging of a gate, a radio playing, a car passing on the road—which served only to heighten the silence within that charmed lens. She felt that she had by some magic entered a world where, because of the silence, nothing human might ever enter again, and even Harry, shouting for his turn, could not disturb it.

Singly, in twos and threes, the horses rose and came on, fleeing across the confining circle until, when they were almost free, she shifted the binoculars and they were caught again. In the silence the billowing colours drummed and shone. She outpaced the running horses simply by moving her wrist and waited for them at the double jump. The first horse rose to it and touched and rose again and was gone; the brush on the hurdle trembled. But before she too could swing away the following horses showered into the lens and, all grace gone, struck and fell, and a jockey in crimson and yellow silks and white breeches made an absurd clash of colour on the green grass.

Only when she took the binoculars from her eyes did the shouting beat up to her, blown, like the music, to shreds, whispering and roaring over the rooftops and the road.

——Can you see anything? Harry asked.

MAURICE DUGGAN (b. 1922)
Race Day

TROUT AT EVENING

A twenty-five-shilling licence thenceforth became for Sam and me a passport to scores of miles of trout-stocked rivers, streams and lakes, virtually unfished waters then, and all within easy range of home. It was to lead us into unfrequented places screened by virgin bush, where fantails tumbled in the air around us and the banks echoed the plaintive, ventriloquistic notes of the first cuckoos of the year resting after their long trans-ocean flight, their delicate yet haunting song becoming associated in our minds as the music of welcome to a new fishing season. It was to let us learn the magic of the evening rise on a bushland river at the end of a sweltering high summer day and, on several of these evenings, to let us experience that truly rare moment which others have described as "nature's hour

A TABOOD STORE-HOUSE AT THE BAY OF ISLANDS

Augustus Earle (1798-1837) came to New Zealand in 1827 and made many sketches of Maori life and customs. In this water-colour of 1827-8, he depicts a typical store-house which has been placed under tapu, or made sacred and untouchable.

SCOUTING PARTY, WANGANUI (c.1865)

One of the most colourful characters in the Maori Wars, Major Gustavus Ferdinand von Tempsky (1828-1868) came to New Zealand in 1859 and led a special corps in bush-fighting until he was killed in the Hauhau risings. He made many water-colours of the New Zealand scene and Maori life.

A HAKA OF WELCOME

Modern Maoris dressed for the occasion in traditional costume perform one of their vigorous dances of welcome during a visit of a Vice-Regal party to Rotorua.

IN CONTRAST

A Maori elder speaks to an attentive audience of fellow-elders at a meeting in the Maori Battalion Hall, Gisborne.

of worship," a moment that seems almost too beautiful to belong to the world of men. It is a moment when the evening is golden in the west and the full fragrance of the cooling bush is on the gentle breeze and the green of the trees becomes more vivid in the aureate glow. Your line, helped by the up-river draught, is snaking out without effort and you watch the fly riding the silver and the shadows with an ever-increasing sense of contentment of mind. All at once, and quite unaccountably, the rise stops completely and the flies of the evening hatch pass over the lies unmolested. The gentle current of the air dies away and the hushing voice of the river seems to soften perceptibly and the birds fall silent. Something within you feels a presence is close by and that time is standing still for a moment in respect to the passing of a day; that all nature around you is indeed worshipping its Creator and that the place of man at this divine moment is surely on his knees. And then as suddenly as it came the moment passes. The fantails and pippits flirt low over the water. The small fish along the edging waters send out rings again from their quick, showy rises, and the big fellows at the edge of the white water resume their unhurried snout, fin and tail action, porpoising gracefully through the eddies. The breeze is cool on the cheek again. Time is under way once more.

Our river-roaming days also taught us something about the characters of the streams; the hustling Gowan River which plunges helter-skelter down on her seven-mile dash to join the Buller; the fighting fish that live in the churning pools and in the shelter of the tangles of timber heaped on the bends by the floods. We came to know the pattern of the long, lazy reaches between the Buller rapids and the fish, silvery with the daylong sun that bathes them, which you will come on lying almost awash at the river's edge on a hot afternoon but which, if you have time to experiment long enough, will usually reward you with a rise. We learned that rivers and fish have moods and that studying these roots their peculiar character much more firmly in the affections.

Neither were the less aesthetic delights of trout fishing overlooked. One of these grew from the conversion of a 600-gallon water-tank to serve as a smoke-house, where, over a bed of smouldering manuka sawdust, with a blending of the green foliage of the same plant, we learned to turn the thick, pink sides of trout into fragrant golden-brown fillets which could be stored for weeks at a time and were an abiding joy to visitors. Another associated art and pleasure was that of fly-tying, an occupation to titillate the memory and the imagination on the long nights of the close season. That it would leave a legacy for later years I didn't then appreciate. Too often has my Sabbatic composure and attention to psalm or sermon been disturbed by a sudden flare-up of covetousness brought on by the sight of a flash of jungle-cock wing or the dancing of the steely hackle feathers of the Old English Game bantam in the hat-mount of a fellow-worshipper in a neighbouring pew.

TEMPLE SUTHERLAND
Green Kiwi

DOWN THE HALL ON SATURDAY NIGHT

I got a new brown sportscoat,
I got a new pair of grey strides,
I got a real Kiwi haircut,
Bit off the top and short back and sides.

As soon as I've tied up the guri,
As soon as I've broomed out the yard,
As soon as I've hosed down my gumboots,
I'll be living it high and living it hard.

I'm going to climb on to the tractor,
I'm going to belt it out of the gate.
There's a hop on down the hall, and
She starts sharp somewhere 'bout half-past eight.

Hey, look at the sheilas cutting the supper.
An' look at the kids sliding over the floor,
And look at the great bunch of jokers,
Hanging round the door.

They got the Teacher to belt the piano;
They got Joe from the store on the drums;
Yeah, we're slick as the Orange in Auckland
For whooping things up and making them hum.

I had a schottische with the tart from the Butcher's,
Got stuck for a waltz with the constable's wife;
I had a beer from the keg on the cream-truck,
And the cop had one, too, you can bet your life.

Oh, it's great being out with the jokers,
When the jokers are sparking and bright;
Yeah, it's great giving cheek to the sheilas,
Down the hall on Saturday night.

PETER CAPE (b. 1926)

ROUGH RIDING

Bill got the mare out in the centre of the ring, touched
the stirrup, and jumped. He was ready for the mare
to buck. Instead she ran sideways at the fence, and he
threw up his leg just in time. Then she put down her
head, and went up into the air, and Bill caught ignom-
iniously at his saddle and rolled off into the dust.

Willing hands dragged him clear, and Jazz ran round
and round the ring until she was captured.

A rough-rider from the Cape mounted her, and she threw herself over backwards and gave him such a shaking that he was too dizzy to mount again. One of the shearers tried, and was thrown heavily, and then Smithson in his immaculate boots and breeches, sauntered into the ring, and announced his intention of riding her.

Valentine held up two fingers at her father.

"Remember my bridle."

Smithson lasted exactly a minute in the saddle, and his immaculate breeches were immaculate no longer. Jazz was beginning to warm up to the job.

"Nobody going to ride this wonderful outlaw?" King rallied. "Come on, some of you rough-riders. I'll give her a try myself."

"No, you won't," Valentine said low and emphatically. "Please! You know you were supposed to take things easily for a while."

"I'll give her a try," Cliff McLeod suggested.

"You?" said Valentine.

"Why not?" said Cliff, gently, with his faint smile.

He ducked under the rail, divesting himself of his blazer as he went out into the ring.

There was a hilarious chorus of cheers.

Cliff stood at the mare's head, clad only in a sleeveless white singlet, and grey flannels, and laced canvas shoes, his uncovered head shining fair in the sunshine.

"Oh, send him a mile, Jazz," Valentine said, low and vindictively.

Jazz waited until her new rider was in the saddle, and then she ran straight at the fence. Cliff threw up his knee, and jerked her head round, and she struck the stout posts in a head-on collision. She staggered back, shaking her head, and the crowd roared.

Up went the mare in the air, head down, and back tucked up, and she pitched. Her legs were stiff; she went up with the force of an uncoiled spring, came down like an iron pile-driver. Cliff rode her loosely, swinging in the saddle, anticipating her every movement.

It was the riding of a master, and Valentine stood at the fence in her breeches and boots, with the scarlet band on her hair, and her flaming, scarlet scarf, and watched, very still.

The end came quicker than anyone expected. Jazz finished her performance by going straight up into the air, and Cliff, as she fell, rolled off, and landed on his feet. When she stumbled up from all-fours he was on her back, and shaking, lathered, twitching, she stood still and swayed.

"There goes my bridle," cried Valentine, in the wholehearted cheer that went up, and Cliff galloped the redoubtable outlaw around the ring, and turned her back into the lane to go out.

JOYCE M. WEST
Sheep Kings

"HE'S OVER!"

The still air had grown chilly. Gordon went on storming. Play had not crossed the half line since the last kick off. They were making sure; they must, by the look of things, score again. By ones, twos, and threes, men detached themselves from the crowd and walked to the gates. 'Varsity was done; not a kick in them. The game was over.

Not five yards from the 'Varsity line, and in front of the right goal posts, two Gordon forwards came at Reilly. He got the ball but they were on him; there was no room to kick. Trevor was standing a yard off, and with a flick Reilly jerked the ball to him. Trevor had half a second in which to kick. He took a step forward and even in this crisis his eye took in the whole

field. Stevens! His opposite wing was slightly out
of position. A chance in a hundred. Trevor kicked
high and hard towards the left touch line. Up and up
went the ball, and for a moment no one noticed Stevens.
He had been waiting his chance all day and disappointment had sharpened his senses. The moment the ball
left Trevor's foot he saw what might happen, and he
was springing up the field and watching its flight.
To kick out was the natural thing for Reilly to do; and
it was not until he saw Stevens nearly under it that he
began to move more quickly. He was just too late.
Stevens and Foggarty raced for the ball. Stevens was
there a shade before the other. He caught it perfectly
in his stride, gave a thrust of his body as he felt Foggarty's hand on his hip, and tore on. Palmer was coming
across, running with that lovely easy motion that
drew men to see him on track and field, made a mark
with his left foot on the turf six inches from the line
as he curved past Palmer, and then the open road!
He glanced back as he ran—he could afford to. Foggarty
was chasing him, but he was safe. So on he ran, like
a slim young deity with victory in his arms while the
world around him seemed to dissolve in uproar. Hats
were in the air, walking-sticks were breaking themselves
against railings, men and women were jumping,
cheering, laughing, crying. And through it all, though
none could hear him, the professor chanted, "'Varsity!
'Varsity!"

The clamour died away. Against the grey arc of
light in the western sky, the ball curved gracefully
as it floated up between the goal posts, and a whistle
from the referee proclaimed "Time!" Another roar of
cheering, and the stream began to move to the gates.
The game was over. Along the footpath of the main
road through the dusk tramped the tired crowd. Horse
trams and buses and cabs filled the roadway. After a
while came the lurching brakes with singing teams.

Oh, Molly Riley, I love you;
Tell me, Molly Riley, that your heart beats true.
Tell me that you love me, I'll die if you say no,
And my ghost will come and haunt you, Molly
Riley.

On the field itself there were nothing but ghosts,
brothers of the memories that the crowd bore home.
In the years ahead they would come not to trouble
joy but to brighten life with the memory of sun and
wind and struggle and possession and the immortality
of youth. Brightest of all to the ageing procession moving on would be the recollection of victory snatched at
the last moment, and the flying figure of beautiful
speed, blazing like a meteor and curving splendidly
across the sky.

ALAN MULGAN (1881-1962)
Spur of Morning

NO JUDGE OF A RUN

I have scored from good bowling and fast;
  I have taken the wicket—to slows;
And long, long ago, in the past
  By fielding to eminence rose.
I have smitten the province's foes;
  Have obtained an analysis—one,
But alas! all my history shews
  I was never a judge of a run.

I have bowled out a crack for an egg
  With sinuous grubber Sydneian;
I once hit a seven to leg
  In combat with bowlers plebeian.
I have practised at eve in the cold,
  Have sweated at noon in the sun,

But alack! when my story is told,
　　It remains, I'm no judge of a run.

I have taken a chance in the slips,
　　And given a great many more,
Have splintered a bat into chips,
　　(It was borrowed) in hitting a four.
I have *pulled* a match out of the fire—
　　Pray pardon the obvious pun—
But this I could never acquire,
　　A notion of judging a run. . . .

When Winter and Football conspire
　　To rage; when the Summer is fled;
When the turf is deep trodden in mire;
　　Then, late, when the house is abed,
They rise, as I sit by the fire,
　　The ghosts of the men I've undone,
And, gibbering, hiss in their ire,
　　"You—you are no judge of a run."

Ye boys who attend to this tale;
　　Who yet have control of your fate,
Beware lest like me ye bewail,
　　When wailing is futile and late;
Play crooked, pull, fumble, or miss,
　　Hard work and not practises shun,
Do *anything* rather than this—
　　Be known as no judge of a run.

WILLIAM PEMBER REEVES (1857-1932)
Colonial Couplets
by G. P. WILLIAMS and W. P. REEVES

EYES ON THE BALL

Rugby football is by far the most popular New Zealand sport and the national touring teams of "All Blacks" have an international rugby reputation. This is an incident from a Ranfurly Shield match, an inter-provincial tournament that attracts huge crowds.

YACHTING AT HAMILTON

Centre of the rich farming area of the Waikato, the city of Hamilton is the sixth city of New Zealand and its largest inland centre. On the 154-acre expanse of Lake Rotoroa in the heart of the city, fresh-water sailing is a popular pastime.

CANOEING ON THE WANGANUI
A favourite sport with many New Zealanders is canoeing the length of
the Wanganui river, 140 miles winding through beautiful country.
Shooting the rapids in rubber boats is one of the thrills of this sport.

SUMMER ON THE BEACH
In the long New Zealand summers, thousands of families spend their
holidays by the beach. During the week-ends, city beaches like this one
at Mission Bay, near Auckland, attract thousands.

A GREAT CRICKETER

Bert Sutcliffe—he was always "Bert"—arrived in England with a ready-made reputation and publicity that included such tags as "best left-hander in the world," "New Zealand's Don Bradman." Great things were expected of him, a current of centuries, and broken records in all directions. It may have been that, in an effort to live up to it, this background weighed unconsciously on his nerves. At all events, after a fine innings to start the tour against Yorkshire, when he hit seventy-two, and a pleasant eighty-three in the first match against Surrey, he entered an indifferent period when nothing would go right for him; either he was beaten by a beautiful ball turning off the seam, or he would break his wicket, or cock up a catch. . . .

During this trying period, Bert proved his great qualities as a cricketer by his calm acceptance of the luck of the game; and his determination to succeed fed upon his lack of success. Though he was naturally disappointed, his sunny outlook and enthusiasm for cricket was never affected; he had self-confidence and guts, and he won the admiration of the team by his self-composure and his cheerfulness. One of his greatest admirers was Frank Mooney, who was convinced during this dull period that Bert would finish with more than 2,000 runs.

And so it proved. Bert ended the tour with 2,627 runs, the highest aggregate of the team, and ranks second in the list of outstanding batsmen of touring teams in England, preceded only by Bradman. He made seven centuries, including 243 against Essex. In that week, which covered two innings in the Fourth Test, he hit 485, and his 110 not out against Middlesex at the end of the tour was probably his best innings, certainly one of the most sparkling of the summer.

Whether he is the best, or second or third best left-hander in the world, I don't know and I don't care. All I know is that he breathes the joy of cricket, and that on his day he is one of the most delightful batsmen you could hope to watch. Many left-handers give the impression of "kack-handedness"; they look awkward, no matter how good they are—and left-handed. But such was Sutcliffe's orthodoxy of stroke and his grace that one was seldom aware that he was left-handed. He had most of the strokes, except a late cut which we saw him use only once or twice during his many innings. His off and cover driving, hooking and pulling were models for a copy book. He seemed always as though he could and would bat for ever.

ALAN W. MITCHELL (b. 1908)
Cricket Companions: The Story of the 1949 New Zealand Tour

Poems, Songs and Ballads

A LOVE SONG

Were you, beloved, to invite me,
Straightway, by way of the hill I would come;
Lest I stray afar, and eagerly I would
Follow the path you trod.
Alas, you are gone, as if borne on high
By some magic enchantment.

Why did you not when first we met
Set about undoing our affection;
Before love had fastened firmly
And become a consuming desire?
Comes it now, I am a derelict canoe,
Stripped to the hull, alas.

Sink down, O sun, presently to set,
Come then copious tears.
False lips you have, thou descendant of Makiri,
Of whose infamy we have already heard!

Of you, dear one, no word is heard,
You are, as a father, quite lost.
Unlike, thou art, the waning moon which dies,
Later, is seen again on high.

translated from the Maori by
SIR APIRANA NGATA

A LULLABY

O son who arose in the winter's morn
Ascend and proceed onward
To your myriad Kinsmen in the heavens.
Will you, O son, survive
These times of bitter strife?
My son, bestir yourself betimes
So that you may reach the sacred mountain waters
    of your ancestors;
And they will unfasten and present you with the
    prized dogskin cloak.
A mantle 'twill be for you in the warriors' ranks.
The plume of the land I have already point fastened
To this trusty weapon;
The plume of the sea I did pluck
From the surging waves;
It was about to disappear in the stormy seas.

NOHOMAITERANGI
translated by Sir Apirana Ngata

SOUTHERLY SUNDAY

The great south wind has covered with cloud the whole
    of the river-plain,
soft white ocean of foaming mist, blotting out, billowing
fast to the east, where Pacific main surges on vaster bed.

But here, on the hills, south wind unvapoured encoun-
    ters the sunshine,
lacing and interlocking, the invisible effervescence
you almost hear, and the laughter of light and air at
    play overhead.

Seabirds fly free; see the sharp flash of their underwings!
and high lifted up to the north, the mountains, the
    mighty, the white ones
rising sheer from the cloudy sea, light-crowned,
    establishèd.

This sparkling day is the Lord's day. Let us be glad and
    rejoice in it;
for he cometh, he cometh to judge and redeem his
    beautiful universe,
and holds in his hands all worlds, all men, the quick
    and the dead.

MARY URSULA BETHELL (1874-1945)

SHE WAS MY LOVE WHO COULD DELIVER

She was my love who could deliver
From paws of pain and melancholy,
And light the lamps that burn forever,
And cleanse a page of screeds of folly,
And with a motion of her hand
Could reap a harvest on my land.

And she could melt an iron mood,
And lashing cords with love were softer,
And she could bring my course to good,
Could renovate with raining laughter,
And eye and heart her beauty brace
When death approached with peering face.

Against a secret shaft of malice
Piercing my solitary isle
She would defend with flying solace,
And visitations of her smile,

And from the spirit's blank occasions,
And from the craft of days and seasons
She was my love who could deliver.

J. R. HERVEY (1889-1958)

LEAVING NEW ZEALAND

I took my hat, I took my gun,
I left the red woods in the sun.
I left the streams that ran with me
Through happy years from hill to sea.

My shadow led me down the track,
The mountain madly called me back,
Where, white as washing hung to dry,
The snow lay up along the sky.

They sang me all the loves I knew,
The lazing sun, the lakes of blue,
The billy boiling at the sky,
But never one remembered I.

For I had read the hand of night
That wrote a thing for my delight,
But not the birches' purple haze
Could hold me to the river-ways.

Not Beauty in the bluest skies
Could hold me with her mountain eyes,
When in the stars I read my goal,
The stars that summon to the soul.

When in the stars I staked my claim
To sluice the shining peaks of Fame,

And seized my gun and seized my hat
And galloped down the tussock flat,

It seemed as though I could forget
The bending grasses, blowing yet,
That carry up from hill to hill
The reinless winds that ride them still. . . .

Ah, mother-land, could I depart
From all that had enslaved my heart,
The bare, bright snow, the woods of green,
The glitter of the sea between,

It was that I would make of them
A banner in the eyes of men,
And far the legend of your name
Would peddle in the marts of Fame;

That I would ride as Beauty's knight
Proud flaunting in the lists of Light
The feather of your foeless seas,
Their lance of thunder on your leas.

And can I win a laurel crown,
Above the green of forest gown,
Above the white of breathing snow,
I live that you should wear it so.

For that it was I took my gun
And left the red woods in the sun,
To sluice the hills that haunt my dreams,
In hunger for the grain that gleams.

WALTER D'ARCY CRESSWELL (1896-1960)

THE TIDES RUN UP THE WAIRAU

The tides run up the Wairau
That fights against their flow.
My heart and it together
Are running salt and snow.

For though I cannot love you,
Yet, heavy, deep, and far,
Your tide of love comes swinging,
Too swift for me to bar.

Some thought of you must linger,
A salt of pain in me,
For oh what running river
Can stand against the sea?

EILEEN DUGGAN

TOM'S A-COLD

Where is my love that has no peer,
    where wanders she, among what brakes,
along what hillside cold and drear
    above the tarns and hollow lakes?
I hear the whirlwind shake the sky,
    I feel the worm within me gnaw,
for she is lost, and lost am I,
    alone upon my bed of straw.

Beyond the door blasts of black air,
    the rain descending on the wind;
I know my love is wandering there
    with ragged clothes and hair unpinned.

I shall not lead her through the door
   and lay my hand upon her wrist,
O she must roam for evermore
   through rain and dark, or moonlit mist.

My love was fairer than the sun,
   her breast beneath my hand was warm,
but she has left me all alone
   in midmost darkness of the storm.
I hear the sleet upon the thatch,
   the thunder by the lightning hurled;
I know she will not lift my latch
   before the ending of the world.

A. R. D. FAIRBURN (1904-1957)

ON THE SWAG

His body doubled
   under the pack
   that sprawls untidily
   on his old back
   the cold wet deadbeat
   plods up the track

The cook peers out:
   "oh curse that old lag
   here again
   with his clumsy swag
   made of a dirty old
   turnip-bag."

"Bring him in cook
   from the grey level sleet
   put silk on his body
   slippers on his feet,
   give him fire
   and bread and meat

"Let the fruit be plucked
and the cake be iced
the bed be snug
and the wine be spiced
in the old cove's nightcap:
for this is Christ."

R. A. K. MASON (b. 1905)

JACK-IN-THE-BOAT

is always ready to row across the boat or lake. Wind up the motor, and watch him dip his blades like a true oarsman—in, out, in, out—with never-tiring enthusiasm.

LEGEND ON A TOY-MAKER'S PACKAGE

Children, children, come and look
Through the crack in the corner of the middle of the
world
At the clockwork man in a cardboard house.
He's crying, children, crying.
He's not true, really.

Once he was new like you, you see
Through the crack in the corner of the middle of the
night,
The bright blue man on the wind-up sea,
Oh, he went so beautifully.
He's not true, really.

O cruel was the pleasure-land they never should have
painted
On the front and the back, the funny brand of weather,
For the crack in the corner of the middle of the picture
Let the colours leak away.
He's not true, really.

One at a time, children, come and look
Through the crack in the corner of the middle of the day
At Jack-in-the-boat where the light leaves float.
He's dying of a broken spring.
He's not true, really.

ALLEN CURNOW (b. 1911)

DISTILLED WATER

From Blenheim's clocktower a cheerful bell bangs out
The hour, and time hangs humming in the wind.
Time and the honoured dead. What else? The odd
Remote and shabby peace of a provincial town.
Blenkinsopp's gun? the Wairau massacre?
Squabbles in a remote part of empire.
Some history. Some history, but not much.

Consider now the nature of distilled
Water which has boiled and left behind
In the retort rewarding sediment
Of salts and toxins. Chemically pure of course
(No foreign bodies here) but to the taste
Tasteless and flat. Let it spill on the ground,
Leach out its salts, accumulate its algae,
Be living; the savour's in impurity.
Is that what we are? something that boiled away
In the steaming flask of nineteenth century Europe?
Innocuous until now, or just beginning
To make its own impression on the tongue.

And through the Tory Channel naked hills
Gully and slip pass by, monotonously dramatic
Like bad blank verse, till one cries out for
Enjambement, equivalence, modulation,
The studied accent of the human voice,

Or the passage opening through the windy headlands
Where the snowed Kaikouras hang in the air like mirage
And the nation of gulls assembles on the waters
Of the salt sea that walks about the world.

M. K. JOSEPH (b. 1914)

NURSERY TALE

My mendicant, caught between two seas
with the world at your elbow for a begging bowl,
brighter than coins your hair, a silken net
to snare my heart; four teeth are more than pearls,
and *sursum corda* in the crowing mouth
babbles my bliss. All summer long my bird
hangs on my gaze his dazzling eye, my nest
of kisses in a thornless tree. I wish
by every star, Orion, the Pleiades,
two centaurs guarding the Cross, by all spells,
by incantation, to keep from harm my thief,
my little dancer on the tightrope of time.
And yet I know that he will prick his finger, the spindle
fall in the well, the impenetrable hedge grow up
like a wall between him and his desire.
The fairy by the cot one day forgets
the luckless godchild with the tarnished spoon.

MARY STANLEY (b. 1919)

THE CLOUD, THE MAN, THE DREAM

The cloud, the man, the dream are locked
forever within one tangible knot of time
where frozen in a huge and ignorant unity
all the divisible units like swans upon
a winter-frozen lake in their death lie.

As images, motionless, held at his world's
centre, charged neither with good nor evil
nor, of these, agents; being only so far
as he is, the white high gesture; and, as he
so far, the fingering sea—these crystal
agents must become the actors of his will.

So from the empty shore looking skyward
the man sees the cloud vacant above him,
the cloud looks down upon the sea below,
the sea approaches with its bright and
leathery hands. Between them he stands.
His dream gazes out on cloud, sea, sand.

When he walks away in the evening through
the friendly bars of the light they will
accompany him lightly across the marram.
                    Forever
at his one hand immense and restless
this sea which agelessly moves with him
weaves a peculiar, webbed dry music.
                    Forever
as nightly he will lie down on his
left side, turning to wind with the planet
he mounts through his dream up to the
cloud's tall, pale, thoughtful edge.

KENDRICK SMITHYMAN (b. 1922)

MOTHER

She sits with a son on her nursery knee
With never a breast to call her own,
More ancient than evil and further from me
Than ever were angels or idols.

A moon to her sun and his star

She walks in a cloud of nesting wings
And no hawk, not I, can pirate there,
In the world the narcotic of infancy brings
Where loneliness has no name.

A moon to her sun and his star

Where did he come from this amorous boy
Who is houses of lovers and satisfied never?
He came from my company lodging with joy
And left me to talk to myself.

A moon to her sun and his star

KEITH SINCLAIR (b. 1922)

MATING CALL

For not in forty years, hunters affirm,
Has there been such an early roaring season.
Nightlong the Ruahines' lower spurs
Tremble with sound, the immense, invisible form
Of an antlered god is risen
Like a wraith above the peaks and given voice.

"Damn them!" the old man mutters, half awake,
And half-dead too, his own sap having quietened,
And all he asks for—Sleep.
Over dark mountain trails where great stags break
Silence in triumph, something has quickened,
Beating the guns and time that hunters keep.

And in the shepherd's hut, stiff, back to back,
The angry man and woman do not speak,
Recalling too-harsh words an hour before

Spilled out of heat. Over their dark
And huddled hurt the rampant echoes break
Like impulse that will turn him round to her.

LOUIS JOHNSON (b. 1924)

ISLAND

Twilight is memoried. A current of cold air
Runs from an offshore island over a green
And nervous stretch of water. Within the stream
Of memories that slip towards these bare
Deserted sandhills there are voices, clear
And ringing over the sea's long curving line;
Voices and murmurs echoing a dream
The world had once, of innocence. Despair
Inherited the dream. Against a yellow sky
The island, rimmed with fire, stands from the sea,
A black uplifted place where embers turn
To tongues and lips of flame and endlessly
Re-echo fire and fortune to this high
Waste shore where dry bones wait to burn.

W. H. OLIVER (b. 1925)

PHIALS

If only to be born were being invented
Merely or, better still, to concoct oneself
From an antique alembic, a receipt. How splendid
To take the phial cleanly from its shelf;

Powders and liquids, all one's favourite hues
Making the being one would be, the looker at stars
Or storks on the spires of Denmark, drinker of dews,
Or an eye simply, peering through deep green trees

With still, black quality, age, settlement. Pictures
Of an idyllic sort immediately come;
But some obstinacy of intellect, demanding structures
Complete, all details carefully trim,

Will take down the last bottle, thick as glue,
Mingle it into the potion, and for all the good
It does, as well had nothing been done. The new
And perfect formula's spoiled, with the taint of
    living blood.

CHARLES DOYLE (b. 1928)

SEA-CALL

Let the radio pip and shudder
at each dawn's news . . .

Let the weatherman inspire
a gaunt meaning to the chill
and ache of bone:
but when the moon's new bowl
is storing rain
the pull of time and sea
will cry to me again . . .

And I shall stuff my longing
in an empty pack
and hasten to the secret shore
where the land's curve lies
clad in vermilion—and the green
wind tugging gravely . . .

There let the waves lave
pleasuring the body's sense:
and the sun's feet
shall twinkle and flex

A SKI-ING CLASS

While mothers watch, their children are given a ski-ing lesson on the slopes of Mount Ruapehu. In the background is the crater of Mount Ngauruhoe.

HIKING

The mountains and valleys of New Zealand attract large numbers of climbers and hikers every year. Here is a band of young climbers in Westland mountain country near the Fox Glacier.

THE WELLINGTON CENOTAPH

On Anzac Day (25th April) each year, services are held to honour the dead of two World Wars. This picture shows the service held at the Wellington Cenotaph in the centre of the city.

to the sea-egg's needling
and the paua's stout kiss
shall drain a rock's heart
to the sand-bar's booming. . . .

HONE TUWHARE

RIVER LAND

In summer-shrinking innocence these waters
Wander through groove and gravel bed,
As idly as a half-formed thought
Tracing the anguish of another's mind,
But the vision enlarged, includes
Those black backwaters smooth as new-laid tar.

Pyres of driftwood (awaiting the martyrs' burning)
And ditches like empty graves.
Fabric for a nightmare,
Or deserted battlefield
Wrecked by ancient grievance.
No one has leased this landscape from the river.

Since death and the first blood, falling like wolves
On the waking meadow, bled it
Beyond the surgery of barb and plough.
Now, children privateer among the ruins,
Old men dig dreams, and lovers feel the rush of wings
Burst from their bodies' ark in search of Ararat.

PETER BLAND (b. 1934)

DAVID LOWSTON

My name is David Lowston, I did seal, I did seal,
My name is David Lowston, I did seal.
My men and I were lost,
Though our very lives 'twould cost,
We did seal, we did seal, we did seal.

'Twas in eighteen hundred and ten, we set sail,
    we set sail,
'Twas in eighteen hundred and ten, we set sail.
We were left, we gallant men,
Never more to sail again,
For to sail, for to sail, for to sail.

We were set down in Open Bay, were set down,
    were set down,
We were set down in Open Bay, were set down.
Upon the sixteenth day
Of Februar-aye-ay,
For to seal, for to seal, for to seal.

Our Captain, John Bedar, he set sail, he set sail,
Yes, for Port Jackson, he set sail.
"I'll return, men, without fail!"
But she foundered in a gale,
And went down, and went down, and went down.

We cured ten thousand skins, for the fur, for the fur,
We cured ten thousand skins for the fur.
Brackish water, putrid seal,
We did all of us fall ill,
For to die, for to die, for to die.

Come all you sailor lads, who sail the sea, who
    sail the sea,
Come all you Jacks who sail upon the sea.
Though the schooner, *Governor Bligh*
Took some who did not die,
Never seal, never seal, never seal!

Old Sealers' Song[1]

THE SHANTY BY THE WAY

It's in a first-rate business section
Where four bush-roads cross and meet;
It stands in a quiet and neat direction
To rest the weary traveller's feet.

Chorus
Rows of bottles standing upright
Labelled with bright blue and gold,
Beer so cold it needs no icing
From the cellars dark, drear hold.

Kerosene lamps are shining brightly,
Cards and lo the billiard balls:
Men and women are dancing lightly
To the music inside those walls.

There's quoits and games and bagatelle
All to suit your fancy-O,
But better far behind the bar
Stands smiling darling Nancy-O.

Nancy's smiles are quite beguiling
To make some fun she's willing-O.
You give a rap she turns the tap
And thanks you for your shilling-O.

[1]This song was collected by Rona Bailey.

Landlord stands with smiling face;
He likes to see your cash forked out;
Landlord stands with smiling face,
Sometimes he will stand a "shout."

Landlord "shouting" is uncommon;
He's kidding you to dance and play;
How the devil can a man keep sober
In those shanties by the way?

When you wake up in the morning
In your thirst without a mag,
You cast around a sad reflection
As you shoulder up your swag.

Penniless you'll have to wander
For many a long and dreary day,
Till you earn another cheque to squander
In those shanties by the way.

Old Swagman's Song[1]

WHEN WE'RE AT THE MATAURA

The folks are a' gaun mad outricht,
The yellow fever's at its height,
And naething's heard baith day and nicht
    But gold at the Mataura.

There'll be some pretty rows we know,
When ladies drive the bullocks O,
And many a loud "Come ither, wo!"
    When we're at the Mataura.

[1]This song, collected in New Zealand by Dr. Percy Jones, in 1940, incorporates a few lines from a poem by E. J. Overbury in *Bush Poems*, published in Victoria in 1865.

They'll make the laws themselves to please,
And set to making Road Trustees,
And nominating M.P.C's.,
    When we're at the Mataura.

Our Tibbies, Bettys, Nellys, Molls,
Will rectify electoral rolls,
And check the bribery at polls,
    When we're at the Mataura.

The land that's waste they'll parcel oot,
In quantities they think will suit,
And sell't to all that's got the hoot,[1]
    When we're at the Mataura.

Otago Gold-miners' Song

THE YOUNG TEETOTALLER

I am a young teetotaller,
And though but six years old,
Within my little breast there beats
A heart as true as gold.

My father and my mother
Are temperance people too;
My sister and my brother,
All to their pledge keep true.

Our little dog named Frisky
Turns up his nose at beer;
Our little cat makes quite a fuss
When drunken folk are near.

[1] *Utu:* Maori word for money.

We have an old canary
Whose voice is very fine,
And he has never all his life
Touched either beer or wine.

How happy all of you would be
If you could say with me,
I am a young teetotaller
And so will always be.

Prohibitionist Song, c. 1895

THE TALE OF DOOM

Here we sit on the isle of Crete
With sweaty socks and blistered feet;
Little wonder we've got the blues,
With feet enclosed in big canoes.
Khaki shorts instead of slacks,
Living like a tribe of blacks,
Except that blacks don't just sit and brood
And wait throughout the day for food.

It was just a month ago, not more,
We sailed to Greece to win the war;
We marched and groaned beneath our load
While Jerry bombed us off the road.
They chased us here, they chased us there,
The bastards chased us everywhere,
And while they dropped their loads of death,
We cursed the ruddy R.A.F.

Yet the R.A.F. was there in force—
They left a few at home, of course—
We saw the whole outfit one day—
A Hurricane, flying the other way.

Then we heard the wireless news,
Old bluff-artist Winston giving his views.
"The R.A.F. is now in Greece
Fighting hard to win us peace."
We scratched our heads when we heard that lot;
It smelled just like an army plot.
For if in Greece the Air Force be,
Where the ruddy hell are we?

Then at last we met the Hun,
At odds of thirty three to one!
Though they made it pretty hot,
We gave the blighters all we'd got.
The bullets whizzed, the big guns roared,
We yelled for ships to get aboard!
At last they came and off we got,
And hurried from that ticklish spot.

Then they landed us in Crete
And marched us off our poor old feet.
The tucker was light, the water was crook,
I got fed-up and slung my hook—
Next day I stopped a heavy fine
And got back that night—full of wine.

My pay book was behind to hell,
So when pay was called I felt quite ill.
They wouldn't pay me, I was sure of that,
And when they did, I smelled a rat.
The next day when the rations came,
I realised their wily game,
So sooner than lie down and die,
I spent my pay on food supply.
So now it looks like even bettin'
A man will soon become a Cretan
And spend his days in black-out room
On Adolf Hitler's isle of doom.

But Adolf one night when "hooped"
Decided to send his paratroops.
They'd shift us from this heavenly spot
Or leave their bodies there to rot.
They gave us hell from dawn to dusk,
We fought for fifteen days, then bust.
The navy rescued us once more
And landed us on Egypt's shore.
So now at night beneath the desert moon
We dream of Hitler's isle of doom.

But do not think that we are done;
We'll soon have him on the run.
On the desert or in the air,
We'll get him somehow—foul or fair.

ANON. 1941
collected by LES CLEVELAND

IT'S NOT THE BEER

They send us to the 'Varsity to tone our spirits down,
They take away our nice short pants just when our
    knees are brown,
They set us forty hours a week and make us fit to learn,
And then we drown our sorrows, for the freshest worm
    will turn.

Chorus
It's not the beer that makes you feel so queer,
Nor the good old long-squash shandy;
But the stuff to make you rock is the sherry and the hock,
Martini, too, and cherry-brandy.
Shell-shock and rum may warm the portly tum,
But they don't leave the head too clear,
So if gin and whisky make you frisky,
Peg along on good old beer.

ROMAN CATHOLIC CATHEDRAL, CHRISTCHURCH

Described by Bernard Shaw as the finest piece of architecture in the
country, the Cathedral of the Blessed Sacrament was completed in
1905. It was designed by F. W. Petre, a New Zealand descendant of the
eleventh Baron Petre, who also designed the Catholic Cathedral of
Dunedin and several other churches.

MT. TARAWERA AND LAKE (1873)

An Englishman, John Barr Clark Hoyte (1835-1913) became drawing master of the new Auckland College and Grammar School in 1869, and left many water-colours of New Zealand scenes. Mt. Tarawera, here in its original state, erupted in 1886, destroying a village and the Pink and White Terraces.

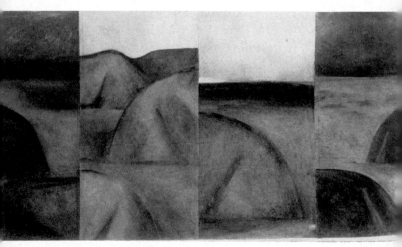

FROM A LANDSCAPE SERIES

Colin McCahon (b. 1919), a prominent modern New Zealand painter, in this work, entitled "Four Panels from a Landscape Series" uses forms abstracted from characteristic New Zealand natural formations.

They sell you wine in bottles and whisky by the flask,
They sell you gin and peppermint whenever you may ask,
They sell you risky cocktails, but please remember that
The first one makes you happy but the last one knocks
    you flat.

They warn us of the primrose path, of women's fatal
    charm,
They tell us if we lay off cards we'll never come to harm,
They say the seeds of ruin lie in foolishness in drink,
So take your fancy brews away and pour them down the
    sink.

University Students' Drinking Song

LAMENT FOR BARNEY FLANAGAN, LICENSEE OF THE HESPERUS HOTEL

Flanagan got up on a Saturday morning,
Pulled on his pants while the coffee was warming:
He didn't remember the doctor's warning,
    "Your heart's too Big, Mr. Flanagan."

Barney Flanagan sprang like a frog
From a wet root in an Irish bog,
May his soul escape from the tooth of the dog!
    God have mercy on Flanagan.

Barney Flanagan, R.I.P.
Rode to his grave on Hennessey's
Like a bottle cork in the Irish sea.
    The bell-boy rings for Flanagan.

B.N.Z.   K

Barney Flanagan, ripe for a coffin,
Eighteen stone and brandy-rotten,
Patted the housemaid's velvet bottom—
    "Oh, is it you, Mr. Flanagan?"

The sky was as bright as a new milk token,
Bill the Bookie and Shellshock Hogan
Waited outside for the pub to open—
    "Good day, Mr. Flanagan."

At noon he was drinking in the lounge bar corner
With a sergeant of police and a racehorse owner
When the Angel of Death looked over his shoulder—
    "Could you spare a moment, Flanagan?"

O the deck was cut; the bets were laid;
But the very last card that Barney played
Was the Deadman's Trump, the bullet of Spades—
    "Would you like more air, Mr. Flanagan?"

The priest came running but the priest came late
For Barney was banging at the Pearly Gate.
St. Peter said, "Quiet! You'll have to wait
    For a hundred masses, Flanagan."

O the regular boys and the loud accountants
Left their nips and their seven-ounces
As chickens fly when the buzzard pounces—
    "Have you heard about old Flanagan?"

Cold in the parlour Flanagan lay
Like a bride at the end of her marriage day.
The Waterside Workers' Band will play
    A brass good-bye to Flanagan.

While publicans drink their profits still,
While lawyers flock to be in at the kill,
While Aussie barmen milk the till
    We will remember Flanagan.

For Barney had a send-off and no mistake.
He died like a man for his country's sake;
And the Governor-General came to his wake.
    Drink again to Flanagan.

Despise not, O Lord, the work of Thine own hands
And let light perpetual shine upon him.

                                    JAMES K. BAXTER (b. 1926)

Traditions, Customs and Beliefs

IN THE BACK COUNTRY

At night, and by a lovely clear cold moonlight, we arrived at our destination, heartily glad to hear the dogs barking and to know that we were at our journey's end. Here we were bona fide beyond the pale of civilisation; no boarded floors, no chairs, nor any similar luxuries; everything was of the simplest description. Four men inhabited the hut, and their life appears a kind of mixture of that of a dog and that of an emperor, with a considerable predominance of the latter. They have no cook, and take it turn and turn to cook and wash up, two one week, and two the next. They have a good garden, and gave us a capital feed of potatoes. and peas, both fried together, an excellent combination. Their culinary apparatus and plates, cups, knives and forks, are very limited in number. The men are all gentlemen and sons of gentlemen, and one of them is a Cambridge man, who took a high second-class a year or two before my time. Every now and then he leaves his up-country avocations, and becomes a great gun at the college in Christ Church, examining the boys; he returns to his shepherding, cooking, bullock-driving, etc., etc., as the case may be. I am informed that he having faithfully learned the ingenuous arts, has so far mollified his morals that he is an exceedingly humane and judicious bullock-driver. He regarded me as a somewhat despicable new-comer (at least so I imagined) and when next morning I asked where I should wash, he gave rather a French shrug of the shoulders and said, "The lake." I felt the rebuke to be well merited, and that with the lake in front of the house, I should have been at no loss for the means of performing my ablutions. So I retired abashed and cleansed myself therein. Under his bed I found Tennyson's "Idylls of the King." So you will see that even in these out-of-the-world places people do care a little for something besides sheep. I was told an amusing story of an Oxford man shepherding down in Otago. Some one came into his hut, and, taking up a book, found it in a strange tongue, and enquired what it was. The Oxonian (who was baking at the time) answered that it was "Machiavellian discourses upon the first decade of Livy." The wonder-stricken visitor laid down the book and took up another which was at any rate written in English. This he found to be Bishop Butler's "Analogy." Putting it down speedily as something not in his line, he laid hands upon a third. This proved to be "Patrum Apostolicorum Opera," on which he saddled his horse and went right away, leaving the Oxonian to his baking. This man must certainly be considered a rare exception. New Zealand seems far better adapted to develop and maintain in health the physical than the intellectual nature. The fact is, the people here are busy making money; that is the inducement which led them to come in the first instance, and they show their sense by directing their energies to the work. Yet, after all, it may be questioned whether the intellect is not as well schooled here as at home, though in a very different manner. Men are as shrewd and sensible, as alive to the humorous, and as hard-headed. Moreover, there is much nonsense in the old country from which people here are free. There is little conventionalism and much liberality of sentiment; very little sectarianism, and, as a general rule, a healthy sensible tone in conversation which I like very much. But it does not do to speak about John Sebastian Bach's "Fugues", or pre-Raphaelite pictures.

SAMUEL BUTLER (1835-1902)
A First Year in Canterbury Settlement

THE OLD YEAR AND THE NEW

We beheld the old year dying,
　　In the country of our birth;
When the drifted snow was lying
　　On the hard and frozen earth,

Where the love of home was round us,
　　By the blazing Christmas fires;
And the love of country bound us
　　To the hearth-stones of our sires.

But our sons will see the glory
　　Of the young and springing year;
Where the green earth tells the story
　　Of a younger hemisphere.

And the eve will lose its sadness
　　In the hopefulness of day—
In a birth so full of gladness,
　　In a death without decay.

But for us the morning's garland
　　Glistens still with evening's dew]
We—the children of a far land
　　And the fathers of a new.

For we still, through old affection,
　　Hear the old year's dying sigh,
Through the sad sweet recollection
　　Of the years that are gone by,

While, through all the future gleaming,
    A bright golden promise runs,
And its happy light is streaming
    On the greatness of our sons.

Pray we, then, whate'er betide them—
    Howsoever great they've grown,
That the past of England guide them,
    While the present is their own!

CHARLES CHRISTOPHER BOWEN (1830-1917)

MINING LINGO

In a diggings-town one sometimes meets with strange
characters—ignorant people with large sums of money
at their command such as would have surpassed even
the wildest dreams of their ancestors, and the mistakes
made by some of them are now and then not a little
amusing. The commonest source of error is the use,
or rather misuse, of words, and in this they beat Mrs.
Malaprop hollow. I once heard a "lady" confidentially
inform a friend that she had made up her mind to get
an "antimonic" dress. Further enquiry elicited that it
was a *moiré antique* that she meditated purchasing.
Another person thought that the mayor of their town
should wear "a scarlet robe lined with vermin" and
could not see the joke when those around laughed.
An enterprising German publican, having obtained for
a public supper something he was pleased to call *puté-
de-fois-gras*, the individual seated opposite this rare dish
insisted on calling them "potted photographs." At a
similar entertainment, a guest loudly lauded the "blue
munge" (*blanc mange*). Besides such outré expressions,
there are many words and phrases current peculiar
to the mining population. Of these, one of the most
inexplicable is the diggers' good-bye, as in place of that

good old Saxon word of parting, they always say
"so-long." There are, of course, many what may be
called technical terms in connection with the pursuit
of mining, but besides these there are words used in
general conversation which would not be found in an
English dictionary. Such, for example, as "duffer" or
"shiser", anything that is useless; "flash", an adjective,
differing in meaning a little according to what it is
applied to, but which may be interpreted generally by
stylish. Some words do not betoken a very exalted origin,
as "scrag", the name given to a digger's blankets and
personal luggage, usually carried in a long bundle
round the body, which is just the thieves' cant for
booty. To treat a person is called "shouting": the
origin of the word is obvious. . . .

One of the greatest social evils in the gold-fields is the
system of "shouting." Two friends cannot meet without
one saying, "Come and have a drink." A business
transaction is seldom concluded without the purchaser
asking, "Are you going to shout?"

ALEXANDER BATHGATE (1845-1930)
Colonial Experiences

THERE'S NAE PLACE LIKE OTAGO YET

There's nae place like Otago yet,
  There's nae wee beggar weans,
Or auld men shivering at our doors,
  To beg for scraps or banes.
We never see puir working folk
  Wi' bauchles on their feet,
Like perfect icicles wi' cauld,
  Gaun starving through the street.

We never hear o' breaking stanes
    A shilling by the yard;
Or poor folk roupit to the door
    To pay the needfu' laird;
Nae purse-proud, upstart, mushroom lord
    To scowl at honest toil,
Or break it down that he, the wretch,
    May feast on roast and boil.

My curse upon them, root and branch,
    A tyrant I abhor;
May despotism's iron foot
    Ne'er mark Otago's shore;
May wealth and labour hand in hand
    Work out our glorious plan,
But never let it be allowed
    That money makes the man.

JOHN BARR (1809-89)
Poems and Songs

ELECTIONS IN A MINING TOWN

The barmaid always knew. She was the miner's source
of information, the policeman's contact, she was part
and parcel of the social fabric of old Thames and the
surest check to insobriety this country has ever known.
She knew, for instance, as the 1869 provincial elections
drew near, that Ned Twohill, licensee of the Brian
Boru, supported Williamson and that Captain Lipsey
of the Bendigo backed Gillies, and that there would be
trouble in the air when Thames turned out to poll.
She was not wrong. Polling day dawned in November,
the signal for unfettered carousal and prelude to events
which have been likened to the chapter in *Pickwick
Papers* where the inn guests were hocussed with lau-
danum so that fourteen were unfit to be polled.

The miners stopped work at noon. Oratory thundered from the hotel veranda-tops. At the polling booth near Butt's inn hecklers jousted with one another, retiring periodically to the public-houses as thirst overcame political ardour. One Williamson supporter repaired to the Brian Boru where he became so attached to the premises that he had to be wheeled back to the poll in a barrow in the cause of provincial democracy. To the Williamson band Ned Twohill's was open house—free meals, free liquor, free cigars, free car rides to the poll. In Lower Shortland the Bendigo succumbed to the blandishments of the Gillies team, likewise the Munster, diagonally opposite the Brian Boru. The air rang with flaming posters, catcalls and cries. The booth rang with the shrill yelps of clerks and scrutineers, hopelessly penned in. It rang also to the crack of Major Cooper's whip as he demanded admittance—men were being blocked from voting, picks and shovels swung into action, so did the Thames Volunteers. Some cried "Stop the poll!"; the returning officer said "Carry on."

They carried on. At four o'clock when the poll closed there was a crowd of three thousand around the booth . . . splashes of rioting broke into waves, Warden Davey was humped shoulder high up to the Brian Boru, Williamson followers marched in a body to the Munster, seized its billowing green flag and continued up the full length of Pollen Street, smashing the windows of known Gillies followers as they went. They came back down the other side, past Twohill's to Captain Lipsey's where his own company of volunteers was drawn up inside. In the ensuing battle the Bendigo lost lock, stock and most of its barrels—windows went, the doors, the veranda palings. And then, quite exhausted, the crowd faded out.

That night, Ned spread a victory dinner "for the delectation of the million" (in Thames Williamson had polled almost double his rival's figures) but the proprietors of the Bendigo and the Munster had the last laugh. The final result was confirmed as Gillies, 2,531; Williamson, 2,479.

JAMES McNEISH (b. 1931)
Tavern in the Town

NOT UNDERSTOOD

Not understood. We move along asunder,
   Our paths grow wider as the seasons creep
Along the years, we marvel and we wonder
   Why life is life? and then we fall asleep
      Not understood.

Not understood. We gather false impressions,
   And hug them closer as the years go by,
Till virtues often seem to us transgressions;
   And thus men rise and fall, and live and die,
      Not understood.

Not understood. Poor souls with stunted vision
   Oft measure giants by their narrow gauge;
The poisoned shafts of falsehood and derision
   Are oft impelled 'gainst those who mould the age,
      Not understood.

Not understood. The secret springs of action,
   Which lie beneath the surface and the show,
Are disregarded; with self-satisfaction
   We judge our neighbours, and they often go,
      Not understood.

Not understood. How trifles often change us!
    The thoughtless sentence or the fancied slight
Destroy long years of friendship and estrange us,
    And on our souls there falls a freezing blight;
        Not understood.

Not understood. How many breasts are aching
    For lack of sympathy! Ah! day by day,
How many cheerless, lonely hearts are breaking!
    How many noble spirits pass away
        Not understood.

Oh, God! that men would see a little clearer,
    Or judge less harshly where they cannot see;
Oh, God! that men would draw a little nearer
    To one another, they'd be nearer Thee,
        And understood.

THOMAS BRACKEN (1843-1898)

THE COLONIAL

Although the New Zealander has preserved, after more than half a century of autonomy, a number of characteristics which make it possible to classify him without hesitation as a member of the great British family, he has not been able to carry with him to the Antipodes, as Aeneas did his Penates, a European atmosphere. Above all, he has not found in his new home the political and economic conditions of an old country like England, rich with accumulated capital and venerable traditions. Thus, much in his environment and much in his nature, has undergone a change, and he has become a member of what is practically a new people.

Indeed, despite the British appearance which makes them seem much more English than the Canadians, the Australians or the South Africans, the inhabitants of New Zealand are nevertheless "colonials", that is to say, a very different type from the islanders of Great Britain. One must hear the Englishman speak with his air of condescending patronage of the colonial, to realise that all the imperialistic ideas in the world will not prevent the citizen of the mother country from regarding the other citizens of the Empire as, in spite of everything, a slightly inferior class; unintellectual, thinks the cultured; rather rough, thinks the snob. One must hear the colonial speak in his turn of the "old country" to realise that with his filial affection, real and touching as it is, is mingled a contemptuous pity for those conservative and prejudiced Europeans, who are afraid of their own shadows when there is any question, as some philosopher has said, "of stirring something in the great reservoirs of the future." Yet in spite of all, there is still a dormant Englishman under the noisy self-assertiveness of the New Zealander. Hence two traits in him which alternately get the upper hand. At times he becomes imaginative, expansive, eager for reforms and new ideas, recking little of vain respect for ancient prejudices. At times, on the other hand, he shows himself, to our great astonishment, a lover of ancient forms and established hierarchies, more than half a snob, and in his way almost a conservative.

The real fact is that, according to circumstances or character, we see before us a man who is either predominantly English or a real colonial free from all European influence.

ANDRÉ SIEGFRIED (1875-1959)
Democracy in New Zealand

NEW ZEALAND ART

We are the wheat self-sown
Beyond the hem of the paddock,
Banned by wind from the furrows,
Lonely of root and head,
Watching the brows of our kith,
Like exiled kings at a crowning,
Mourning through harvest moons
Our hope of holy bread.

We are the wistful woman
Who sees another unswaddle
The bloom of a small ripe body
While windows blaze in the west,
Mourning the waste of her womb
Like barren queens at a chrism,
Praying for life to seed,
And a mouth to hurt her breast.

EILEEN DUGGAN

THE COMING RACE

So far as the natural features of a country tend to
produce a fine race of men, New Zealand has the advantage of Australia. Australia, too, has hills and rivers,
woods and fertile lands, but unless in the heated plains
of the interior, which are sublime in their desolation,
it has nothing to touch the imagination, nothing to
develop varieties of character. In New Zealand there
are mountain ranges grander than the giant bergs of
Norway; there are glaciers and waterfalls for the hardy
hillmen; there are the sheep-walks for the future
Melibœus or shepherd of Salisbury Plain; there are

the rich farm-lands for the peasant yeomen; and the coasts, with their inlets and infinite varieties, are a nursery for seamen, who will carry forward the traditions of the old land. No Arden ever saw such forests, and no lover ever carved his mistress's name on such trees as are scattered over the Northern Island; while the dullest intellect quickens into awe and reverence amidst volcanoes and boiling springs and the mighty forces of nature, which seem as if any day they might break their chains. Even the Maories, a mere colony of Polynesian savages, grew to a stature of mind and body in New Zealand which no branch of that race has approached elsewhere. If it lies written in the book of destiny that the English nation has still within it great men who will take a place among the demigods, I can well believe that it will be in the unexhausted soil and spiritual capabilities of New Zealand that the great English poets, artists, philosophers, statesmen, soldiers of the future will be born and nurtured.

JAMES ANTHONY FROUDE (1818-94)
Oceana

THE TRUMPET-BLOWER

The New Zealander among John Bulls is the most John-Bullish. He admits the superiority of England to every place in the world, only he is more English than any Englishman at home. He tells you that he has the same climate—only somewhat improved; that he grows the same produce, only with somewhat heavier crops; that he has the same beautiful scenery at his doors, only somewhat grander in its nature and more diversified in its details; that he follows the same pursuits and after the same fashion—but with less of misery, less of want, and a more general participation in the gifts which God has given to the country. He reminds you that at Otago in the south, the mean temperature is the same as at London, whereas at Auckland, in the north, he has just that improvement necessary to furnish the most perfect climate in the world. . . . All good things have been given to this happy land, and when the Maori has melted, here will be the navel of the earth.

I know nothing to allege against the assurance. It is a land very happy in its climate; very happy in its promises. The poor Maori, who is now the source of all Auckland poetry, must first melt; and then if her coal fields can be made productive, and if the iron which is washed to her shore among the sands of the sea can be wrought into steel, I see no reason why Auckland should not rival London. I must specially observe one point on which the New Zealand colonist imitates his brethren and ancestors at home—and far surpasses his Australian rival. He is very fond of getting drunk. And I would also observe to the New Zealander generally, as I have done to other colonists, that if he would blow his own trumpet somewhat less loudly, the music would gain in its effect upon the world at large.

ANTHONY TROLLOPE (1815-82)
Australia and New Zealand

COUNTRY HOSPITALITY

In some parts, however, farm homesteads were separated by many miles, by hills, by heavy bush, swamps or dangerous rivers. For the women living in such circumstances, social life consisted largely in the hospitality which they offered to chance travellers. It was a hospitality which almost literally knew no bounds. In the complete absence, or prolonged scarcity, of accommodation houses, the little houses "up country" seemed sometimes to have walls of some substance more elastic than cob or than slabs of timber. As many as seven or eight young men might turn up at one time, more rarely there might be a woman in one party of travellers; and they came nearly always unexpectedly—necessarily when no regular means of communication existed. The difficulties and trouble of accommodating such numbers, though they might be great, were cheerfully accepted by the women, being more than compensated by the pleasure of fresh companionship after it might be months of comparative isolation. If there were maids, they were as much pleased as their mistresses with the sight of new faces. Space was as a rule the main problem, but one which seems never to have been found insoluble; except in rarely unfortunate instances, the food supply presented no difficulty. It was only if stores happened to be drawing to an end, and the weather made the procuring of fresh supplies impossible, that hardship of this sort was occasioned by, and for, the travellers; and Lady Barker's classic experience in "the great snow-storm" of 1867 was happily most unusual.

Sometimes, of course, these travellers, who might be weather-bound at a station for three or four days or longer, were friends or at least acquaintances, of the host and hostess. Often, however, they might be complete strangers. This appears to have made no difference to the hospitality offered; letters of introduction were not required; one's necessity was enough to open doors and ensure a welcome. In the earliest days of the Canterbury settlement the Deans' home at Riccarton was especially noted for its generous hospitality. Ten or twelve people to lunch, some of whose names even might be unknown, was no unusual thing, and on occasion these numbers were doubled or even trebled. "You just walked in," said a Canterbury woman, "and were treated with warm hospitality." As years went on, and hotels and accommodation houses were built, the need for this tax on the earlier settlers,

and on the men and women of the back country farms
and stations, though so willingly and freely paid, was
reduced. In 1891 a visiting Englishwoman spoke of
hospitality as " almost a ruling passion in New Zealand."
Long after the more urgent necessity had ceased to
exist, women in the country were still liable to be
called upon without notice to provide bed and breakfast,
at the least, for the wayfarer. The habit of " turning up"
unannounced, even in places where every facility exists
by which due warning may be given, the New Zealander
has never entirely outgrown; and he, or she, is apt by
it sorely to disconcert his English cousins when fortune
takes him overseas.

HELEN M. SIMPSON (1890-1962)
The Women of New Zealand

PRAYER FOR A YOUNG COUNTRY

Leave the nest early, child. Our climate's changing,
Snow has a stiffer grip on every part:
Fingers of ice, about their treasons raging,
Too soon shall set their purchase on your heart.

But where to turn? Feathered in what delusion
Sing the fierce swan-song, stride this cataract
Of one world's deadly purpose, one's confusion,
The noble dream turned cruel in the act?

I see the road sick centuries have tramped
Dying in scorn, by novel ways and bleak;
I see the earth beneath us cut and stamped
For new inheritors, but not the meek.

And gods born blind to lightning, deaf to thunder,
Whose evening is abyss and avalanche,

Shall teach you (youth, made clean to love and
    wonder!)
Under new names the oldest arrogance.

Also, brow lifted for the wind's white greeting,
I see the blind man, trusting to his stick;
I hear the children laugh . . . and know that fleeting
Echo of joy on earth is not a trick.

And dreaming near, too vast for rage or mirth,
I see where woman-breasted ocean lies;
One hand for her horizons, one for earth . . .
The green Pacific, with her waiting eyes.

ROBIN HYDE (IRIS WILKINSON) (1906-1939)

THEY SHALL TAKE AND HOLD

There is want in the homes of the People,
    The children are crying for bread,
And the Church sweeps the sky with a steeple
    That shadows the graves of our dead.

There's a wail in the wind at the dawning,
    A sound of a sob in the sea,
There's an evil that shudders when morning
    Flings mantles of gold o'er the lea.

There is hate betwixt toiler and toiler,
    And malice and envy and strife,
Labour lengthens the rule of the Spoiler
    With the plunge of the fratricide's knife.

But there's hope in the hearts of the Teachers,
    Their gospel rings clear through the night—
Fair Freedom's brave army of Preachers,
    Who're learning Life's lessons aright.

And the wage-slaves are waking from slumber
  Where the lowlands are washed by the seas,
And each day-spring is swelling the number
  Who'll fling their red flags to the breeze.

O the war-drums of Labour are throbbing
  Their call from the depths of the years,
And they'll end the young children's wild sobbing
  And sorrow of sad mothers' tears.

They shall take all the earth and its treasure,
  They shall tear down the banners of Wrong,
They shall hold all their wealth in full measure,
  And gladden the world with their song.

HENRY EDMUND HOLLAND (1868-1933)
Red Roses on the Highways

INCENTIVE AND INDEPENDENCE

In 1868 C. W. Dilke thought that in the North Island the "winterless and moist climate" had led to "a certain want of enterprise shown by the Government and settlers." A good many people since then have fancied that the Polynesian way of life was spreading to the Europeans, though the change has been more commonly attributed to the relative lack of rewards, and hence of incentive, or to the sapping of individual initiative by the state, than to the climate.

Such a change cannot be substantiated by any objective evidence. The farming industry, judged in terms of production, is easily the most efficient in the world, and secondary industry stands high in this respect. A small population, efficient methods and favourable circumstances may, however, have enabled men to achieve a high level of productivity without working too hard. There can be little doubt that the New

Zealanders, job for job, do not work as hard as the Germans or Americans. On the other hand, the persistence of European and Puritan attitudes towards work limits any excessive addiction to leisure or pleasure. The moral attitudes of society were moulded, perhaps more decisively than in Australia or the United States, by puritanical forms of Christianity and by the evangelism which permeated most Christian churches last century. Many a "Kiwi" drinker must look into his nine-ounce glass, only to discover there the disapproving face of his Primitive Methodist ancestor.

It would be misleading to imply that the New Zealanders are a very religious people—some of them go to church when they are christened, many when they marry, and more when they die. The prevailing religion is a simple materialism. The pursuit of health and possessions fills more minds than thoughts of salvation. The most respected personage in the community is the doctor, who is often regarded as both aristocrat and priest. The New Zealanders surpass all Europeans and rival the Americans in their love of motor-cars and washing machines. Acquisitiveness, like Puritanism, provides a strong incentive to work.

There is a popular New Zealand saying that a man works five days a week for the boss and two for himself. Any fine week-end a large part of the population seems to be engaged in digging the garden, building a shed or a house. "Do-it-yourself" was a national pastime long before the Americans rediscovered its joys and penalties. The New Zealanders certainly work hard for themselves. They are a practical people, good at improvising; the pioneer is but a generation or two away.

The small population, the large gardens, leave room for a sense of independence and a varied individual life. There is, as yet, no "mass-society", and little of the anonymity of life in great cities. For this reason the state has not become Leviathan. It is not yet quite impersonal. For twenty years parliamentary debates have been broadcast. Ministers, even the Prime Minister, are easily accessible to the voter. The people participate to a high degree in their democracy; over ninety per cent habitually go to the polls. The state is still, in a practical sense, the people in action. The New Zealanders have not, then, become either lotus-eaters or slaves of the modern state.

KEITH SINCLAIR (b. 1922)
Pelican History of New Zealand

THE COLLAPSE OF MATERIALISM

When, during the course of this century, the thinking public become aware of the collapse of materialism, and the new ideas which are replacing it spread out from the small circle of mathematicians and physicists, what will be the effect? The influence of the old notions was on the whole not good, because in their popular form the limits of their applicability, fully understood by those who knew, were ignored in the interests of simplicity. And I fear that the new ideas may also be used for base ends. Allied with modern psychology with its stress on emotional causation and with certain social doctrines with their stress on economic causation, they could easily produce an atmosphere unfavourable to objective unemotional thought and favourable to superstition, propaganda and brutality. If, men may say, things are so delusory, and truth so elusive, let us believe what is comfortable; those in authority may say, as they have always been tempted to do, let us induce, and if we cannot induce, let us compel others to think what is useful to us. Thus the most sinister developments of to-day may acquire powerful allies. It will be the duty of every child of light to emphasize that the conclusions which have been reached, are tentative and subject to modification, and that they are the results of the severest logical and mathematical thought and the most painstaking observations and experiments; that they are the triumphs of rational objective thinking, of an attempt to see things as they are. We must exalt the claims of reason and make clear that the modern views have been reached by intellectual processes and not by emotional conditioning or economic or political compulsion. Last century the poet, the artist, the idealist and the philosopher acted as the check and counterpoise to the scientific materialist. This century the rationalist, the believer in detached and unprejudiced thinking, must provide the remedy for emotionalism, propaganda, superstition and hysteria.

We have seen that it is possible that this universe had a beginning in time and that it is passing away; we at least are ephemeral spectators of the scene; many of the fundamental things, photons, electrons, also have a transitory existence. Photons arise and pass away, electrons lose their identity; newly created electrons are reborn. The world is a world of flux, its constituents are transitory, and it is growing old. Is there a more stable, a permanent world behind the play whose stage is space and time? Many have thought that in pure mathematics man has a vision, obscure and partial, of the deeper underlying reality, of which this fleeting scene is a faint and imperfect copy, and that the reason which guides us in the mathematical world is a reflection in our minds of the life and light of that Reason which manifests itself in created things. *In principio erat Verbum.*

H. G. FORDER (b. 1889)
"Science and Philosophy"
1840 and After

SECULAR LITANY

That we may never lack two Sundays in a week
One to rest and one to play
That we may worship in the liturgical drone
Of the race commentator and the radio raconteur
That we may avoid distinction and exception
Worship the mean, cultivate the mediocre
Live in a state house, raise forcibly-educated children
Receive family benefits, and standard wages and a
    pension
And rest in peace in a state crematorium
    Saint Allblack
    Saint Monday Raceday
    Saint Stabilisation
      Pray for us.

From all foreigners, with their unintelligible cooking
From the vicious habit of public enjoyment
From kermesse and carnival, high day and festival
From pubs, cafés, bullfights and barbecues
From Virgil and vintages, fountains and fresco-painting
From afterthought and apperception
From tragedy, from comedy
And from the arrow of God
    Saint Anniversaryday
    Saint Arborday
    Saint Labourday
      Defend us.

When the bottles are empty
And the keg runs sour
And the cinema is shut and darkened
And the radio gone up in smoke

When the tote goes broke
And the favourite scratches
And the brass bands are silenced
And the car is rusted by the roadside
 Saint Fathersday
 Saint Mothersday
 Saint Happybirthday
  Have mercy on us.

And for your petitioner, poor little Jim,
 Saint Hocus
 Saint Focus
 Saint Bogus
 And Saint Billy Bungstarter
  Have mercy on him.

          M. K. JOSEPH (b. 1914)

PLAYING TO WIN

Our main pursuits were only cultural in the broadest
sense. They were horse-racing, playing Rugby football,
and beer-drinking—especially playing football. There
were other minor interests like yachting, mountaineer-
ing, politics. Religious meetings of a faith-healing
kind had a considerable following; faith-healers never
lacked an audience. A simple people, after all, to whom
much poetry was denied, the New Zealanders took
their romance in the form of bucket-shops, gold-bricks,
and companies who claimed to make petrol out of water.
Gentle grafters who could raise the fare from Sydney
or San Francisco praised our simplicity and treated
New Zealand as a holiday ground.

 Rugby football was the best of all our pleasures;
it was religion and desire and fulfilment all in one.
Most New Zealanders can look back on some game
which they played to win and whose issues seemed to

them then a good deal more important than a lot that has happened since. This phenomenon is greatly deprecated by a lot of thinkers who feel that an exaggerated attention to games gives the young a wrong sense of values. This may well be true, and if it is true, the majority of New Zealanders have a wrong sense of values for the whole of their lives. But to be frank, and since we live in a hard world, and one that has certainly not in my time got any softer, I found in war-time that there was a considerable virtue in men who played games like professionals to win, and not, like public-school boys and amateurs, for exercise. So that perhaps it would be more correct to say that the virtues and values of New Zealanders were not so much wrong as primitive, and to this extent useful in the current collapse of civilisation.

New Zealanders, when they went to war, found it easier to get down to the moral plane of a German soldier, and were even capable of thinking a ruse or two ahead in the game of total war. Englishmen spent some time and casualties in finding war ungentlemanly before they tossed the rules overboard and moved in on the same basis. I don't know that the cunning and professionalism of my fellow countrymen is to be commended on abstract grounds, but these are comfortable qualities to have about in war-time. Oddly enough, I don't think these things affected their natural kindliness, nor the kind of ethics that they expect from people in private life. It was only that they looked on war as a game, and a game to New Zealanders is something that they play to win, against the other side and the referee. Personally, I still prefer games that way and find them more interesting.

JOHN MULGAN (1911-1945)
Report on Experience

BURIAL OF A BARD

The people in front had begun to throw handfuls of earth in on the coffin. One by one the whole crowd about the grave filed past it and slowly Ned and his father began to move forward.

" 'Tis a bit of the old Galway sod I have here," said Pat Conroy, taking a large envelope from his side pocket as he walked and spilling out a clot of blackened earth into his large hand. "I took it with me the day I said good-bye to my poor old father forty years agone and him in his grave not long after. Keeping it for myself, I was. And then when I looked at it this morning I thought to myself; 'Twould be a mean thing not to spare a crumb for old Larry, God have mercy on him, and him bringing back the taste and tales of Ireland and the very smell of the old sod itself this many a long year."

He stepped forward and threw his handful on the coffin. Ned's father followed. And then Ned, too, stooped and took his own handful of crumbling cool earth to cast it into the grave. Father Casey's eye rested for a moment on him, still there by the grave, murmuring prayers, patient like Larry while the mourners passed.

The priest and the poet, two solitaries, apart and measured against struggles that were not like other men's. Scapegoats both but in our time rivals, however devoted in their passion for first and last things. *Tantum religio potuit suadere malorum.* There was a Latin to rival the Church's. Curious that Larry should have been spared the clash; especially in a community for which work was not merely a virtue but a condition of life. But perhaps not so curious; for in a nation oppressed both in its patriotism and in its belief priest and poet have a common cause, as in Poland, as in Ireland. And here in this transplanted Ireland where the old folk-pattern was only now beginning to languish, the tradition of persecution died harder than the reality, religion and nationalism were still one. And so priest and poet still had the same cause. Their differences were still mute in the bonds that kept both slave. And so to this Larry owed his safety from disdain, from starvation; to this and to the accident that the emigrant Irish had kept for one or two generations the peasant tradition of hospitality, the memory they owed to the bard, their sense of debt to the man who dealt in words. He helped them to remember their Zion; and not to forget too quickly that poverty which is still hospitality's best soil.

Fortunate in his death, then. For the generation was changing! The men growing now from the soil being flung back upon his coffin were not the men whom Paddy Conroy's black handful had bred. The last false summer of the poet was dying. Conflict with the priest, isolation from his fellows, awaited whoever might be bold enough to take up Larry's shrivelled laurel.

For it had been his role to recreate the past as it might have been. And now men were interested at most in the past as it must have been. Larry had lived in the past and the past had lived in him; and so long as the life of his neighbours had resembled, however wretchedly, that life gone by, the flickering faces about the fire, the rapt eyes, the old women turning the burnt log and muttering: Sha, weren't they the grand times? all these had been possible. But now that past was dead; dead as the castles, the round towers, the cottages, dead as the forms of its life, dead and far. And with it, too, were dead the forms of its fancy, the white sparrows presaging grief, the black hound upon the hills, the sons of Finn. The life men were to live now had too little left, was truncated, could give people neither light nor darkness. There was asphalt between the new life and the soil; and even myth would be able to survive only as fact, that superstition of the newer times.

DAN DAVIN (b. 1913)
Roads from Home

IN THE YOUNGER LAND

This stubborn beach, whereon are tossed
white roses from the sea's green bough,
has never sheathed a Norman prow
nor flinched beneath a Roman host;

yet in my bones I feel the stir
of ancient wrongs and vanished woes,
and through my troubled spirit goes
the shadow of an old despair.

A. R. D. FAIRBURN (1904-57)

A CLASSLESS SOCIETY

Even marked differences of wealth, the appearance of a substantial moneyed group and the advance of residential segregation do not appear to establish two classes. For different economic grades to be transformed into social classes, it is necessary that separate patterns of life be established for each class. Nobody contemplating New Zealand in the fifties, could accuse the upper grades of neglecting to try; nor could an observer accuse the lower grades of failing to imitate what they could. In a land without servants this has been a busy decade for "upper" wives, turning from the dish-master to drive the children to the private preparatory school and hurrying back to preparations for entertaining. Item by expensive item the equipment in the roomier

homes of the prosperous has drawn ahead. The acquisi-
tion—while young—of a permanent holiday house at
certain resorts sets a more obvious barrier. Travel
overseas after marriage, regular dinner in restaurants,
expense account living and frequent holidays are all
signs of differentiation.

But the substance will lie in a combination and
perpetuation of these and other things; a nearly
exclusive course from cradle to grave which can incor-
porate talented outsiders but cannot be duplicated
outside. Accordingly it is significant that private
preparatory and secondary schools are multiplying, at
least in the north, existing facilities are being extended
and the staffing brought up to the State standards where
it lagged. Certain notable old State grammar schools,
drawing on "the better areas" are being pressed in to
serve the trend and Roman Catholic colleges are by no
means immune.

Nevertheless the gaps in class formation are as obvious
as the achievement. The English style of club is rare and
the more appropriate American country club is a thing
of the future. No widespread merger between the
well-to-do of the city and country has been effected.
Education is still, on balance, definitely an equalising
force, though an undue prolongation of secondary
schooling and juggling with bursaries and university
fees could alter that balance. Marriage, always an acid
test, seems to have retained much of its random colonial
sweep. What we are confronted with is a suddenly-
enlarged pile of pieces—some of them interlocked—for
the jigsaw puzzle of class society. Mercifully we do
not yet have to gaze at the assembled picture.

ROBERT CHAPMAN (b. 1922)
"Politics and Society"
Landfall (*September, 1962*)

SUBURBAN TRAIN

The man with prominent, aggressive eyes
Grates words at his companion on the train
In tones like rain on tin; he shies
Curds of pipesmoke out—a belching blame—
And tells of one who will not rise
Further in the department, having found
No proper channel for his qualities,
No clever way to walk on special ground.

And slowly ebbs the listener's sorry pulse
Receding behind silence and the cloud
Of nicotine and adjectives; how else
Combat the arrogant urgency this loud
Destructive storm would utter, leaving spent
All that it passes over? Coming up
The station of escape: he was not meant
To drink of the immortal's thunder-cup.

But this one, with assertion in his lids
Retamps his pipe and measures in his mind
Steady progression up the grading list;
Savours the satisfaction he will find
Soon walking up that street of ordered hedges
Where roofs like polished filing-cabinets glisten.
Well-fed he'll settle back and talk of ledgers
To the woman washing dishes, who just listens.

LOUIS JOHNSON (b. 1924)

LIBYA, 1941

Brigadier Hargest represented Awarua, the southernmost electorate
in the world, for 14 years in the New Zealand Parliament. He won
the M.C. and the D.S.O. in the 1914-18 war. In January 1940, he
left New Zealand as commander of the Fifth Infantry Brigade.
Captured in Libya in 1941, he escaped from the Generals' Camp
near Florence, and returned to England in 1943, being the highest-
ranking British officer to escape in either war. He was awarded the
C.B.E. and the M.C. and two bars to his D.S.O. Returning to France
on D-Day, he was killed by a shell on August 12, 1944.

Brigadier Hargest's book *Farewell Campo 12* is dedicated "To my
son Geoffrey who died of wounds in Italy, March 1944".

After a while a tank drew up beside me and a be-spectacled
German officer spoke to me from the turret top where
he was standing.

"Are you the commander?"

"Yes.

"I am General Kramer and I speak English. Will you
please come up beside me."

I told him that I had received a blow on the hip from
a shell and I could not manage the climb. Someone
assisted me and I got up somehow. He was courteous
and most anxious to please.

"Your men fight well," he said, "and fight like
gentlemen. So do we; but I have been in Russia where
that is not so."

From the top of the tank I could see that my men
had been herded into a group near the dressing station
not far away and we drove over to them. I asked
Kramer if, in view of his opinion that we were gentlemen, he would allow me to send my men to their
respective slit trenches to get their coats, blankets and
food, as they had not breakfasted. He consented at
once. When one of his officers pointed out that I still

OTIRA GORGE
Petrus van der Velden (1837-1913) came to New Zealand from Holland in 1890, and painted and taught in Christchurch. He was the first serious painter in the country and his widespread influence, especially in his use of oils, helped to shape one of the main traditions of New Zealand art.

PIPIWHARAUROA, LATE SUMMER
Don Binney (b. 1940) has based many of his paintings on native bird-
life. In this oil he shows the Pipiwharauroa, as the Maoris name the
shining cuckoo, in flight and repose.

carried my revolver, he refused to disarm me; but the moment his back was turned I was rapidly deprived of it and of my field glasses.

There was a little stir among the Germans and another officer appeared. It was Rommel. He sent for me. I bowed to him. He stood looking at me coldly. Through an interpreter he expressed his displeasure that I had not saluted him. I replied that I intended no discourtesy, but I was in the habit of saluting only my seniors in my own or Allied armies. I was in the wrong, of course, but had to stick to my point. It did not prevent him from congratulating me on the fighting quality of my men.

"They fight well," he said.

"Yes, they fight well," I replied, "but your tanks were too powerful for us."

"But you also have tanks."

"Yes, but not here, as you can see."

"Perhaps my men are superior to yours."

"You know that is not correct."

It was a perfunctory conversation. He asked me if he could do anything for me, and I said that I would be glad to have access to my kit for some clothes. He agreed and appeared to give the necessary orders; but nothing transpired, and I never saw a particle of my kit again. . . .

I wanted to go to the dressing station nearby to see our wounded, so approaching a German sentry, I asked him to come with me and I set off, the sentry following faithfully behind and never leaving me. I kept him until I was sent to Bardia.

The dressing station was full of wounded, our own and German, and the three New Zealand doctors there were hard put to it to cope with the situation. One gunner as well as being wounded was badly shell-shocked. His condition was pitiable. The ammunition and mines were still exploding and at each burst the poor fellow sprang as far off his stretcher as his wounds would allow, then fell back in terror. I stayed by him a little while and tried to talk him into quietness, not very successfully.

Then I came upon my great friend and parliamentary colleague, Major Arthur Grigg. He was fatally wounded and unconscious. I sat beside him for a little while until the Germans came to take me off to Bardia. He was a loyal comrade and a very gallant gentleman, and our country suffered a great loss when he died. In Parliament for a period preceding the war he had charmed New Zealand by his sincerity and his gentleness. Members of all parties liked and admired him. He had come away with me, in the artillery, and after a period as staff captain to Brigadier Miles, had been given the job he wanted, with a battery, as second in command. On this day he had been in command of the twenty-five pounders and when ammunition had run low had himself gone to get more. He had just driven up to the gun in a truck when a shell burst on the gun, killing and wounding most of the crew. Grigg jumped down and, running to the gun, began serving it as Number Two when another shell scored a direct hit, putting it completely out of action and mortally wounding him. Gunner comrades carried him down to the dressing station, but he did not regain consciousness.

As I walked away I realised for the first time what the day's catastrophe meant. Defeat, loss, grief; and the prospect of months, perhaps years, in prison. So great was my misery that I envied Arthur his quiet sleep in the sun.

JAMES HARGEST (1891-1944)
Farewell Campo 12

WALK PAST THOSE HOUSES
ON A SUNDAY MORNING

Walk past those houses on a Sunday morning
with a piano stumbling in the front room,
where the mechanic freed from tools takes shears
to clip his hedges, talk of politics.

Or move along the lake, or down the track
sit under butts of logs and watch the mangroves,
the chips, the pottery shards; there distant farms
grow out of fog to sun; for it was here
that pedant summer rose to teach us fate.

Think how the threads were coming close together:
remember the month, the day, the hour, and the
ungainly kitbag dragged off home in the tram and two
    days after
set in the hot Waikato close to the river—
bell tents, new straw, and uniforms everywhere.

Leave was a chance to take the bike
and go crawling into the ranges. Here were places
not to be seen as before, and places to visit:
a house with oaks where there was one
was quick with sympathy but did not understand.

Remember all these things: the League ball punted
    across the park
processional the sails of eighteen footers
and a cold salad at five.

Somewhere there is value to them. As the piano stumbles
something grows into being. It will take shape in the
end.

KENDRICK SMITHYMAN (b. 1922)

STATE CONTROL

The relation of the New Zealander to the State is a
very interesting one. He is far less suspicious of State
interference than the Western European is apt to be,
far more ready to turn to the State when a job needs
to be done. This difference of attitude is not due to
any deepseated difference of temperament. I think it
is purely the result of historical and geographical facts.
The history of government in Europe is filled with
memories of tyranny and oppression; the New Zealander
has been more lucky, simply because his community
and its government only came into existence in the
nineteenth century. That is the historical factor. The
geographical one is this. New Zealand is a fair-sized
country inhabited by an incredibly small number of
people, often scattered in tiny villages and solitary
homesteads; consequently, many of those people
wouldn't get common services if they were not centrally
planned and largely financed from central taxation;
it wouldn't pay private enterprise to provide such
services. Thus a certain amount of central planning
in New Zealand is inevitable, and there is no dark history
to give warning of the dangers of too much centralised
control. So the New Zealander takes government
control for granted, and whenever a new task is called
for he looks to the Government to take it on.

D. D. RAPHAEL (b. 1916)
New Zealand Listener, Nov. 12, 1948

NEW ZEALAND PAINTING

In New Zealand, circumstances of geography and cultural tradition are constantly snagging on each other. Obviously, the only cultures thoroughly at home in the Pacific are those of the indigenous peoples. How, then, can an intrusive culture continue its traditions in an environment thoroughly foreign to it? How can this culture fit into the pattern of the native cultures which in conception and application are so different? Up to the beginning of the last war one would imagine the culture of European New Zealand to be in static condition, unable to advance because the practitioners of that culture looked upon themselves merely as so many stranded voyagers, clutching to them their books, pictures and music, the while searching the horizon for the smoke of the ship which was to carry them back to civilisation. There was, then, this endless belt process of refreshing the mind at the European faucets of culture before returning, still panting with thirst, to the deprivations of the bush. There were few, in fact, who kept up the cycle. Many remained in Europe unable to face the return to what was, they imagined, a land where no bird sang.

No man with his face bent over his grubber, hacking out manuka roots, is concerning himself with culture, but at least in his shack there are certain humble indications of the European cultural tradition. A few books, the occasional print, a piece of silver lustre, a book of songs constitute a microcosm of civilisation, and the fine arts are merely extensions of these simple things. Although these may be sufficient for most men, the creative artist demands about him greater evidence of his own culture, not only in static collection, but in active creation. Neither does reproduction give him the necessary impetus or encouragement. The long-playing record, the facsimile reproduction, the taped broadcast drama are no substitute for the concert hall, the original picture and the living theatre. With reproductions there is no sense of communication, visual or sensory, and the artist, whatever his medium, cannot exist in a vacuum; he must be constantly aware of a stream of consciousness along which the current of his ideas will be directed towards receptive minds. The artist must be cherished, not materially, but spiritually, so that his feeling of creative isolation is not augmented into a feeling of social isolation. It is when the artist perceives his social isolation that he must, like a bird, remove to a warmer climate.

This migratory instinct on the part of the New Zealand artist of the first decades of this century has now developed into a psychological compulsion which might be termed *Drang nach Europa*. This compulsion, however, was negatived during the last war when this annual lemming-like rush to the sea of Europe by young artists was prevented for six years, and it would seem that the work of the artists of this generation has a quality of virility totally lacking in the work of previous generations. It seems, in fact, that where artists had to stay at home they came to terms with the characteristics of New Zealand. That they came to see the relationship between corrugated iron and the pohutukawa tree; that the wide, bright Pacific light bleached out the colours and threw the contours of forms into sharp relief; that no human being can live in the middle of so much ocean without land and the structure of its shape becoming for the perceptive mind something of overwhelming significance.

Now, despite the resumption of artistic emigration, there is a greater awareness amongst the younger artists of their land, and the relationship of man to

that land, and there is also evidence of a greater dependence on the sensations at hand, rather than seeking for
others elsewhere.

P. A. TOMORY (b. 1922)
New Zealand Painting

SOCIAL CLIMBING

The New Zealander, expecially of the middle class, has
a two-faced attitude to social climbing. We all dimly
hope to rise, yet we are afraid of rising above the common level. We become righteously indignant when anyone tries to impose on us by reason of money or birth.
"Who does he think he is, Lord Muck?" Think of the
sneers we have for the clipped polite speech of the
English middle class—which we confuse with the
speech of aristocracy—or for the visiting English
aristocrat, the giggles of young girls at his manner,
the cold shoulder of the worker. We can only stand it
when he speaks from a platform; we fear direct human
contact; he is the occasion of Rotarian oratory, a column
in the press, but we are awkward in his presence as if
our weakness were exposed. Because our vaunted pride
in being as good as he is, is in fact a sense of inferiority.
That is why so many New Zealanders, when they come
to England, try to get to a royal garden party and
conduct themselves like teen-agers in the presence of a
film-star. Being middle-class we fear and sneer at
royalty and aristocracy, yet we hanker after them
because an aristocrat's goodwill confers security on
our self-esteem. But on the other hand we feel superior
to some workers, especially those of the strong left-
wing unions—miners, watersiders and freezing workers;
and, as tourists, to foreign menials, workers and peasants
we adopt attitudes we wouldn't dare at home. I have
heard New Zealanders in London say "Cockney" and

"Irishman" in the same tone of voice as adults in my boyhood used to say "night-man." Generally the sense of inferiority makes us all the more determined to enforce the level; it is fear of social climbing that brings the dread uniformity all artists in New Zealand have to contend with. This too is at back of our two-faced attitude to England. It is a boast to be *going* to England; but not to come back is desertion, like crashing your way into another class. We like to be told we are the Dominion most like England, yet an English educated accent makes us feel we are being imposed on. If it crops up in someone's talk that he has been to England his listener will at once suspect that he only raised the subject as an occasion for mentioning his travels. We sneer at English customs, yet from every visiting Englishman we exact words of praise and are offended if he criticises us. We crave for commendation from those we feel inferior to. Remember how flattered we used to be to read those digest articles about New Zealand the Social Laboratory, the experiment watched by the whole world?

W. H. PEARSON (b. 1922)
"Fretful Sleepers"
Landfall, (*September, 1952*)

RUSH HOUR IN THE PUB

The noise beats at my eardrums. The bar is crowded, for the five to six rush is in full swing. It's part of the ritual, the New Zealand Way of Life. See the game from the bank and then replay it in the bar. Tell your cobbers what they should have done on the paddock, what the referee should have seen, why your team should have won. I'm jammed into a corner, hemmed in by a talking drinking throng. Glasses of beer jerk precariously above their heads to eager hands stretched up as if from lineout, men push in and men push out with cries of mind ya backs and make way for a naval officer. The glasses stand in platoons on the slopped bar and the barmen pounce about with plastic hoses browned with beer squirting them full again from chromium beaks, the same again and fill em up Bill, in goes your eye out, let's get crackin, fill em up. Those with a hard-won beach-head on the bar and a foot on the rail stand firm elbowing out and the rear files hem them in and the walls echo the talk talk talk, everyone stating his opinion loudly to defeat the tumult and drinking beer in the rapid, round, New Zealand style.

More push in the swinging door and the schools grow and men who came in for a coupla three beers find themselves involved into taking out the wallet for a school of ten or a dozen and some on spirits, unknown blokes introduced unheard in the din, and the meaningless unheeded toasts are drowned by the noise. Here's health. Cheers. All the best. And the glasses go up for the New Zealander swallow, down the hatch, and here comes Herbie. How'd ya get off the chain, Herbie? One for Herbie. Join our school, Herbie. Be in, it's ya birthday, Herbie. And the man in the chair pushes through the mob with hands decked with glasses and the bubbles run in the clear plastic tube and down they go again. Although the bar is packed tight the joker raffling the beer always gets through waving his card with the triangles of chance and wriggling away again as I shake my head. And the beer pours through the plastic and they are hurrying up the slower drinkers in the school and down they go again and Herbie's wife at home curses as she puts his tea in the oven.—Ya father's boozin again. Him and his back soon. Just a coupla beers with the boys he says.

In the bar, this masculine retreat, this refuge from wifely domination and household chores, this man's world, the talk goes on and on. Female gossip in a male world. Titbits of conversation, half heard, half imagined, as I stand there amongst all the talk talk talk—She was a pretty fair sort of game. Thought I'd conk out with excitement. You haven't got that on your own, sport. Bastards crawling around the boss. There's a swag of them in our joint. He's a hard shot. Yeah, he's a woopkacker all right. You'll go down the road if ya don't wake ya ideas up, I said. Was gonna give him a buncha five but I flogged off instead. Yeah innit stupid. Got a snitch on me and put me in crook with the boss. Tried to cut me out with me sheila. Hadn't jerried to it before. Put the kybosh on that smartly. You'll come a gutzer son I sez. You'll haveta shake ya shirt and get down to some hard yakker. Cunning as a Maori dog. Too right he is. Got the pricker with me. Slinging off at me he was. You're up the boo-ay he told me. Muggins that's me. Stop dragging the chain and have one with me. Kill or cure that's me. The man who rode the bull through China that's me.

And it's always me me me in these pubs. I can imagine them all through the bar, all talking about themselves. All those busy mouths slopping back the suds and talking about themselves. Why don't they shut up for a change?

GORDON SLATTER (b. 1922)
A Gun in my Hand

NEW ZEALAND FOR ME

I love bonnie Scotland, and England's blest shore,
But I love the new land of the Maori more,
Where labour's a blessing, and freedom's supreme,
And peace and contentment endears every scene.

With its flax, and its fern, and rare cabbage tree,—
Its freedom,—its blessings,—New Zealand for me.

Like a child of old Ocean, surrounded by sea,
Is the land of New Zealand, the home of the free:
Its wide-spreading valleys, and cloud-capped hills;
Its beautiful rivers, and blythe-sounding rills.
    With its flax, etc.

The land of the goi tree, mapu, and pine,
The stately totara, and blooming wild vine;
Where the birds, sporting cheerily all the day long,
Make the woods ring and echo the voice of their song.
    With its flax, etc.

Where the Englishman's cot rises sweet to the view
Surrounded with flowers of each varying hue;
And his fields, waving yellow with earth's golden spoils,
Make his home circle happy and sweeten his toils.
    With its flax, etc.

Bright land of the south! fairest gem of the sea!
Like branch from the stem of old England the free,
May thy name be enrolled in the annals of fame,
And spread a halo around the old English name.

    With its flax, and its fern, and rare cabbage tree,—
    Its freedom,—its blessings,—New Zealand for me!
JOHN BLAIR

ANY COMPLAINTS?

"We live in the best country in the world and we have little to complain about . . ." New Zealand M.P. on return from a United Nations conference.

Hooray for You, Hooray for Me,
Hooray for Us, with huge Ovations!
Alas for Them, Alack for Those
Who are not We, poor Other Nations!
The ragtag Rest, who are not blest
Like Us, with Nothing but the Best!

"WHIM-WHAM" (b. 1911)

CHILDREN'S GAMES

Wallflowers, wallflowers
Growing up so high.
And all the pretty maidens
Have got to die.
Except Mary,
For she's the fairest flower.
For she can dance and she can sing,
And she can turn round in a ring.

Two more weeks and we shall be
Out of the gates of misery.
No more writing, no more French,
No more sitting on a hard board bench.
No more walking two by two,
Like the monkeys in the Zoo,
No more spelling, no more sums,
No more teachers to whack our bums.

Paddy on the railway,
Picking up stones,
Along came an engine,
And broke Paddy's bones.
Oh, said Paddy,
That's not fair,
Oh, said the engine-driver,
I don't care.

I am a Girl Guide dressed in blue,
These are the actions I can do.
Stand at ease, bend my knees,
Salute to the King, bow to the Queen,
Never turn my back on the Union Jack,
Under the archway,
One, two, three.

There was a man and he went mad,
He jumped into a biscuit bag.
The bag it was so full,
He jumped into a roaring bull.
The bull it was so fine,
He jumped into a bottle of wine.
The bottle of wine it was so clear,
He jumped into a barrel of beer.
The barrel of beer it was so thick,
He jumped into a walking stick.
The walking stick broke,
And gave him a poke.
And that's the end
Of my gentleman's joke.

Yesterday at three o'clock in the morning,
An empty house full of furniture caught light.
The fire brigade came and put it out before it started,
Ran over a dead cat and half killed it.

Two naked men came running down the stairs,
With their hands in their pockets.
Two dead men went to the hospital all right.

Mr. Low is a very good man,
Who tries to teach us all he can.
Singing, spelling, arithmetic,
He never forgets to give us the stick.

Mr. Low is a very good man,
He goes to church on Sunday.
He prays to God to give him strength
To whack the kids on Monday.

quoted in *The Games of New Zealand Children*
by BRIAN SUTTON-SMITH

IN MY COUNTRY

In my country at this time of the year,
The wind of summer fans
The sombre bush into flower,
And tames wild water from the mountains.
Brief is the blossom, the river stone dry and bare.

He stands close to the earth,
My obdurate countryman,
Drawing from the wind's breath,
The arid sweetness of flower and mountain;
Knows no green herb for the heart's erosion.

COLIN NEWBURY (b. 1929)

A RIDDLE: OF THE SOUL

I cannot give
Unless I have
I cannot have
Unless I save
Unless I have
I cannot save
Unless I give
I cannot have.

Unless I live
I cannot be
Unless I am
I cannot seem
I cannot be
Unless I seem
I cannot live
Unless I am.

I cannot be
Unless I give
I cannot have
Unless I die
Unless I grieve
I cannot love
Unless I die
I cannot live.

M. K. JOSEPH (b. 1914)

NATIVITY

They were set for the home, but the horse went lame
And the rain came pelting out of the sky.
Joe saw the hut and he went to look,
And he said, "She's old, but she'll keep you dry."

So her boy was born in a roadman's shack,
By the light of a lamp that would hardly burn.
She wrapped him up in her hubby's coat,
And laid him down on a bed of fern.

Then they came riding out of the night,
And this is the thing that she'll always swear;
As they took off their hats and came into the light,
They knew they were going to find her there.

She sat at the edge of the fernstalk bed,
And she watched, but she didn't understand,
While they put those bundles by the baby's head;
That river nugget into his hand.

Then she watched as they went through the open door,
Weary as men who have ridden too far.
And the rain eased off and the low cloud broke,
And through the gap shone a single star.

                                        PETER CAPE (b. 1926)

SEMINAL YEARS FOR LITERATURE

"Would they had come a century or two earlier" to
prepare the way in the mid-nineteenth century for a
New Zealand Hawthorne and his drama of Calvinist
frustration set, it would be fitting, in the stern hinterland

of Otago; for a Melville to interpret those sordid, picturesque, ennobling, barbarous decades in the Bay of Islands; for an Emerson to weave his philosophy in the cloisters of Canterbury, or a Thoreau to muse and write—again it would be fitting—on the lakeside at Tutira. . . . The dreams dissolve, and we are left with— what? Nothing remotely comparable with the flowering of New England, it is true, but with a miscellany of prose and verse that is not discreditable to its authors, given the circumstances.

The circumstances—how large and how limiting a part they have in New Zealand's early years as a British colony! In six small settlements were gathered a few thousand people drawn from every quarter of the British Isles and set down, often with scant preparation, in surroundings whose very grandeur held the promise of isolation, physical danger, and hard toil. There were forests to clear, homes to build, farms to break in, exploration and surveying to be undertaken; a native people to be understood and conciliated; constitutions, regulations, laws—all the machinery of men in society— to be fashioned and applied. Then there were painful adjustments to be made by people, some of them deluded seekers after the New Jerusalem, who were forced into a new and utterly uncongenial way of life. Can we wonder that there was no great efflorescence of litera- ture in these foundation years? The real question is how so much, relatively, came to be produced.

For there is another side to this picture of struggle and privation. Granted that the "six colonies of New Zealand" were small and isolated; yet they were in a real sense communities—associations of people welded together into some sort of whole by a common origin, by common aims, and often, it must be admitted, by common grievances. "We are," runs the manifesto of an early periodical, "a community of brethren, having common objects in view—to reclaim and occupy the waste places of this land . . . to cultivate the arts and sciences, and the practice and extension of the amenities of civilised life." In nostalgic moments one wonders whether so positive a statement could have been made in any later period of history; whether, in fact, Port Nicholson and Nelson and Dunedin in their early years were not, apart from the centres of ancient Maori life, the first and last genuine communities in this country. What is clear is that the New Zealand of Domett, FitzGerald, Grey, and Barr did provide some of the necessary conditions for the writer—an interested audience, a sense of direction, and, in a new country and a new people, an inexhaustible theme.

E. H. McCORMICK (b. 1906)
New Zealand Literature

GLOSSARY

*This brief list contains both New Zealand slang and Maori words,
the latter indicated by* (m).

Aue! (m). Exclamation of astonishment or distress.
Buncha five. Fist.
Cabbage-tree. A tree belonging to the Lily family. *Cordyline australis.*
Conk out. To break down or faint.
Creek. A small stream.
Get the pricker. To become fed up.
Guri. Dog (from Kuri. m.)
Gutzer. A heavy fall.
Haere mai! (m). Welcome!
Haka (m). A dance or song.
Hapu (m). A section of a large tribe or a secondary tribe.
Hop. A dance.
Jerried. Recognised.
Joker. A man.
Kowhai (m). A tree bearing golden-yellow flowers. *Sophora microphylla.*
Kumara (m). Sweet Potato.
Kybosh. Calumniate.
Mag. Halfpenny.
Mere (m). Short flat stone weapon used for close fighting.
Morepork. Small owl, so named for its cry.
Pa (m). Stockade, fortified place.
Pakeha (m). European.
Pipi (m). Small shell-fish.
Poi (m). Small ball with string attached, swung rhythmically in accompaniment to a song.
Raupo (m). Bulrush. *Typha augustifolia.*
Rimu (m). A tree. *Dacrydium cupressinum.*
Sheila. A girl.
Sling off. To utter abuse.
Snitch. To inform upon.
Strides. Trousers.
Taiaha (m). Broadsword-like weapon, about five feet long, of wood.
Tangi (m). Lamentation or dirge.
Totara (m). A tree. *Podicarpus totara.*
Up the boo-ay. In the country or all astray.

Utu (m). Payment or prize.
Walk his chalks. To move away or escape.
Whare (m). House, hut.
Weka (m). Woodhen.
Woopkacker. Anything excellent or astonishing.
Yakker. Hard work.

DATES IN NEW ZEALAND HISTORY

A.D.

1642   European discovery of New Zealand by Abel Tasman.

1769   Lieut. James Cook, R.N., in the *Endeavour*, on his first of five visits to New Zealand, leads the first European party ashore.

1792   A gang of sealers land at Dusky Sound. About the same time whaling vessels begin to operate in New Zealand waters.

1814   Rev. Samuel Marsden, of the Church Missionary Society, brings first cattle to New Zealand, and, at Christmas, preaches the first Christian sermon in the new land.

1822   Wesleyan Mission arrives.

1826   First band of 60 English colonists at Bay of Islands.

1833   James Busby established at Bay of Islands as first official British Resident.

1835   William Colenso publishes New Zealand's first book, a Maori translation of St. Paul's *Epistles*.

1838   French Catholic Mission under Bishop Pompallier establishes Catholicism. At this time about 2,000 Europeans in New Zealand.

1839   Col. William Wakefield arrives in the *Tory* to purchase land for New Zealand Company settlement.

1840   First New Zealand Company settlers at Port Nicholson. Country annexed by Great Britain. Captain Hobson appointed Lieutenant-Governor of the country. Treaty of Waitangi signed, ceding Sovereignty of the Maori chiefs to Queen Victoria. Hobson takes up residence in Auckland.

1841   Second New Zealand Company settlement at Nelson. Settlement at Taranaki by the Plymouth Company.

1842   Bishop Selwyn (Anglican) arrives. Governor Hobson dies.

1844   Hone Heke cuts down British flagstaff at Kororareka and sacks township. Maori Wars begin.

1845   George Grey appointed Lieutenant-Governor.

1848   Otago founded by Scottish Company under the auspices of Free Church of Scotland.

1850   Foundation of Canterbury by Canterbury Association in conjunction with the Church of England.

1852   New Zealand Constitution Act, passed by British Parliament, divides the country into six provinces, each with a Provincial Council.

1853   Ordinance by Grey lowers price of Crown land to ten shillings an acre.

1854   The first Parliament meets at Auckland as the General Provincial Assembly.

1858   The first Maori King elected as head of Maori "Unity" Movement by the Maori chiefs in reaction against European domination.

1861   Otago gold-rushes follow discovery of gold at Gabriel's Gully. First police force organised.

1863   First railway opened—Christchurch to Ferrymead. New Zealand Settlements Act confiscates Maori land.

1864   Action by Grey against Maori rebels in Taranaki and Waikato.

1865   Wellington chosen as seat of Government. Peace with the Maori tribes proclaimed by Governor Grey.

1867   Four Maoris admitted to Parliament as representatives of the Maori people.

1869   New Zealand's first University founded at Otago. Secret ballot for Parliamentary elections.

1870   Sir Julius Vogel's works programme for roads and railways. University of New Zealand established by Act of Parliament.

1873   Forty-eight-hour working week for women established.

1876   Vogel abolishes Provincial Councils. Cable opened between New South Wales and New Zealand.

1877   Sir George Grey becomes Premier. Education Act provides for free, secular and compulsory elementary education.

1879   Manhood suffrage and three-year Parliaments introduced.

1882   First shipment of frozen meat to England.

1886   Tarawera eruption destroys Pink and White Terraces.

1891   Ballance leads Liberals to power, inaugurating much reformist legislation.

1893   Ballance succeeded by Seddon. Franchise extended to women.

1894   Industrial Conciliation and Arbitration Act introduces world's first compulsory state arbitration. Advances to Settler's Act.

1895   The Bank of New Zealand guaranteed by the State.

1898   Old Age Pensions Act.

1899   Volunteer troops sail for South African War.

1901   Forty-eight-hour working week for men. Cook Islands annexed. Captain Scott sails from Lyttleton in the *Discovery* for the Antarctic.

1907   New Zealand a Dominion by Royal Proclamation.

1908   First through trains from Auckland to Wellington.

1910   First Labour Party established. Nation Provident Fund Act.

1911   Miners' strike at Waihi, broken with considerable violence.

1912   William Massey (Reform Party) begins thirteen years as Prime Minister.

1914   Main Expeditionary Force leaves for Egypt. Western Samoa occupied by New Zealand Advance Expeditionary Force.

1915 Anzacs (Australian and N. Z. Army Corps) land at Gallipoli.
1916 New Zealand Division transferred to Western Front.
1918 Arbitration Court empowered to fix minimum wages for all industries.
1919 Women eligible for seats in Parliament.
1920 New Zealand admitted to League of Nations.
1922 Government Meat Board established.
1923 Government Dairy Board established.
1928 Kingsford Smith makes first successful flight from Australia.
1930 Economic depression begins.
1933 Mrs. Elizabeth McCombs first woman Member of Parliament.
1935 First Labour Government, led by M. J. Savage, embarks on the first of fourteen years of power.
1936-8 New Zealand transformed into a Welfare State.
1936 Forty-hour week. System of guaranteed prices for butter and cheese. Radio stations nationalised.
1938 Social Security Act initiates National Health Scheme, increases pensions and extends family allowances.
1940 First contingent of 2nd N. Z. Expeditionary Force takes part in North African campaign.
1941 N. Z. Division in Greece and Crete, and Second North African campaign.
1944 Canberra Pact of mutual defence between Australia and New Zealand.
1945 Final assault on Italy; end of war in the Pacific. New Zealand joins United Nations. Bank of New Zealand taken over by State.
1947 Statute of Westminster (1931) adopted by New Zealand Parliament.
1949 National Government takes office.
1950 New Zealand represented at Colombo Conference. Combat force in Korea.
1951 ANZUS Mutual Defence Pact between United States, Australia and New Zealand.
1953 Hillary and Tensing climb Mount Everest.
1954 New Zealand elected to U.N. Security Council.
1955 New Zealand sends air force to Malaya.
1956 Colombo Plan Conference at Wellington.
1961 First television transmissions. University of New Zealand dissolved, and replaced by four autonomous Universities at Auckland, Wellington, Christchurch and Dunedin. Census shows total population of 2,414,064.
1962 Control of radio handed over to New Zealand Broadcasting Corporation.

FIRST LINES OF POEMS

345

LIST OF AUTHORS

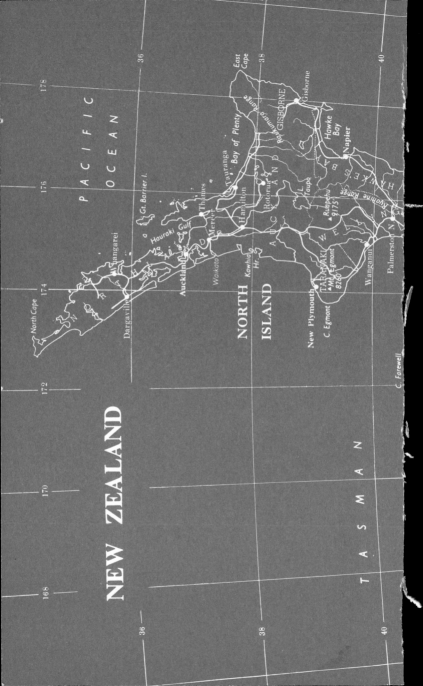